THE
SUPREME
COURT

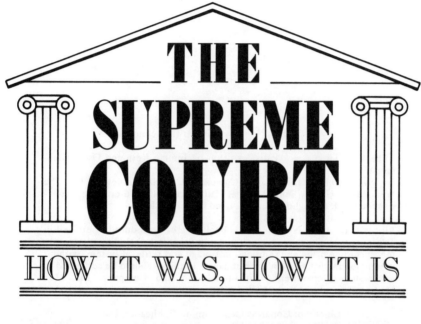

THE SUPREME COURT

HOW IT WAS, HOW IT IS

WILLIAM H. REHNQUIST

Quill
William Morrow
New York

Library of Congress Cataloging-in-Publication Data

Rehnquist, William H., 1924–
    The Supreme Court : how it was, how it is / William H. Rehnquist.
        p.   cm.
    Bibliography: p.
    Includes index.
    ISBN 0-688-08668-3 (pbk.)   ISBN 0-688-05714-4 (hard cover)
    1. United States.   Supreme Court—History.   2. Judges—United
States—Biography.   I. Title.
[KF8742.R47 1989]
347.73'26'09—dc19
[347.3073509]   88-29737
                                                              CIP

Printed in the United States of America

First Quill Edition

1 2 3 4 5 6 7 8 9 10

BOOK DESIGN BY LINEY LI

To Nan

PREFACE

*A*lexander Hamilton, writing in No. 78 of *The Federalist Papers*, described the Supreme Court of the United States as "the least dangerous" of the three branches of the federal government. Whether or not the passage of time has proved this assessment correct, it has most assuredly proved that the Supreme Court is the least understood of the three branches. This book is designed to convey to the interested, informed layman, as well as to lawyers who do not specialize in constitutional law, a better understanding of the role of the Supreme Court in American government.

Most of us have been exposed in either high school or college to a descriptive summary of the place of the Supreme Court in our system of government, but it is quite evident that this is not enough to convey any but the most rudimentary understanding of the nature of the Court's work. There are literally dozens of works dealing with one or more aspects of constitutional law, but almost all of them are written for lawyers and are too detailed and too technical to be easily comprehended by a nonlawyer. There are excellent biographical studies of some of the justices, and the Holmes Devise History of the Supreme Court, when complete, will treat its subject comprehensively. But these volumes are intended for the serious scholar and not the interested citizen trying to find out more about how the government works.

I have tried in this book to fill what seems to be a hiatus between the descriptive material and texts in American government and the comprehensive historical works. I have been guided by the view that placing the work of the Court in the context of American history, and sketching the lives and personalities of some of the most influential justices, would be more apt to whet the reader's interest than would an exposition of the constitutional doctrine expounded by the Court. The first part of the book, dealing with the first few months of my service as a clerk for Justice Robert H. Jackson in 1952, is designed to give the reader some feel for what the Court building is like physically, what it is like to work in that building, and the sort of work that law clerks do. The second part, dealing with the history of the Court from the time of John Marshall to the middle of the twentieth century, is an effort to follow a trail on the borderland between American history and constitutional law, and to give some idea of how the Court has responded to important developments in the history of our country. I have tried to briefly portray the lives of some of the important justices of this period, because the individuals who comprise the Court at any particular time have a great deal to say about the kind of decisions that the Court makes. The third part of the book is a description, from the point of view of a member of the Court, of how the Court today goes about its business of deciding cases.

To say that I have not attempted a treatise on constitutional law is an understatement. Several dozen cases at most are discussed, and whole areas of very important constitutional doctrine are not even touched upon. I have quite deliberately ended my discussion of the substantive doctrines developed by the Court at the time that Chief Justice Fred M. Vinson died in 1953, because I wanted to avoid any discussion of the cases and doctrines in which any of my present colleagues have played a part. I have been quite willing to sacrifice completeness in my treatment of all of these subjects in the interest of putting together within manageable limits a synthesis which I hope will leave the reader feeling that he knows considerably more about the Supreme Court when he puts the book down than he did when he picked it up.

The subjects of some of these chapters were tried out on the road, so to speak, as speeches at various law schools, and I am grateful to these law schools for having afforded me the opportunity to develop these subjects. Robby Lantz of the Lantz Office encouraged me in the conception and writing of this book far more than I would have expected a literary agent to do. My editor at William Morrow and Company, Lisa Drew, has seemed to me to have exactly the right touch necessary to improve an author's work.

My secretary, Janet Barnes, has with unfailing willingness and good humor typed the manuscript for the book and Mark Miskovsky, also employed in my office, has been both willing and able to ferret out errant scraps of information for me. The staff of the Library of the Supreme Court of the United States, now headed by Librarian Stephen Margeton, has been more than cooperative in filling my requests for a wide number of volumes. Gail Galloway, the curator of the Supreme Court, has offered her valuable help in the obtaining and selection of pictures for the volume.

My wife, Nan, has been a true factotum throughout the preparation of the book. She has always encouraged me to go ahead with it, even though it meant more of my time spent in my study and less with her and the family. She has been the editor of first resort, and nearly every chapter bears the imprint of one or more suggestions which she made. When I have thought of the interested, informed, nonlawyer for whom I am writing, I have had her in mind.

CONTENTS

THE
SUPREME
COURT

1

A LAW CLERK COMES TO WASHINGTON

*I*t was the morning of January 30, 1952, in Wooster, Ohio. I had spent the night in a tourist home, where, despite the inflation resulting from the Korean War, one could still get a room for four dollars. I was en route from my parents' home in Milwaukee, Wisconsin, to Washington, D.C. I was due there two days later to report for duty as a law clerk to Robert H. Jackson, one of the eight associate justices of the Supreme Court of the United States. It was a highly prized position; I was surprised to have been chosen for it, and I did not want to be late for the start of my work.

I was sitting at the counter of a diner, trying at the same time to eat three rather soggy pancakes covered with a mysterious kind of syrup and scan the weather report in the Akron *Beacon-Journal*, which I had purchased for a nickel from the cashier. I was very fond of pancakes and was still at an age where I could eat them without worrying about my waistline, but I did like the syrup I put on them to have some hint of maple flavor. I knew perfectly well that at an Ohio lunch counter I would have almost no chance of getting 100 percent pure maple syrup, but I didn't insist on that; all I asked was that the syrup be what was described on the label as "maple-like" or that it contain a certain amount of maple sugar or maple syrup, however small. I had very pointedly inquired of the woman who served me whether the syrup was indeed maple, and she had replied in the affirmative. Reflecting on its taste now, I decided there probably was at least a trace of maple flavor in it, and I had no claim for breach of warranty.

Concern with the weather for the remaining part of my trip to Washington became more acute as I read the weather report. It had apparently been snowing farther south in Ohio yesterday and that storm was expected to move eastward across the Appalachians today. The morning in Wooster was overcast, and there was snow on the ground, although none was falling at present. Since my transportation for this trip consisted of a 1941 Studebaker Champion, a good little car but eleven years old, I decided that I had best be on my way as soon as possible. Driving through the Great Lakes states in the middle of winter I had become acutely aware of a seasonal shortcoming of my car. It had no heater. Looking back from the present time, it is hard for me to believe that even as long ago as 1941 a heater would have been optional equipment on a car sold in Milwaukee, Wisconsin. But I know from occasionally bitter memory that the car did not have a heater, and therefore I certainly did not want to be on the road after sundown if I could avoid it.

Finishing up my pancakes, I paid the check and stepped outside. From the looks of the sky to the southeast, it appeared that I might be heading into the storm. The drive from Wisconsin to northern Ohio had been familiar to me because I had gone to school for a short time in Ohio before entering the army and had then been stationed there while in the service. But from here on I would be covering new territory: through eastern Ohio to Wheeling, West Virginia, and across the northern panhandle of West Virginia, through southwestern Pennsylvania and thence southeastward through Maryland to the Nation's Capital. I patted my little blue Studebaker's fender and thought, "Don't let me down, baby." I started it up and headed toward New Philadelphia and Wheeling.

I was a twenty-seven-year-old bachelor, somewhat late in completing my education because of three years' service in the military during World War II. By going through two summer sessions, I had managed to finish Stanford Law School in December 1951. The clerkship with Justice Jackson would be my first job as an honest-to-goodness graduate lawyer.

A large element of luck seemed to me to have entered into my selection as Justice Jackson's law clerk. Through studying about constitutional law in law school, and picking up bits of information here and there, I of course knew that justices of the Supreme Court had law clerks. Indeed, two recent Stanford graduates, Warren Christopher in the class of '49 and Marshall Small in the class of '51, had been clerks to Justice William O. Douglas. But Justice Douglas himself had western roots, and had arranged for the committee that chose his clerks to interview applicants on the West Coast. The chance of getting a clerkship with one of the other justices seemed remote indeed to a Stanford student such as I was, in a day when one did not fly across the country except in the event of a major emergency, and when one did not spend one's small savings on transcontinental train trips for interviews that seemed to have little prospect of success.

But, as fate would have it, Justice Jackson came to dedicate the new Stanford Law School building in the summer of 1951, when I was attending my second summer session. Phil Neal, my administrative-law professor, had himself clerked for Justice Jackson several years before. Shortly before Justice Jackson was due to arrive for the dedication ceremonies, Professor Neal asked me if I would be interested in clerking for the justice; the suggestion came to me out of a clear blue sky, but I naturally said that I would be. Neal then arranged for Justice Jackson to interview me for the position while he was at Stanford.

It cannot be difficult to imagine the fear and trembling with which I approached the interview. My academic record at Stanford Law School was excellent, but Stanford at that time did not enjoy as much national prestige as it now does. I first tried to bone up for my meeting with the justice by reading some of his opinions, and by trying to steep myself in constitutional law. After a few hours, however, I decided that it was utterly futile; if I had not learned enough constitutional law in my course on the subject to qualify for the position, I would probably not learn it in a few additional hours of cramming.

I met with Justice Jackson in one of the faculty offices, and his pleasant and easygoing demeanor at once put me at ease. After a few general questions about my background and legal education, he asked me whether my last name was Swedish. When I told him that it was, he began to reminisce about some of the Swedish clients he had had while practicing law in upstate New York before he had moved to Washington. I genuinely enjoyed listening to the anecdotes, but somehow I felt I should be doing more to make a favorable impression on him. He, however, seemed quite willing to end the interview with a courteous thanks for my having come by, and I walked out of the room sure that in the first minutes of our visit he had written me off as a total loss.

I was naturally surprised, therefore, to receive a letter from him in November 1951, telling me that his efforts to get by with only one law clerk that term were not working out well, and that both he and the clerk felt that some added assistance was in order. I had told him that because of my going through the summers I would graduate from Stanford in December, and he requested that I come to Washington on February 1, 1952, and plan to serve as his clerk from then until June 1953. I was surprised and delighted to receive this offer, and accepted it immediately.

As I noted the steady lowering of the southeastern sky, I thought to myself that a Swedish surname might have helped in the interview last summer but it wasn't going to help me perform the presumably demanding tasks associated with my new job. I crossed the Ohio River at Wheeling, West Virginia, and by the time I was in Pennsylvania, it had started to snow. An hour or so later, when I angled south across the Pennsylvania line into western Maryland, it was snowing hard. I was following United States highway number 40, the old "national road," which would take me to within forty miles of Washington.

I pulled up at a Shell station on the outskirts of Cumberland, Maryland, bought some gas and had the oil checked, and took another look at the weather. I guessed that the visibility was no more than a quarter of a mile, so I decided to pull over on the side of the road until things improved a little. A snowstorm in the mountains is a good deal more hazardous than a snowstorm on level ground, especially when you are not familiar with the road.

After a few minutes the visibility seemed to improve, and I decided that I was hitting the tail end of a weather system moving eastward over the Appalachians. I started up my car and headed east again on Route 40. I held my speed down, which wasn't hard to do in my 1941 Studebaker, because I didn't want to catch up to the storm any more than was necessary to make progress toward my destination. I came over the Appalachians, went through Hagerstown, and climbed back over the Blue Ridge without much more improvement in visibility. But when I finally turned south toward Frederick the skies began to brighten some, and the snow first let up and then stopped. During the last forty miles from Frederick to Washington the sun emerged from behind the clouds, and I had the feeling that it was personally welcoming me to the Nation's Capital.

I was fortunate enough to have a hospitable great-aunt who lived in the Northwest part of Washington near Chevy Chase Circle. She had been widowed four years previously, and had generously undertaken to put me up until I found a permanent place to stay. She gave me a very pleasant bedroom in her house, and I spent the day after my arrival getting my bearings in the city and working out a route to cover the rather long distance between her house and the Supreme Court building. The following day, February 1, 1952, I proceeded to follow that route—south on Connecticut Avenue to Dupont Circle, then southeast on Massachusetts Avenue to Capitol Hill. I found a parking place for my car on the street, realizing for the first of many times what an advantage a small car was in a city where parallel parking was *de rigueur*. From Maryland Avenue, where I had parked, one sees the north wing of the Supreme Court building. I walked around to the plaza in front of the main entrance to the building, and stood for a moment to admire it. I had been in Washington only once before in my life, when I came with my cousins from Iowa between my junior and senior year in high school. But I had absolutely no recollection of ever having seen the Supreme Court building; as I looked at it now, I felt sure that I would have remembered it if I had seen it before.

Behind me and across the Capitol plaza was the United States Capitol building, with its familiar dome thrusting up into the chilly gray February sky. In front of me was the main portico that provided entrance to the Supreme Court building, flanked on either side by two large, seated, marble figures. The portico itself is supported by sixteen massive Corinthian marble columns. Above these on the architrave is inscribed in large letters the familiar phrase "Equal Justice Under Law." Capping the entrance is a pediment with a sculptured group in bas-relief. The whole impression is of a magnificent Greek temple of white marble, flanked by two low wings extending outward on each side.

Later that spring I would learn that the glare of the sunlight on the plaza and the steps could make one's eyes smart unless he wore sunglasses, but today the gray skies and the few piles of shoveled snow on the plaza gave no hint of that. I climbed the seemingly endless steps leading up to the front entrance of the building, opened the large door, and walked through a vestibule. Beyond the vestibule I entered the Great Hall, and here again paused to feast my eyes on the sight. The ceiling looked to be at least twenty feet high, and on each side were double rows of marble columns. Arrayed along each side of the hall in niches designed for that purpose were busts of each of the eleven former Chief Justices of the Court, from John Jay to Harlan F. Stone.

But the fact that impressed me as much as the architecture was how quiet the Great Hall was. With the exception of the guard on duty, I was the only person in the hall. I explained to the guard my mission—to report for work to Justice Jackson—and he directed me to the Marshal's Office. From there I was taken by messenger down a corridor, just as deserted as the Great Hall, through some brass gates and down another corridor to a door where a bronze plaque contained the black letters MR. JUSTICE JACKSON. The messenger opened the door, walked into a reception room, and presented me to Mrs. Elsie Douglas, Justice Jackson's secretary.

Mrs. Douglas was a handsome, urbane woman who had been

notified by telephone from the Marshal's Office that I was en route. She welcomed me cordially, told me that Justice Jackson had not yet arrived at his chambers, and proceeded to show me into a smaller room adjoining the reception room, which contained two desks, piles of briefs and papers, and stacks of law books. At one of the desks was seated George Niebank, who had been clerking for the justice since the beginning of the term in the fall. He arose quickly when I entered the room, and I got the impression that he was delighted to see me, if for no other reason than that he would now have some help in processing the stacks of briefs and papers on the desks. It was now about 9:30 A.M., and George told me that Justice Jackson ordinarily arrived about 10:00 in the morning.

George and I made small talk for a few minutes, during which time Harry Parker, the justice's elderly messenger, came in and I met him. Despite the age difference between Harry and the law clerks, he insisted on calling the clerks nothing but "Mr. Smith" or "Mr. Jones." Unfortunately, Harry found my last name just too much of a tongue twister even to try, though I often encouraged him and told him if he could just get it out once, it would be easier the next time. George was "Mr. Niebank," but I remained "Mr. (pause)."

Elsie Douglas stuck her head in the door to tell me that Justice Jackson had arrived, and would like to see me. Although I had only the pleasantest recollection of our interview the preceding summer, I found myself wondering whether he might be a good deal fiercer on his home territory than he had seemed on the Stanford campus. But as I knocked and walked into his chambers, which adjoined the reception room on the opposite side of the clerks' office, he greeted me with the affability I remembered.

Robert H. Jackson had been born sixty years earlier in a hamlet in northwest Pennsylvania, but at the age of five his family moved north across the New York state line to the village of Frewsburg.

Because he adhered to the political faith of his fathers, he was one of the few Democrats in otherwise staunchly Republican upstate New York. Combining service to his party, to his state, and to his profession with his practice, he was known throughout the state when at the age of forty-two President Franklin Roosevelt appointed him general counsel for the Bureau of Internal Revenue in Washington. Jackson rose rapidly in the legal hierarchy of the New Deal; that rise culminated in his appointment as an associate justice of the Supreme Court in June 1941. As I stood before him on this February morning in 1952 he was in the midst of his eleventh year on the Court.

He was a friendly-looking man, a little on the stout side, with thinning dark hair that came to a widow's peak. His face was broad, his complexion somewhat florid, and his eye had an incipient twinkle. He was, I would judge, five feet nine inches or ten inches in height.

He greeted me warmly, and after an exchange of pleasantries, I told him that I supposed I ought to go to work. He allowed as how this was so, but said that we first had to do an even more important thing—have me put on the federal payroll. After signing the appropriate form, I became a GS-9 at a salary of $6,400 per year. While this doesn't seem like a lot of money today, it was far and away the most I had ever earned in my life. Justice Jackson then remarked rather casually that he supposed I had a general idea of how the Supreme Court operated. Actually, I had only the foggiest notions of how the Supreme Court operated, but I was naturally loath to volunteer this fact. He told me that he would be "on the bench" beginning at noon that day, and was now engaged in reading some briefs for the cases that would be argued that afternoon. He suggested that I let George Niebank fill me in on the details of the clerk's job, and that he would discuss my responsibilities with me at greather length when he had more time.

I had taken a course in constitutional law in my second year of law school, but had done no work at all in the field called "federal jurisdiction," which dealt with the niceties of when a case might be brought in federal court, as opposed to state court. I decided that I would have to work hard, keep my eyes and ears open, and hope to benefit from what was obviously going to be on-the-job training. Back in the law clerks' office, I confided some of my self-doubt to George Niebank while he was explaining to me what Justice Jackson expected of his law clerks. George assured me that his law-school education at the University of Buffalo Law School had not included any course in federal jurisdiction either, and although it might have been nice if it had, he had since been able to pick up whatever knowledge was necessary in that field. He went on to explain that the principal tasks of the law clerks were to write short memoranda on each petition for certiorari, and to help edit or make suggestions on Court opinions or dissents that Justice Jackson had written.

I was glad that, after I received the letter from Justice Jackson in November, I had done a little outside reading on the way the Supreme Court does its business. I did know the difference between petitions for certiorari and Court opinions. Petitions for certiorari was a term applicable almost exclusively to practice in the Supreme Court of the United States, and had its origin in the way the docket of the Supreme Court had grown from the time that our nation first began.

After the necessary states had ratified the Constitution in 1789, among other bills that the First Congress enacted was one called the Judiciary Act of 1789. That act provided that the Supreme Court of the United States should consist of a chief justice and five associate justices, and then went on to create federal trial courts in each of the thirteen states, and specified how appeals should be taken from those courts to the Supreme Court. The Supreme Court from its very first day was essentially an appellate court: a court that sits not to hear witnesses and to decide facts, but one that hears appeals on questions of law from decisions of trial courts that do hear witnesses and decide facts.

Since the Supreme Court was primarily an appellate court, it started out with very little to do because the principal source of its appeals—the lower federal courts—had not been in existence long enough to decide any cases that could be appealed to the Supreme Court. There was obviously no docket congestion in the Supreme Court of the United States for the first few years of its existence. But all of this changed in the next sixty years, as the United States expanded its territory. First the Louisiana Purchase in 1803 and then the Mexican Cession in 1848 established a nation whose boundaries extended from the Atlantic Ocean to the Pacific Ocean. In 1789, the population of the United States had been 3 million; by 1850, that population had increased to more than 23 million.

As might be expected, the increase in population meant new courts in the new territories and states, and thus more business for the Supreme Court. By 1850, the Supreme Court, which had always been very much up-to-date with its docket, was gradually falling behind. The situation worsened until 1891, when Congress stepped in and created the federal circuit courts of appeals, which were placed between the federal district courts and the Supreme Court of the United States to siphon off many of the appeals that had previously gone directly to the Supreme Court. This measure alleviated the docket congestion until after World War I, but in 1925 Congress stepped in again and passed what is commonly called the Certiorari Act. This act provided that in most cases there would be no right to appeal from a lower court to the Supreme Court of the United States; instead, review of a lower-court decision would take place only upon the agreement of the Supreme Court to hear the case. An application for such review was called a petition for certiorari. A petition for certiorari initiated the first of two steps by which the Supreme Court reviewed the decision of a state supreme court or of a federal court of appeals. The Supreme Court had to affirmatively agree to review the decision, and it did this by granting the petition for certiorari filed by the party that had lost in the court below. After the Supreme Court granted certiorari in a case, the parties each filed briefs supporting their positions, and within a few months after certiorari had been granted the Supreme Court heard the case argued orally by lawyers for both sides while the justices were on the bench in the courtroom.

During the term of court in which I came to work for Justice Jackson, about thirteen hundred petitions for certiorari were filed. Sitting there and talking to George Niebank, I suddenly realized that about thirty or forty of these petitions were currently stacked on my desk. George explained that he thought we should divide up the petitions equally between us as soon as I got the hang of the work, but that he would be glad to take the lion's share until I felt I had gotten my sea legs. This generous arrangement suited me fine.

George explained that the justice wanted a typed memorandum both describing the legal questions presented by the petition for certiorari and giving the clerk's judgment as to whether the issues were serious and important ones. He then wanted the clerk's recommendation as to whether the petition for certiorari should be granted or denied by the Court. I told George that this seemed like a lot of responsibility for a brand-new law clerk, but George told me that the justice felt perfectly free to disregard a recommendation with which he disagreed, and so I should concentrate on the descriptive part of the memorandum. He suggested that I look over a few of his recently prepared memoranda to get an idea of what was expected. Doing so gave me something of a feel for what I should be doing, and whetted my appetite to begin hoeing my own little plot of ground.

With some trepidation I picked up the certiorari papers on the top of the stack on my desk, and began reading through them. I was relieved to find that when I came to grips with an actual real-life petition, many of the abstract problems as to how a memorandum should be written faded away. The set of papers on which I was now working consisted of a petition for certiorari, printed and bound in the traditional form of a legal brief, and a memorandum in opposition from the prevailing party in the lower court. The petitioner in my case—that is, the party who had lost in the court of appeals and wanted the Supreme Court to review his case—had been indicted in the federal district court in Philadelphia on a narcotics charge, and after trial a jury had found him guilty. He had then appealed to the Court of Appeals for the Third Circuit, which sat in Philadelphia, and that court had handed down a written opinion upholding his conviction. I dutifully noted the numerous contentions raised by the petitioner: The government had not produced sufficient evidence at his trial to support the verdict of guilty, several of the trial judge's rulings on the admissibility of evidence had been wrong, and the trial judge's charge to the jury, in which he advised the jury of the governing law which they should apply to their deliberations, had incorrectly stated that law. Each of these three points was covered in a petition containing sixteen pages, and after reading only the petition I thought that perhaps there was some merit to the claim that the trial judge hadn't properly stated the law in his instructions to the jury.

But reading the memorandum in opposition filed by the United States, I got a totally different picture of what had been going on in the lower courts. The government pointed out that in all probability the trial judge's charge to the jury did correctly state the law, but that even if it didn't, the defendant's lawyer had made no objection to it at the time the trial judge informed the parties that he would charge to that effect. The government also made the point that even if there had been an isolated misstatement of the law in the judge's instructions, it was very likely "harmless error": That is, the evidence of guilt presented to the jury was so overwhelming in this case that an isolated misstatement of the law could not possibly have affected the conclusion reached by the jury. Finally, the government pointed out, in the best tradition of the advocate, that *even* if the instruction to the jury had been wrong, and *even* if it did not constitute merely harmless error, this was simply not the kind of case that the Supreme Court typically decided to review. In the government's view, the case was of no general importance, no new principles of law were involved, and if the wrong result had been reached in the lower courts, they had at least gone through the right motions in reaching it.

This last argument by the government troubled me considerably as I sat there pondering it, and I more or less put it to one side to think about for a while. I then turned to the opinion that had been written by one of the judges of the Court of Appeals for the Third Circuit in Philadelphia. I realized as I read the opinion that much of the government's memorandum in opposition to the petition for certiorari was based on this opinion, and it seemed to be a thoughtful, workmanlike job. As I made this observation, I mentally asked myself the question, "Who are you, two months out of law school, to give such a patronizing evaluation of an opinion written by a judge of a United States court of appeals who was appointed to his office by the president of the United States and confirmed by the United States Senate?" While the question may have been a good one, I rapidly realized that I must cast aside such modesty if I was to get through my share of the hundreds of certiorari petitions that had to be processed between February 1 and the time that the Court adjourned in June.

The petitioner who had been convicted of the narcotics offense in Philadelphia relied on two Supreme Court decisions which he claimed had not been followed by the lower courts in his case; the government in opposition said that these two cases weren't applicable, and that a third decision, which had not even been cited by the petitioner, was controlling. I dutifully read the opinions in each of the three cases and concluded that the government was probably right. I now tentatively decided that my recommendation to Justice Jackson should be that he vote to deny this petition for certiorari. The rule followed by the Supreme Court ever since the Certiorari Act of 1925 was that the votes of four of the nine justices were required in order to grant certiorari in a case; if Justice Jackson and at least five other members of the Court voted to deny certiorari in the case I was working on, the effect would be to leave standing the opinion of the Court of Appeals for the Third Circuit in Philadelphia, leaving the petitioner to serve his time in prison.

I decided I would write all but the last paragraph, which gave the reasons for the recommended action, now, and think about the recommendation a little more. I pulled out two sheets of blank loose-leaf paper which were supplied for composing the memos and a sheet of carbon paper to insert between them. George had told me that typing was required for the job, and I was concerned about my lack of any systematic typing skill. I was about as good as the next man with what was called the hunt and peck system, which required using only the index fingers of each hand. But even at my best, though I could go fairly rapidly, I was prone to make mistakes. Feeling some uneasiness as I placed the blank sheets in the typewriter, I listened briefly to the clatter of

George's typewriter across the room. I was sure from the sound of it that he must be an expert typist, but then I remembered the appearance of the memos he had given me to read: They contained a number of strikeouts and erasures with which I felt I could compete on even terms.

I composed as I went along, summarizing what had happened in the trial court, what the court of appeals had said in its written opinion, the defendant's contentions, and the government's response to them. I then sat at the typewriter for a few minutes, wondering if I should compose the final paragraph now or wait until later.

At that point George interrupted to ask if I had ever seen the Court in session. I said no, and he observed that since it was now ten minutes before noon, if we were to go down and sit in one of the cubicles off the main part of the courtroom, which were allotted to the law clerks, we could see them come on the bench at noon and then get in the employees' lunch line before the Court cafeteria opened to the general public at 12:15 P.M. At this time the Court sat from noon until 2:00 o'clock, took a half-hour break for lunch, and then came back on the bench from 2:30 until 4:30 in the afternoon. George's idea sounded good to me, and so I followed his lead from Justice Jackson's chambers to a door that opened into the courtroom from the back. We entered and seated ourselves on two small wooden chairs in one of the cubicles. I had studied a current photograph of the nine members of the Court, and had made myself a rough diagram of where they would sit on the bench in accordance with the seniority system. But while waiting for the opening ceremonies, I took a good look at the courtroom itself.

It was essentially a square, flanked on each of its sides by four pairs of Ionic columns, which looked to me to be at least thirty feet high. Between the pediments atop the columns and the intricately inlaid ceiling were four bas-relief friezes, showing what I assumed must be great moments in the history of the law. Stretching across the front of the courtroom and covering the entire side of the room was the bench at which the nine justices sat. When the justices eventually came on the bench, they, like every other human being in the room, seemed dwarfed by the architecture. No wonder that former Chief Justice Stone was said to have remarked, when the justices first moved into the new building in 1935, that he felt like a beetle entering the temple of Karnak!

The courtroom itself was divided by the traditional "bar"—this one of ornate brass—separating the part of the room reserved for lawyers admitted to practice before the Court from that to which the general public was admitted. Men who were obviously attorneys were seated at two sets of counsel tables within the bar. Several of the attorneys were dressed in morning coats, and I later learned that all lawyers representing the United States before the Supreme Court, and some private attorneys as well, made their arguments in formal morning wear.

Thirty or forty spectators were seated on the upholstered benches provided for the general public. They looked as if they were impressed, as I was, by the magnificence of their surroundings. There couldn't be very many public buildings like this in the United States, I thought to myself. Above the spectators at the rear of the courtroom was a large clock, hanging by a thick metal cord from the pediment.

Just then the marshal of the Court, who was sitting at a desk to the right of the bench, rose, pounded his gavel, and called out, "All rise!" Simultaneously, three groups of three justices each came on the bench—three through an opening in the middle of the red velvet curtain behind the bench, three from around the left end of the curtain, and three from around the right end of the curtain. When each was standing by his chair, the marshal intoned his familiar words:

> "Oyez, oyez, oyez. The Honorable, the Chief Justice and the Associate Justices of the Supreme Court of the United States. All persons having business before this honorable Court are admonished to draw nigh and give their attention, for the Court is now sitting. God save the United States and this honorable Court."

This ceremony moved me deeply. It was a ritual that had been used to open Anglo-Saxon courts for many centuries. A year and a half's exposure to it on a regular basis as a law clerk, and now fifteen years' exposure to it as a member of the Court, have convinced me that it is not only a stirring ceremony with which to open the Court, but that it is also one of the best tourist sights in Washington. Today, of course, the Court comes on the bench at 10:00 in the morning, rather than at noon, but nothing else has changed. I know of no other regularly scheduled occasion on which strangers to the Nation's Capital can be guaranteed a view of so many persons responsible for the functioning of one of the three branches of the United States government. Boredom may soon set in when the Court gets down to the business of hearing the cases that are to be argued that morning, but the opening ceremony is first-rate.

When each of the justices was standing beside his chair, the marshal again pounded his gavel, the justices sat down, and the spectators and lawyers were seated. The justices were seated in black upholstered chairs of varying sizes, which enabled them to rock back and forth as they sat. Behind the justices, and immediately in front of the wine-red drapes between the pillars, stood four young pages dressed in knickers. By virtue of my seating chart and previous study of a Court picture, I found that I was able to identify all nine members of the Court. Seated in the center chair was, of course, the Chief Justice, Fred M. Vinson of Kentucky. He had been appointed by President Truman in 1946, and was now sixty-two years old. He was regarded as a member of the "conservative" wing of the Court, believing that Congress and the president should have considerable authority not only in matters of economic affairs but with respect to civil liberties as well. In physical appearance Vinson had deteriorated a good deal from his early days when he played football for the famous "praying colonels" of Centre College, Kentucky. He was overweight, jowly, and had multiple bags under his eyes.

Seated to the right of the Chief Justice was Hugo L. Black of Alabama, the senior associate justice in point of service. Black had been elected a United States senator from Alabama in 1926, and in his thirteen years of service in that body had developed a reputation as a champion of populist causes and a formidable antagonist in debate. In 1937 President Franklin Roosevelt had proposed what he described as a "Court-reorganization" plan—those who opposed it described it as a "Court-packing" plan—which was roundly defeated in the Senate. But Senator Black had stood with the President all the way. Only a few weeks after the final defeat of the Court-packing plan, Roosevelt made Black his first appointee to the Supreme Court. Black was regarded as a member of the Court's "liberal" wing—a wing that conceded to the government great authority under the Constitution to regulate economic matters, but which sharply circumscribed that power when it was pitted against claims of individual rights. The "conservative" wing on the other hand, was inclined to sustain governmental action pretty much across the board. There are obviously grave deficiencies in any system of one-word adjectives when used to describe a judge's judicial philosophy, but those were the words in use at that time. Hugo Black's tight lips and piercing eyes gave him, I thought, an ascetic look.

Seated on the left of Chief Justice Vinson was Stanley Reed, Franklin Roosevelt's second appointment to the Supreme Court. Reed, like Vinson, was from Kentucky; this was one of those unusual periods where one medium-sized state could claim two of the nine members of the Court as native sons. Reed, like Vinson, had been active in Democratic politics in Kentucky. After an academic career that included a bachelor's degree from Yale, a law degree from Columbia, and a year's study at the Sorbonne, he had practiced law in Mayville, Kentucky. His initial appearance on the Washington scene had been as President Hoover's appointee as counsel for the Federal Farm Board in 1929. He then became general counsel for the Reconstruction Finance Corporation, and in 1935 was named solicitor general of the United States by President Roosevelt. Three years later he became an associate justice of the Supreme Court.

Stanley Reed wore rimless glasses at a time when they were not fashionable; he was almost completely bald now, with a large round face. He, like his fellow Kentuckian, was considered a member of the conservative wing.

Next to Reed was William O. Douglas, a native of the state of

Washington, who had "gone East" to study law at Columbia, then to teach at both Columbia and Yale, and later to become first commissioner and then chairman of the Securities and Exchange Commission. From the latter position Franklin Roosevelt elevated him to associate justice in 1939. He was fifty-three years of age, the youngest member of the Court, and a champion of social reform in general and civil liberties in particular.

Harold H. Burton, the only member of the Court who had been active in Republican politics, sat to Douglas's left on the bench. He had been born and educated in New England, but ultimately settled in Cleveland, Ohio, to practice law. He had been elected mayor of Cleveland in 1935, and United States senator from Ohio in 1940. While in the Senate he had served on a committee investigating the conduct of the Second World War, a committee chaired by then Senator Harry S Truman. Shortly after Truman became President, he named Burton as his first appointee to the Court. Burton was regarded as an eminently fair-minded justice, whose basic instinct allied him with the conservative wing of the Court but who was on occasion unpredictable. In looks he reminded me of the sort of supremely cultivated English butler one might see in a movie.

Seated at the far left of the bench next to Burton was Sherman Minton, the Court's newest member. Minton had been elected a Democratic senator from Indiana in 1934, and had been assigned the seat next to Truman in the Senate chamber. He was an ardent New Dealer, not only championing President Roosevelt's social legislation but also the latter's Court-packing plan. Defeated for reelection to the Senate in 1940, he had been appointed to the federal circuit court of appeals in Chicago by Roosevelt in 1941, and in 1949 Truman had appointed him an associate justice of the Supreme Court.

For all his enthusiasm about New Deal social legislation when he was in the Senate, that was the outer boundary of Sherman Minton's liberalism, and he was a marked conservative with respect to claims of civil liberties. He and Vinson shared the distinction of having played professional baseball in the minor leagues at an earlier stage of their careers, and both remained enthusiastic baseball fans. Minton had a rather square face, with a jutting chin, set on a large, well-built body.

Felix Frankfurter of Massachusetts sat to the right of Hugo Black. The picture of the Court I had examined before taking my seat in the cubicle had shown the justices seated, and comparisons of height were difficult to make. But when I saw the justices coming on the bench, I realized how short Frankfurter was. He had keen, piercing eyes, something of a beak for a nose, and always looked very alert. He, too, wore rimless glasses. If any one member of the Court typified the New Deal of President Franklin Roosevelt, it was Felix Frankfurter. Frankfurter had served as a member of the Harvard law faculty from 1919 to 1939, and during that time had been responsible for placing many of his students in important legal positions with the New Deal agencies. He himself had been a close personal adviser of President Roosevelt, and it came as no surprise when the latter elevated him to the High Court in 1939. Frankfurter was born in Vienna and came with his family to the United States at the age of twelve; he loved the United States and its system of government with the zeal of a convert. Though not always predictable, he tended to side with the Court's conservative wing in most matters.

Next to Frankfurter sat Justice Jackson, and to Jackson's right sat Tom C. Clark, known for his Texas drawl and his penchant for bow ties. Tom Clark came to the Department of Justice in 1937, and headed in succession the Antitrust Division and the Criminal Division of the department. When Truman became President in 1945, he named Clark as his attorney general, and Clark had served in that capacity for four years when in 1949 Truman named him to the Supreme Court. Clark was regarded as a staunch supporter of the government in all matters, and was considered a part of the Court's conservative wing.

As I was assessing each of these justices in the flesh, so to speak, for the first time, George Niebank tapped me on the shoulder and suggested that it was time to go to lunch. As we stood waiting for our trays, George explained to me that all the law clerks who were eating in the building on a given day usually ate together in a dining room set aside for them just across the hall from the cafeteria proper. When we had paid the cashier, he led the way to the clerks' dining room where the rest of the law clerks, ahead of us in the lunch line, had already made their way.

I was naturally an object of some curiosity, since all the rest of the clerks had come to work sometime during the preceding summer and had gotten to know one another pretty well by this time. I was fortunate in knowing Justice Douglas's single clerk, Marshall Small, because he had graduated from Stanford Law School a year ahead of me, and I was looking forward to renewing my acquaintance with him. Unfortunately, Marshall was not there that day, and I was told by the other clerks that Justice Douglas's demands on his law clerk were frequently such that the clerk could not go to lunch at the time that the other clerks did.

At this time Chief Justice Vinson had three law clerks, and each of the associate justices except Justice Douglas had two. Justice Douglas preferred to use only one clerk. There were probably ten or twelve of us seated around the clerks' dining table that noon, and I made an effort to size up the others. The majority came from a very few law schools—Harvard, Yale, Columbia, Pennsylvania, Chicago, and Northwestern. We all seemed to be roughly of an age, since it was almost impossible to have finished law school in 1951 or 1952 without having spent some time in the service during the Second World War or immediately afterward. I was not surprised by the fact that of all the clerks that term only Marshall Small and I came from law schools west of the Mississippi River, but sitting there at the lunch table I began to feel a little bit defensive about it.

The conversation turned to a proposed opinion for the Court which Justice Jackson had authored and, unbeknownst to me, circulated to the other justices the preceding day. Opinions for the Court were issued after the Court had heard arguments in a case in which certiorari had been granted, and the opinion was supposed to be based on the discussion among the justices at their conference on the case in question. The justices sat on the bench in the courtroom from noon until 2:00 P.M. and from 2:30 until 4:30 P.M., Monday through Friday during each week of oral argument. They then met in conference on Saturday morning to discuss and vote on the cases they had heard argued during the week. The Court's schedule generally called for two one-week sessions of oral argument, and then two weeks of recess in which opinions could be prepared and considered by the justices. At the end of each two-week session of oral argument, the Chief Justice would assign the writing of the draft opinion in a particular case to one of the members of the Court who had voted with the majority, and it then became the task of that justice to draft an opinion that would explain the reasons why the Court was deciding the way it did.

The case about which the law clerks were now talking was entitled *Sacher* v. *United States*, 343 U.S. 1, and it had been orally argued to the Court during the second week of January. I was vaguely aware that the case involved the actions of Judge Medina, who had presided at the trial of the Communist party members in New York a few years earlier, in citing several of the defense lawyers for contempt of court. Judging from the discussion among the clerks, the Court had been sharply divided in voting on the case at conference, and Justice Jackson's opinion upholding the contempt citations was not very popular at this particular lunch table.

George, who knew about the case and had apparently helped Justice Jackson with it, stoutly defended the result, but he seemed to have few supporters. There were dark predictions of stirring dissents from justices who disagreed with the majority of the Court, and I became quite uneasy about what would happen to Justice Jackson's opinion. Only later did I come to realize that it would be all but impossible to assemble a more hypercritical, not to say arrogant, audience than a group of law clerks criticizing an opinion circulated by one of their employers. Their scorn— and in due time it became my scorn too—was not reserved for Justice Jackson, but was lavished with considerable impartiality upon the products of all nine chambers of the Court.

When I returned to my office, I debated whether I should go ahead and type the last paragraph of the memorandum I had been working on before lunch, or whether I should read through some other petitions to get more of a feel for how the merits of the various claims stacked up against one another. I began thumbing through another petition in a rather desultory manner, but found my mind wandering back to the earlier memo. I finally decided to take the bit in my teeth and go back and finish it up. I thereby began to teach myself a lesson that most law clerks and most judges have to teach themselves somewhere along the line. Ideally speaking, one never knows as much as one ought to know about the particular matter being judged, whether it be a law clerk trying to make up his mind what recommendation to make with respect to a petition for certiorari, or an appellate judge making up his mind whether to vote to affirm or reverse the decision of a lower court. After immersing oneself in the materials at hand in order to reach a conclusion, albeit a tentative one, the crucial question is "When will I know more than I do now?" Perhaps it is just my own way of working, but I have always preferred where possible to go through one thing from beginning to end, do what I had to do with it, and move on to the next thing.

As a result of this newfound determination to forge ahead with my "cert" memos, I managed to finish several more that afternoon. There seemed to be a customary coffee break around the middle of the afternoon, at which time the cafeteria reopened and many of the clerks went down to get a snack. My snack—which seems incredible to me now at my present age and in an era of calorie counting—was cherry pie à la mode. With two people in one office, some kind of an understanding either acknowledged or tacit has to be worked out about time for work and time for conversation. It seemed to me that first day that George and I were both operating on pretty much the same wavelength—small talk just before going to lunch and just after we got back, and at snack time. But otherwise it was pretty much business unless one of us was really bothered by a legal question with which he thought the other might assist him.

The first day on the job, of course, is a time for feeling out as deftly as possible some of the contours of one's employment. Having served three years in the army, and held the usual college summer jobs as a factory worker and ditch digger, I was familiar with the regimen of that kind of work: You are told exactly at what time to report in the morning, or at the beginning of the shift, and you are told exactly what time you can leave. Although my clerkship with Justice Jackson was my first really professional job, I sensed even in my first day that it would not do simply to ask point-blank what time I was expected to be in in the morning or what time I was to be permitted to leave in the evening. That would show me up to be a "time server" rather than a true professional determined to do the job assigned to me.

I was, of course, fully determined to do the job assigned to me, but I was also curious as to the normal daily schedule which Justice Jackson kept, because I assumed I was expected to be in my office during the time that he was in his chambers or on the bench. Conversely, I guess, I assumed that I was free to absent myself if I was current with my work before Justice Jackson arrived in the morning and after he left in the evening. I didn't actually want to ask even George Niebank about what hours I should keep, because it somehow seemed to indicate less than complete devotion to the job.

I solved part of the problem that first evening by simply staying until everyone else had left. Mrs. Douglas left shortly before 6:00 o'clock, Justice Jackson left around 6:00 o'clock, and George Niebank left around 6:15. I departed at about 6:20, and felt that I could probably set my minimum hours around Justice Jackson's schedule. I proved correct; morning rush-hour traffic in Washington was bad even in 1952, and it seemed to me that most of my clerk colleagues tried to get into the office about 9:30 A.M. Justice Jackson almost invariably arrived around 10:00 A.M. and left about 6:00 P.M.

As I turned out the lights and locked the door of my office, I had a feeling of almost complete satisfaction with my first day on the job. The work interested me greatly, I enjoyed the people I had met, and I felt very enthusiastic about the immediate future.

2

THE
STEEL SEIZURE CASE
IN THE LOWER COURTS

I had not been in Washington more than a few days before I realized how important the daily newspapers were in the lives of most of its inhabitants. The ten years since I had graduated from high school had been spent almost entirely in the service, at college, or at law school, and none of these experiences had made me an avid newspaper reader. But because so much of the small talk in Washington related to events in the political world, one had to read the newspapers or else feel completely deprived of the common denominator of most conversations. I therefore became a newspaper reader, and it was just as well that I did; for one of the most celebrated cases ever to be decided by the Supreme Court—the Steel Seizure Case—emerged virtually full-blown that spring from events that were described from beginning to end on the front pages of the city's daily newspapers.

During that winter of 1952, there were two morning papers in the capital, *The Washington Post* and *The Washington Times-Herald*. The *Post* was generally thought to have better news coverage, but the *Times-Herald* had better comics and features; their editorial policies were poles apart. The dominant newspaper in terms of circulation was *The Washington Evening Star*, and the presence of these three dailies made Washington a lively newspaper town.

The fact that 1952 was a presidential election year made politics the dominant national news story. There was a good deal of uncertainty as to whom each of the two major political parties would put forward as its standard bearer in this contest. President Truman had succeeded Franklin Roosevelt upon the death of the latter in 1945, and had been elected in his own right in 1948. He had not yet committed himself as to whether he would be a candidate for the Democratic nomination for president again in 1952, but he was entered in the New Hampshire primary to be held in March. The Republican candidate was also as yet undetermined. The party's traditional, conservative wing lined up behind Senator Robert A. Taft, and its moderate or liberal wing hoped that General Dwight D. Eisenhower could be persuaded to be a candidate. Charges of corruption in the Truman administration had been surfacing more and more frequently, and when I opened *The Washington Post* on the morning of February 2, 1952—my second day on the job as a law clerk—a front-page story announced that Newbold Morris, a New York lawyer, had been appointed to investigate the "depth and scope of official misconduct" in the government.

A second major fact of life in the United States during the winter and spring of 1952 was the Korean War. Though news of it was no longer regularly on the front pages as it had been when major battles were raging in 1950 and 1951, it remained in the back of most everyone's mind. I was not aware of it at the time, but it seems to me in retrospect that the peculiar national mood with respect to the Korean War played a significant part in the outcome of the Steel Seizure Case.

In June 1950, without any warning or provocation, the armies of Communist-dominated North Korea had invaded South Korea, and within four days the South Korean capital of Seoul had fallen to the enemy. The United Nations Security Council met in special session and called upon member nations to give whatever assistance they could to the beleaguered Republic of South Korea, and by early July, American infantry troops had begun landing in South Korea. Other members of the United Nations—Great Britain, Canada, Australia, and New Zealand, for example—also responded to the call of the Security Council, but the United States furnished the vast majority of U.N. troops. President Truman consulted with both Democratic and Republican leaders of Congress, but even though they expressed general approval of the government's actions, he and his advisers consciously decided not to ask Congress for a declaration of war. Truman, queried by the press, had characterized the United States' engagement in Korea as a "police action," rather than a "war," and so the Korean "War" got off to a rather strange start.

Nearly fifty thousand United States troops were landed in South Korea to fight alongside the South Korean Army, but throughout the summer of 1950 these forces had been relentlessly driven back by the North Korean Army into what was called the Pusan perimeter, based on the south-coast port of Pusan. Then in September General MacArthur, the Commander in Chief of American forces in the Far East, led a brilliantly conceived amphibious invasion of the west-coast port of Inchon, and simultaneously the allied troops defending the Pusan perimeter in the south had broken out and begun pursuing the fleeing North Koreans back toward the thirty-eighth parallel. Seoul was recaptured, and by October 1 virtually all of South Korea was in allied hands and the North Korean Army appeared to be a shattered force.

During October and November, however, several hundred thousand troops from mainland China, performing an incredibly disciplined march, moved from Manchuria into North Korea. By late October, these troops were fighting alongside the North Korean Army. The United States and its South Korean allies were once again badly outnumbered, and the tide of battle had shifted against them as swiftly as it had shifted in their favor after the Inchon landing. By January 1951, the allies had been forced once more to give up Seoul, and to fall back to a line that lay well south of that city. During the next few months the allies succeeded in retaking Seoul, and had established their lines somewhat to the north of that city. But at this point major military movements ceased.

General MacArthur, after publicly expressing his displeasure with President Truman's decision not to permit planes of the

United States Air Force to pursue enemy fighter planes north of the Yalu River and into Chinese territory, had been relieved of his command by the President. MacArthur's return to the United States brought forth remarkable shows of support for him, culminating in a New York City ticker-tape parade where he received nearly twice as much of that ultimate measure of celebrity status as Charles Lindbergh had received twenty-five years earlier. In the summer of 1951, armistice negotiations had commenced, but they were still proceeding at what seemed a snail's pace in the winter of 1952 with no apparent end in sight.

I don't think the peculiar flavor of the Korean War can be properly understood unless we consider the fact that it broke out less than five years after V-J day had signaled the end of hostilities in the Second World War. In the latter conflict, the United States had had fourteen million men and women under arms, Congress had declared war on the Axis powers, and the nation was single-minded in its view that winning the war was far and away the number-one national priority. If there was little of the idealism reflected in First World War slogans such as "make the world safe for democracy," there was nonetheless a more practical determination to see the conflict, which had begun with the Japanese attack on Pearl Harbor, through to a victorious conclusion.

The Korean War was quite different. Though the naval, air, and ground forces sent to fight there engaged in hotly contested battles, there were probably less than one hundred thousand United States troops in Korea at any one time. Instead of starting at a low point and working gradually up to greater and greater successes, as the United States forces had done in the Second World War, the Korean combat proved to be a roller coaster of initial defeat, then stunning success, then defeat, then regrouping, and finally stalemate. There had been no declaration of war to formally signal the national commitment in Korea, and the civilian population at home never gave the sort of disciplined support of the war effort that it had given during the Second World War.

To me these differences are epitomized in the comparison of a verse from a song written to commemorate the fall of Paris to the German armies in June 1940, and a parody of that song coined by some of the United States troops who had broken out of the Pusan perimeter to retake the railroad junction of Taejon. The song commemorating the fall of Paris was called, appropriately enough, "The Last Time I Saw Paris"—memorializing the occupation of Paris, the City of Light, by Adolf Hitler, the Archangel of Darkness.

It concluded with this verse:

The last time I saw Paris
Her heart was warm and gay.
No matter how they change her
I'll remember her that way.

The Korean War parody used these words to the same tune:

The last time I saw Taejon
It was not bright and gay.
Today I go to Taejon
To blow the place away.
(*Time*, October 9, 1950)

Congress had given the President considerable authority to regulate wages and prices during the Korean War, but the authority was limited in some respects and was employed in a rather halfhearted way. As winter turned to spring in 1952, what started as a labor dispute between the steelworkers' union and the major steel producers suddenly blossomed into a major constitutional crisis. The existing collective-bargaining contract between the United Steel Workers and the steel companies had expired on December 31, 1951. The union demanded a substantial wage increase for the workers it represented, but the steel companies were unwilling to grant such an increase unless they had assurance from the appropriate government agency that they would be allowed to raise steel prices to cover the added labor costs.

In late March, the Wage Stabilization Board had recommended a wage increase satisfactory to the union, but the Office of Price Stabilization refused to agree to the sort of price increase the steel companies had said would be necessary to cover the cost of the wage increase. A strike appeared imminent, with all the consequences it would have on the effort of the American forces in Korea. A special mediator was appointed to meet with the companies and the union, but his efforts were not successful. Finally the President, after considering other alternatives and finding them either ineffective or unpalatable, announced to the nation in a radio and television address on April 8, 1952, that he had ordered Secretary of Commerce Charles Sawyer to seize the steel mills from their owners as of midnight. The battle was now joined.

Earlier that day President Truman had signed an executive order directing the secretary of commerce to take possession of the steel mills, reciting as his authority for doing so "the Constitution and laws of the United States, and as President of the United States and Commander in Chief of the Armed Forces." Less than an hour after the President had finished his late-evening address to the nation, attorneys for two of the steel companies had gone to the home of Judge Walter Bastian in Washington and requested him to issue a temporary restraining order to prohibit the President's seizure until a court hearing could be held on the question. Judge Bastian, one of the judges of the United States District Court for the District of Columbia, refused to consider the motions without giving the government attorneys a chance to be heard, and so set a hearing for the next morning.

Another judge of the district court, Alexander Holtzoff, presided at that hearing. Attorneys for the steel companies sought to show that the President, without any enabling legislation from Congress, had no authority to seize private property, and that the steel companies were entitled to an injunction ordering the President to return the property to its owners. The government argued to the judge that he needn't decide whether or not the President's action was lawful in the abstract, because well-established legal principles required that the steel companies show, before an injunction would issue, both that their injury from the President's action would be "irreparable" and that they had no adequate remedy other than an injunction. Judge Holtzoff heard the attorneys argue their case, and then ruled almost immediately that because the President appeared to be acting to prevent the sort of national emergency that would result if the steelworkers went out on strike, he would not at this stage of the lawsuit issue an injunction against the President. The next stage of the case was set for hearing on April 24, 1952.

Lawyers and laymen alike joined in the immediate surge of speculation about how this Steel Seizure Case should and would be decided.

The government's first-line argument was that the courts need not decide whether or not the President's seizure of the steel mills was constitutionally valid because the so-called "equitable arguments," which had persuaded Judge Holtzoff, should prevent the issuance of an injunction against Secretary Sawyer. But the government also argued that if the courts were to reach the constitutional question, the powers conferred upon the president by Article II of the Constitution—powers to "take care that the laws be faithfully executed," and those that resulted from his designation as Commander in Chief of the Armed Forces of the United States—were enough to justify the seizure in this sort of emergency when United States troops were engaged in armed combat on foreign soil.

The steel companies attempted to focus the argument away from the equitable considerations relating to when an injunction would issue, and on to the constitutional issue in the case. Their basic contention was that only Congress could authorize the seizure of private property for public use, even if the property owner was ultimately to be paid the fair value of the property seized. But the companies were quick to assert that the courts need not go this far in order to sustain their position; they need only conclude that when Congress had specifically dealt by statute with the very situation that had arisen in this case, and granted the president several kinds of authority but not the authority to seize plants, the president's actions were unauthorized.

This latter argument of the steel companies was based on the provisions of the Taft-Hartley Act enacted by Congress in 1947 over President Truman's veto, and sure to be a bone of contention in the 1952 presidential campaign. In considering the passage of the act, Congress had taken up the question of what ought to happen when a possible strike threatened a national emergency, and it had very specifically set out the procedure to be followed: The government was authorized to go to court and obtain an injunction against the strike for a period of eighty days. This was known as a cooling-off period, during which time there was to be a secret ballot among the members of the union upon the employer's final offer of settlement. If the labor dispute that led to the strike had not been settled during the eighty-day period, the act required the president to submit to Congress a report and recommendation as to what steps Congress should take to deal with the national emergency.

As might be imagined, these issues were hotly debated in the lunch-table conversation of the law clerks, who at that stage of their careers like nothing better than to discuss and refine abstract legal issues. I think the consensus among the law clerks, and perhaps of other people trained as lawyers with whom I spoke at the time, was that the courts would probably never reach the constitutional issue of the President's authority to seize the steel mills under these circumstances. This view was based on the same set of reasons that seem to have moved Judge Holtzoff in denying a temporary restraining order to the steel companies on April 9. In order to persuade a court to "enjoin" or prohibit the executive from doing something, the victim of an executive action which is claimed to be illegal must show not only that it is illegal but also that he will suffer "irreparable injury"—that is, injury that could not be compensated for by the recovery of damages in an ordinary lawsuit tried before a jury—and that he has no "adequate remedy at law."

These technical-sounding terms boil down to something more understandable when valued in their historical context. When the English court system originated in the Middle Ages, the first set of courts to be developed were called "courts of law," where there were jury trials and awards of damages, and where the governing legal rules were applied in a rather hard-and-fast manner. To ameliorate the harshness of some of the results reached in the common-law courts, the king's chancellor began dispensing a second brand of justice known as "equity." An injunction—which is nothing more than a court order directed to a party and requiring the party either to do something or not to do something—was a creature of the courts of equity, and because of this, one was never automatically entitled upon a showing of a particular set of facts to obtain an injunction; it was a matter of discretion with the court, based on a careful weighing of all the surrounding circumstances. The facts that had moved Judge Holtzoff in denying the temporary restraining order—the President was acting to forestall a national emergency; courts did not lightly interfere with a considered decision of the President; very likely the steel companies could recover whatever damages they suffered from the seizure, even if it was unlawful, by a suit in the court of claims—all weighed against the likelihood that the courts would rule on the legality of the President's action in seizing the steel mills.

The law clerks batted these arguments back and forth even before the district court "downtown" had made a final ruling in the case. We went about our daily tasks of helping our bosses with their work, but from the very first day of the hearing before Judge Holtzoff in April, I think most of us kept something of a weather eye on the Steel Seizure Case, and wondered whether it might come to the Supreme Court.

We were naturally alert to the progress of the hearings of the second stage of the case in the district court, which began on April 24, 1952, before Judge David A. Pine. It was at this stage that the case underwent a rather dramatic transfiguration from the posture it had presented before Judge Holtzoff earlier that month. Judge Holtzoff had accepted all of the established arguments for denying any relief to the steel companies without ever having to decide the question of the President's authority to seize the companies. Perhaps shaping their request at the second hearing in accordance with Judge Holtzoff's response at the earlier hearing, the steel companies did not ask Judge Pine to enjoin the entire seizure, but only to enjoin the government from raising the wages of the steelworkers while the government was in possession of the mills. Judge Pine closely questioned steel-company attorneys on this point, however, and indicated that he was willing to hear extended arguments on the constitutional question in the case—that is, was the President authorized by law to seize the steel plants?

Apparently both the steel-company lawyers and the government lawyers were surprised at Judge Pine's attitude, but the former proceeded to argue their views on the constitutional question. The government attorney, Holmes Baldridge, sought to urge upon Pine the sort of prudential considerations he had successfully urged upon Judge Holtzoff, but to no avail. Judge Pine admonished Baldridge to be prepared to discuss the constitutional issue when court reconvened the following day.

The following day Baldridge advanced to the court the theory that the limitations on governmental power placed in the Constitution—provisions such as the Bill of Rights—limited only the powers conferred upon Congress, and not the power conferred upon the president. While this may have been a plausible or at least interesting legal argument in the abstract, it was not the sort of argument to be emphasized in a case on which there was as much public attention focused as in this one. The government had made a serious mistake, at least in a public-relations sense.

U.S. ARGUES PRESIDENT IS ABOVE COURTS trumpeted *The Washington Post* on the morning of Friday, April 25, 1952. The text of the story contained more of the same:

> [Judge David A. Pine] repeatedly interrupted [Assistant Attorney General Holmes] Baldridge as the government attorney claimed broad "inherent" powers in the President.
>
> "Are you saying that the President claims no statutory power for this seizure?" Pine asked, and Baldridge acknowledged this was true.
>
> "When an emergency situation in this country arises which is so important to the public welfare that something had to be done now, it is the President's duty to step in," Baldridge replied.
>
> Then, the judge asked, "Do you mean that the President can determine whether an emergency exists and that the courts cannot review it to see whether there is really an emergency?"
>
> "That is correct," Baldridge said.

On the following morning, the story was the subject of a banner headline on the first page of the *Post*. Under the headline

JUSTICE DEPARTMENT REPEATS ITS CLAIM PRESIDENT HOLDS
"UNLIMITED POWER," the text of the story read:

The steel seizure case was taken under advisement yesterday
in District Court after the Justice Department contended the
Constitution gives "unlimited power" to the President.

Judge David A. Pine said he would study the case "to the
exclusion of all other court business." He said he hopes to
announce his decision in less than a week.

The two-day hearing reached a climax when Assistant Attorney General Holmes Baldridge declared:

"It is our position that the President is accountable only to
the country, and that the President's decisions are con-
clusive."

At this point, what had been a contest over President
Truman's seizure of the Nation's steel industry shifted into a
conflict over principles of constitutional government.

When Baldridge advanced the theory of absolute power,
Judge Pine interrupted with, "Is that your concept of government?"

Baldridge said that it was.

"Then the Constitution limits Congress and it limits the
Judiciary, but does not limit the Executive?" asked the judge.

"That is the way we read the Constitution," replied the
Assistant Attorney General.

"I have never heard that expressed in any authoritative
case before," said Judge Pine.

The same edition of *The Washington Post* also weighed in on
the editorial page with its views of the government's position, saying under the caption SPEAKING OF HOOEY:

If the President is found to have such authority, we shall no
longer have a government of laws enacted by representatives
of the people. In this era of perpetual emergencies, we shall
have an all-powerful President. And if the courts are not allowed to curb such abuses of executive power, all rights will

be valid only at the discretion of the President. Mr. Truman
may regard the public concern over this issue as a lot of hooey,
as he remarked at his press conference, but citizens bred in
the tradition of freedom and in the need for vigilance in sustaining freedom cannot so regard it. They are more likely to
see the hooey in the fantastic doctrine that in time of stress
the President is a law unto himself.

Nor was the *Post* alone in its editorial censure; the previous
day the American Newspaper Publishers Association had passed a
resolution of censure directed at President Truman for his seizure
of the steel industry. The resolution was adopted at a closed session of the annual meeting of the association with only four dissenting votes among the five hundred publishers attending.
(*Washington Post*, April 25, 1952, page 23).

On these notes, Judge Pine adjourned the two-day hearing
on Friday, and the parties and the nation anxiously awaited his
ruling.

Two days later, on April 29, Judge Pine advised the clerk of
the district court that his decision would be ready at 4:45 P.M.
that day, and the five hundred copies of the opinion that had
been mimeographed were barely adequate for the crowd of lawyers, reporters, and others who were there at the appointed hour
to obtain a copy of the decision. Judge Pine's opinion, occupying
fifteen typed pages, gave the steel companies the "whole hog,"
which one of their attorneys had requested: Unlike Judge
Holtzoff, Judge Pine went directly to the question of whether the
President had the constitutional authority to seize the steel mills.
Judge Pine concluded that he did not have any such authority,
and only later in the opinion were the collateral equitable arguments taken up and rejected.

Judge Pine's decision against the President was not a crippling
setback for the government in a strictly legal sense because the
government had the right to appeal that decision to the federal
court of appeals in Washington, and even if it lost there it could
seek further review in the Supreme Court. But the Pine decision
had an effect on what might be called the political or governmen-

tal climate in Washington, one that was virtually unique in the case of a decision rendered by a single district judge. The Washington newspapers signaled their view of its importance on Wednesday, April 30, the day after Judge Pine had made his ruling. *The Washington Post* proclaimed in a rare double banner headline on page 1:

COURT VOIDS STEEL PLANT SEIZURE;

WORKERS BEGINNING TO WALK OUT

Two front-page stories undergirded the headline, one describing the judge's ruling, and one dealing with the commencement of the strike of the steelworkers following the ruling. In between these two stories, on page 1, was the full text of Judge Pine's fourteen-page opinion. Editorially, the *Post* opined:

> Judge Pine's decision restraining the government from acting under the President's order seizing the steel mills sweeps away the extraordinary arguments about "inherent power" and public necessity with fine majestic strokes. It is an opinion that will long be remembered in the annals of free government. For the Court has grappled with the fundamentals of our constitutional system and come up with a fearless and, in our opinion, unanswerable conclusion, namely, that the President is not the whole Government and that he must act within the law.

The Evening Star had its own banner headline that afternoon, announcing PINE REFUSES TO DELAY ORDER ON STEEL, which likewise led to two front-page stories on the consequences of Judge Pine's decision. The *Star* also carried a story on page 3 entitled BALDRIDGE EXPLAINS BALDRIDGE ON POWERS OF THE PRESIDENCY, describing a memorandum issued the preceding day by the attorney for the government in the Steel Seizure Case. He there explained that his arguments to Judge Pine had been "misunderstood." Editorially, the *Star* praised Judge Pine's opinion for its rejection of the notion of inherent powers in the presidency and its reestablishment of "a rule of law in this country":

These are the broad constitutional principles upon which
Judge Pine has taken his stand. And his stand is one which, if
upheld on appeal, will return this country to constitutional, as
distinguished from personal, government.

The government immediately sought from the court of appeals
a stay of Judge Pine's rulings. But I remember thinking at the time
that whether the government won or lost later rounds in the dispute, Judge Pine's decision and its treatment by the press gave that
dispute a momentum as it worked its way toward the Supreme
Court that it simply would not have had if he had chosen to decide
the case differently. For Judge Pine had taken what was truly a
dramatic step for a district judge. Had the view Judge Holtzoff
expressed after the first hearing ultimately prevailed in the district
court, there might still have been editorial and congressional denunciations of presidential usurpation, and paeans of praise for the
idea of a "government of laws," but these statements would have
been difficult to tie in to the opinion of the court. Somehow, a
holding that an injunction is not a matter of right but a matter of
discretion, or that a plaintiff is not entitled to an injunction if he has
an adequate remedy of law, simply does not set the rafters ringing
the way Judge Pine's decision on the constitutional issue did. Having been in Washington only three months, I knew none of the
lawyers working on the case for the government; but I felt that had
I been they, there would have been a couple of creases more in my
brow after Judge Pine's decision. The public reaction to the ruling,
as much as the ruling itself, suggested that the government was in
more trouble in the case than might have originally been thought
when it commenced only three short weeks ago.

On the day after he issued his ruling, Judge Pine refused to
grant the government's request for a stay. That same morning,
the government asked the court of appeals to grant a stay, and
argument was set on the stay motion for 3:15 that afternoon. Even
more important than the government's motion for a stay, however, was the representation contained in the stay application:
The government was choosing to invoke a rarely used form of
application to the Supreme Court by which the court of appeals

would be bypassed. The government's request to the court of appeals was merely for a stay of Judge Pine's injunction against the steel seizure until the government had time to make application to the Supreme Court for what is called "certiorari before judgment in the court of appeals."

Ordinarily, the government, like any other losing party in the district court, must seek relief from a judgment by appeal to the court of appeals; only if it has invoked that remedy and lost may it petition the Supreme Court for certiorari. But the rules of the Supreme Court provided then, as they do now, that a losing litigant in the district court could immediately seek review from the Supreme Court without going through the court of appeals. The rule went on to state, rather forbiddingly, that a writ of certiorari under such circumstances "will be granted only upon a showing that the case is of such imperative public importance as to justify the deviation from normal appellate processes and to require immediate settlement in this Court."

The government's request for this extraordinary form of review gave the case a momentum that even Judge Pine's decision had not imparted to it. Ordinarily, one appealing a decision from a district court to a court of appeals could expect to wait many months between the time that the appeal was first begun and the time that an opinion deciding the case was handed down by the appellate court. The losing party in the court of appeals could then petition the Supreme Court for a writ of certiorari, but even if review as granted, another period of many months would again go by between the time that review was first sought in the Supreme Court and the time that that body handed down an opinion on the merits of the case. Processed through customary channels of appeal, Judge Pine's opinion might have been stayed by either the court of appeals or the Supreme Court in a matter of hours or days, but a final decision on the merits from the court of appeals would have been months in coming, and a final decision from the Supreme Court would have been at least a year away. But now, because of the government's choice to seek immediate review by the Supreme Court, all of these time sequences were telescoped.

I remembered that sometime during the war there had been

front-page headlines about the government's seizure of the Montgomery Ward headquarters building in Chicago. Out of curiosity I checked through old newspaper files and court decisions to find out what had happened there. Sure enough, *The New York Times* had carried a Chicago-dateline story under a three-line banner headline on the front page of its edition of April 28, 1944.

CHICAGO, APRIL 27—In a specified and virtually unprecedented night hearing, Judge William H. Holly of the Federal District Court at 10:50 o'clock tonight granted a temporary injunction to the Government restraining officials of Montgomery Ward Co. from interfering with the Government's operation of the plant, which was seized with the help of soldiers yesterday. . . .

The Attorney General's action followed by a few hours the forceable eviction of Sewell L. Avery, Chairman of Ward's, from his office and building on the near North Side. He was carried out bodily by two soldiers after refusing to yield control of the properties to [Under-Secretary of Commerce Wayne C.] Taylor and other Government officials in compliance with President Roosevelt's order.

Mr. Taylor became Operating Manager of Ward's Chicago facilities when the Government took them over last night with the aid of forty-four Army troops after Mr. Avery had twice refused to obey the President's order. Soon after today's ejection of the company's chairman, announcement was made that tomorrow or Saturday suit for an injunction would be filed in Federal Court, demanding the ouster of the Washington officials on the ground that they are trespassers. The action presages litigation which probably will go to the Supreme Court for a test of the President's powers.

But in that case the final disposition in the district court in Chicago did not occur until an opinion was filed by Judge Phillip Sullivan on January 27, 1945, nearly nine months after the seizure. The district court held that the War Labor Disputes Act did not authorize the President to take over an essentially retail establishment engaged solely in distribution, and that the President had no authority independent of congressional authorization which would permit him to do so (*United States* v. *Montgomery Ward & Co.*, 58 F. Supp. 408 [1945]).

The government immediately sought review of the district court's adverse decision in the Supreme Court of the United States, seeking to bypass the United States Court of Appeals for the Seventh Circuit in Chicago, just as the government sought to bypass the court of appeals in the Steel Seizure Case. But in the Montgomery Ward case the government had been unsuccessful; six weeks after the decision of the district court the Supreme Court denied the government's petition for certiorari "for the reason that application has been made prior to judgment of the circuit Court of Appeals" (324 U.S. 858).

The court of appeals in Chicago heard the government's appeal from the district court's ruling, and in June 1945, reversed the judgment of the district court and ruled in favor of the government by a vote of two judges to one (*United States* v. *Montgomery Ward & Co.*, 150 F.2d 369 [1945]). The following day Montgomery Ward asked the court of appeals to stay its judgment for thirty days while the company sought a writ of certiorari from the Supreme Court. The district court had earlier stayed its order, so that representatives of the government had remained in possession of the property which they had seized over a year earlier. The court of appeals granted this motion later the same month, and Montgomery Ward filed its petition for certiorari in the Supreme Court on September 7, 1945. The government responded to the petition by pointing out that Montgomery Ward's properties had been returned to it the day before the government's response was filed in the Supreme Court. The government asked that in accordance with Court practice the entire proceedings be dismissed as moot, and although Montgomery Ward opposed this disposition, the Supreme Court did just that by an order dated November 5, 1945 (326 U.S. 690 [1945]). So far as I could tell from the newspaper files, very little publicity had attended the court rulings in the case, perhaps because they had occurred many months and even years after the seizure.

It was by no means certain that the Supreme Court would

grant certiorari before judgment at the government's request in the Steel Seizure Case. But if it did it was conceivable that the Court could hear the case at its next officially scheduled argument session in October, or that the Court might even hear the case argued on an expedited basis before it adjourned for the summer in June. The typical lawyer, when he has finished the trial of a case and gets a verdict or judgment from a trial court, has almost a time-capsule view of an appeal in that case; it is something that will come about eventually, but there are lots of other pressing matters in other cases that can be taken care of before any attention need be given to the substance of the appeal in the case just decided. But now, almost for the first time, it dawned upon those who had been watching the progress of this case that its final judicial disposition might be only a matter of weeks away.

It is probably some indication of the general importance that was attached to this case by the quidnunc element in Washington that half a dozen of us who were law clerks to justices of the Supreme Court went to the court of appeals courtroom that afternoon to hear the government and the steel company argue the government's stay motion. We all had plenty to do for our individual bosses, and would have to make up the time some other way, but this was a "happening" that we did not want to miss. The court of appeals, in which stay motions such as this were normally heard by a panel of two or at the most three judges, did its part to contribute to the feeling that the hearing that afternoon was indeed a happening; all nine judges of the Court sat en banc in the courtroom to hear the government's application. Solicitor General Philip B. Perlman, who had rather conspicuously replaced Holmes Baldridge as the government's oral advocate, and the attorneys for the steel companies argued their respective positions for nearly three hours. Finally, Chief Judge Harold Stephens announced from the bench that the court would retire to consider the motion. I can't remember whether any of the other law clerks who had come to hear the arguments left at this point, but I am sure that most of us wanted to hear how it all ended, and so we milled around the halls of the courthouse with the other lawyers and spectators awaiting the return of the judges to the bench.

Forty minutes later—it was now about 7:00 P.M.—they came back, and Judge Stephens announced that the "court was in division." Judge Henry Edgerton at that point read the court's order granting a stay of Judge Pine's order for forty-eight hours so that the government could petition the Supreme Court for certiorari. The vote in the court of appeals was five to four in favor of the government, and one cynic walking out of the courtroom expressed the view that President Truman's three appointees to the court of appeals had already amply repaid him for their appointments, since each of them voted in favor of the government.

While the government prevailed in the court of appeals, the time limits on the stay gave added momentum to the case. Ordinarily, even where the government seeks review of a district court judgment directly in the Supreme Court by asking for certiorari before judgment, it has sixty days from the date of the district court's decision to file its petition for certiorari. But since this stay was to last only forty-eight hours, the government in effect was required to file its petition for certiorari three days after Judge Pine had ruled. The petition for certiorari would not have been late under the rules if it had taken the full sixty days, but at the expiration of forty-eight hours Judge Pine's injunction against the seizure would have gone back into effect, and this was a consequence the government could not permit. It filed its petition for certiorari on Friday morning, May 2, only to find that under a little-known provision of the rules, the steel companies an hour earlier had filed their own petition for certiorari before judgment. Both parties agreed, in other words, that it was desirable for the Supreme Court to allow them to bypass the court of appeals and obtain immediate review of Judge Pine's decision in the high tribunal.

The regular weekly conference of the Court took place on Saturday, May 3. Again, there was expedition; ordinarily a petition for certiorari does not come before the conference until several weeks after it is filed, but the petitions in this case were taken up the day after they were filed. Late that afternoon word went out over the ticker tape that the Supreme Court, by a vote of 7 to 2, had granted the petition for certiorari before judgment. It had also set the case down for argument nine days later, on Monday, May 12. Finally, while it had continued the stay of Judge Pine's injunction, which had been granted by the court of appeals, it had attached to the stay the very important condition that the government make no unilateral changes in wages or working conditions until the Supreme Court had decided the case.

Matters had now indeed come full circle. The constitutional question of whether the President had authority to seize the steel mills had seemed only a mountain peak seen from afar when the steel-company lawyers had gone to Judge Bastian's home on the night of April 8 to seek a temporary restraining order. Now, less than a month later, it dominated the national legal horizon. It was not merely Judge Pine, or the lawyers in the case, or the newspapers that thought the case was of first magnitude, but the Supreme Court had added its imprimatur to this view. And by imposing upon the government the condition requested by the steel companies in granting the stay, and setting the case for almost immediate argument, the Court had diminished the incentives of the parties to settle their economic dispute.

3

THE
STEEL SEIZURE CASE
IN THE SUPREME COURT

The Court's order granting certiorari and setting the case for oral argument required that the briefs of both parties be filed posthaste, rather than at the more leisurely pace usually countenanced by the Court's rules. Justice Jackson suggested in a somewhat offhand way that both George and I should familiarize ourselves with the briefs in the case when they came in, but he certainly gave no indication at that point, to me at any rate, of any leanings he might have had. I found this to be his practice in the great majority of cases that the Court decided; while the law clerks were frequently called in at least for editing, and less frequently for drafting, after the opinion in the case was assigned, Justice Jackson more often than not did not discuss cases with his law clerks before oral argument and conference.

Naturally George and I devoured the briefs, talking with one another about them, and debating the merits pro and con with law clerks from other chambers. Never was a case more made to order for a group of Supreme Court law clerks, all of whom fancied themselves to be legal whiz kids, than this one which like Minerva seemed to have sprung full-blown from the Washington environment in which we lived and worked. As I recall, in fact, during one lunch hour we even took a formal vote of the clerks on how the case should be decided. The result was an even division between eighteen law clerks, nine voting for the government and nine voting for the steel companies.

There was a certain amount of shadowboxing in a lot of this discussion, since we were painfully aware that it was the justices, and not the law clerks, who were going to decide the case. Most of us were fairly panting to learn how it would be decided, and of course, because we were confidential assistants to the very men who were going to decide the case, one might have thought that we had a good deal of inside information as to how it would come out. If we simply exchanged that information, it would be relatively easy to know in advance of the conference vote how the various justices were leaning.

But whatever one might have thought, at least Justice Jackson's law clerks had no indication from him as to his feeling about the case. The government in its brief relied rather heavily on an opinion that he had written while he was attorney general, shortly before Pearl Harbor, upholding the right of the President to seize the North American Aviation Plant, which had been struck and was therefore unable to deliver government orders for defense materials. Would the justice feel that this precedent was close enough to incline him toward the government's position?

George and I would of course have liked to know, and so would all the other law clerks, just as we would have liked to know of any straws in the wind with respect to the inclinations of the justices for whom they worked. We had no straws in the wind from Justice Jackson, and I suspect that most, if not all of our colleagues were pretty much in the same position. Yet one did not like to admit this fact openly. It was one thing not to be intimately involved in the decisional process, but quite another not even to be the recipient of an occasional confidence as to the result the decisional process was producing. So our exchanges with one another were somewhat guarded when it came to what was going on in our respective chambers; I don't believe anyone claimed to be privy to his justice's thinking, but there were veiled references to "work being done" in the various chambers.

My instincts favored the position of the steel companies, though I can't give any very cogent explanation of why. I think that during my year as a graduate student in government at Harvard, and my three years of law school, I had gotten the impression that the balance of power within the federal establishment had shifted markedly away from Congress and toward the president during the preceding fifteen years, and that this trend was not a healthy one. But when I asked myself how I felt the *Court* would decide the case, rather than how I *wished* it would be decided, I thought the odds were rather heavily in favor of the government.

First there were all the equitable arguments, which had very little drama or newsworthiness to them but which if adopted by the Court would enable it to avoid having to decide whether the President had the constitutional power to seize the steel mills. Six months out of law school and thoroughly confident of my own abilities, I strongly hoped that the Court would strike a blow for freedom and dismiss all these technical arguments, but I certainly couldn't deny that on the basis of existing law the government had made a very strong case respecting them.

But even if the Court should dismiss these equitable arguments, I had the uneasy feeling that a majority would surely vote to uphold the President. My feeling was not based on any detailed survey of the justices or of the law clerks; as I have said, I had no idea how Justice Jackson planned to vote in the case, to say nothing of how any of his colleagues would vote. But any recent law-school graduate knew that during the second term of President Franklin Roosevelt in the late 1930s, a tremendous change had been wrought in the Supreme Court. The "nine old men" who faced President Roosevelt from their judicial bastion on Capital Hill had during Roosevelt's first term held several important New Deal measures unconstitutional; Roosevelt had sought to retaliate by seeking enactment into law of his Court-packing plan, whereby he would have been allowed to appoint additional justices up to the number of fifteen. Congress refused to enact this plan, and Roosevelt lost that battle; but he won the war by virtue of attrition, and during the succeeding four years he had named seven new members to the Court.

These new justices had swept aside past decisions that had limited the power of government, whether federal or state, to regulate economic and social affairs. There had been no decision sanctioning the sort of authority President Truman had sought to wield in the Steel Seizure Case, but the entire decisional trend for fifteen years had been in the direction of aggrandizement of the powers of the president and Congress, with a strong disinclination on the part of the Court to hold the other branches on any sort of a short leash.

When I contemplated the nine individuals who would make this decision, the thought uppermost in my mind was that all nine of them had been appointed by two Democratic presidents, Roosevelt and Truman. Eight of them had been at one time or another active in Democratic politics. I was sufficiently new as a law clerk that I had not had a chance to form an opinion as to whether these sorts of considerations entered into a decision, but I had the suspicion that at the very least a tie would count for the runner— the runner in this case being President Truman. At more than one point in my thinking about the case, I sat back and pondered, just as I am sure lots of other people very interested in the case did, as to what manner of men were these nine justices who were now called upon to decide a very important constitutional question of presidential power.

Fred Vinson was now sixty-two years old, and had served as Chief Justice for six years. He received his law degree in 1911, and after that practiced first in Louisa, Kentucky, and then in the larger city of Ashland, for the next twenty-seven years. He had been active in Democratic politics in Kentucky, and was elected to Congress in 1924 and successively reelected from then until 1938. In the latter year President Roosevelt appointed him to the United States Circuit Court of Appeals for the District of Columbia, where he sat for five years. He resigned in 1943 to accept a series of increasingly responsible executive positions in connection with the war mobilization effort: director of economic stabilization, federal loan administrator, director of war mobilization and reconversion.

When Harry Truman succeeded Franklin Roosevelt as President in April 1945, he began working closely with Vinson, and at his first opportunity brought him into the Cabinet as secretary of the treasury in July 1945. Less than one year later, Chief Justice Harlan F. Stone was fatally stricken while presiding over the Court, and it fell to Harry Truman to pick his successor.

The Court at that time had among its members several strong personalities, and friction among them based on at least one prior incident became the subject of Washington gossip immediately upon the death of Chief Justice Stone in 1946. This friction had its roots in an incident that had occurred in the year preceding Stone's death.

This incident arose out of a petition for rehearing filed by the losing party in a case called *Jewell Ridge Coal Corp.* v. *Local 6167, U.M.W.* There the Court had decided by a vote of 5 to 4 that the union's construction of the Fair Labor Standards Act was correct, and the coal company's contentions to the contrary were rejected. The decision on the merits had provoked unusually acerbic disagreement between the justices in the majority and Justice Jackson, who wrote a dissenting opinion.

The losing party in any decision by the Court is entitled under the Court's Rule to file a petition for rehearing within a stated amount of time; these petitions are very rarely granted, and their denial is usually a matter of form. But in the *Jewell Ridge* case the coal company claimed in its petition for rehearing that Justice Black should have disqualified himself in the case because the mine union's side was argued by a lawyer from Birmingham named Crampton Harris, who for a short period of time twenty years earlier had been the justice's law partner. Justice Black had voted with the majority. Chief Justice Stone, rather than preparing the usual "order list" denial of the petition, drafted a short opinion stating that the question of disqualification of an individual justice is never open for consideration by the full Court. Justice Black insisted that the petition be denied without any explanation, as was the custom in orders denying petitions for rehearing.

The battle lines were now drawn up. Only a justice in the majority, under the Court's rules, would have had standing to vote to grant the petition for rehearing, and none of these five justices wanted it granted. Justice Jackson and Justice Frankfurter, while recognizing that the petition for rehearing itself should not be granted, said that they were unwilling to give "blind and unqualified approval" to Justice Black's having sat in the case. Tempers apparently flared, and at this conference it was decided to postpone decision for a week. During that week, the Chief Justice proposed a compromise draft which he thought "all could join without embarrassment." The Chief Justice's draft simply stated that the Court "is without the authority and does not undertake to pass upon the propriety of the participation, by its members, in the decision of the cases brought here for review." Justice Black responded curtly: "If the *Per Curiam* goes down in this case, as you have today suggested, please put on the names of the Justices who agree to it, and leave mine out."

Those who had sided with Black in the merits of the case also lined up with him against Stone's proposed *Per Curiam*. The Chief Justice then proposed that only the dissenting justices join in the views expressed in his draft, and he, Justice Roberts, Justice Frankfurter, and Justice Jackson agreed.

The petition for rehearing was discussed at conference a second time the following week, and tempers again flared. The result was that Chief Justice Stone backed off from his proposed statement by the four dissenting justices, and with Justice Roberts joined in a simple order of denial desired by Justice Black. Justice Frankfurter joined in a short statement by Justice Jackson explaining that he concurred in the denial of rehearing because only a justice to whom a request for disqualification was addressed was empowered to decide that request.

This rift among the justices received no public attention at the time because the action on the petition for rehearing was buried in a long list of orders and a number of opinions that were announced the same day. But similar friction manifested itself only a few months later, on the occasion of Justice Roberts's announced retirement from the Court. Chief Justice Stone drafted a farewell letter for signature by Roberts's eight colleagues as was customary on such an occasion. Aware of the acrimonious feelings still hanging over from the *Jewell Ridge* petition for rehearing, Stone's letter was by no means effusive, but it was still too effusive for Justice Black, to whom it was first sent because he was the senior associate justice. Black requested that portions be deleted, including the statement that "you have made fidelity to principle your guide to decision."

The Chief Justice, desperately seeking unanimity, told Black to redraft the letter to his taste and circulate it. Black did so, but passed along his revision of the letter as if it had come in this form from the Chief Justice. Justice Reed, the next senior justice, signed, but Justice Frankfurter by the time he received the letter had learned from Stone of Black's objections to the Chief's original draft. Stone now circulated to all members of the Court but Roberts his original draft of the farewell letter together with Black's revised version. Thus the Chief Justice and seven associate justices of the Supreme Court of the United States were once more at loggerheads—this time not about any official business of the Court, but about the wording of one of the amenities traditionally accorded to a departing colleague. Further barbed exchanges took place and the upshot was that when the Court reconvened in the fall of 1945, the justices decided to send no letter at all. This rather peculiar decision, like the denial of the petition for rehearing in the *Jewell Ridge* case the preceding June, evoked no public comment or interest at the time.

The preceding May President Truman had appointed Jackson chief prosecutor for the United States at the Nuremberg trials of the Nazi war criminals. In June 1945, Jackson flew to Europe to help lay the groundwork for this event, and returned to the United States in early September. A week later he returned to Europe and spent the next nine months away from the Supreme Court as the chief prosecutor for the United States in the Nuremberg trials. He was engaged in his duties as prosecutor when the news of Chief Justice Stone's death became public in April 1946. Rumors began to circulate as to whom President Truman might select as a successor, and one newspaper columnist wrote of the internal fracas over the *Jewell Ridge* petition for rehearing under the heading:

SUPREME COURT FEUD—INSIDE STORY OF JACKSON-
BLACK BATTLE LAID BEFORE A HARASSED PRESIDENT

Six weeks after Stone's death, on June 6, 1946, Truman named Fred M. Vinson as Chief Justice of the United States. There seems to be no question that Truman had considered Jackson for the position. It seems quite clear that Franklin D. Roosevelt had virtually promised Jackson the chief justiceship when Jackson was attorney general and Charles Evans Hughes was about to retire from that position. But because war clouds were on the horizon and it was thought desirable to give a bipartisan flavor to appointments at the time, Roosevelt in 1941 elevated Harlan Stone to the chief justiceship and appointed Jackson an associate justice. Whatever Roosevelt might have promised Jackson as to the future was obviously in no way morally binding on President Truman. Truman was very much aware of the controversy between Jackson and Black, and apparently settled upon Vinson in part because of the latter's reputation as a conciliator of diverse factions.

But there is no doubt that Jackson was deeply disappointed by Truman's failure to appoint him, and four days after Vinson's nomination he issued a prepared statement to the reporters covering the Nuremberg trial; the statement was nominally addressed to the chairmen of the Senate and House Judiciary Committees. Far from Washington where the decision would be made as to who should be appointed chief justice, he had apparently been brooding about the events that had taken place within the Court, and about the rumors then circulating about those events. The statement went into great detail about the discussion at conference in connection with the petition for rehearing in the *Jewell Ridge* case, and gave his version of the events in lugubrious detail. Justice Black chose not to respond, Fred M. Vinson was confirmed as Chief Justice, and Justice Jackson resumed his duties as an associate justice beginning with the October term, 1946. But obviously events such as these leave a mark on future relationships.

Chief Justice Vinson, brought in as a conciliator among these feuding factions, largely failed in the task of conciliation. The work of the Supreme Court has enough intellectual meat to it that a justice who is either unable or unwilling to do a certain amount of the cutting of that meat is not apt to emerge as a leader simply on the strength of his abilities as a conciliator. But even if Fred Vinson had had the executive abilities of Charles Evans Hughes or the devotion to the law of Harlan F. Stone, neither he nor any other person in his place would have been able to end the ideological differences on the Court. The bitter personal animus gradually dissipated under his leadership, but the ideological differences remained.

Two important cases involving the power of government to deal with Communism on the domestic front had arisen within a few years after Vinson became Chief Justice. He had written the opinions for the Court in both *American Communications Association* v. *Douds,* decided in 1950, and in *Dennis* v. *United States,* decided in 1951. These cases had upheld respectively the government's victory in the trial of the Communist party leadership before Judge Medina in New York, and an act of Congress requiring non-Communist affidavits from labor-union officials.

The Chief Justice's extensive experience in government—first fourteen years in Congress, and then three years of high-level executive-branch service during a critical time in the nation's history—undoubtedly gave him a feel for the way government works that some of his colleagues did not possess. Three of his colleagues on the bench were veterans of the Department of Justice, and were thus no strangers to government service in the executive branch. But the attorney general to a large extent, and the solicitor general to an even larger extent, remain primarily lawyers rather than executives. They are, to be sure, lawyers for the government, and one who serves in a policy-making position in the Department of Justice is apt to see a far wider range of important legal issues during a given time than he could possibly see if he were engaged in the private practice of law. But the issues he sees are nonetheless legal issues. Vinson's experience in the executive branch had not been as a lawyer, but as an executive and manager.

It seemed to me as I pondered how the justices might vote in the Steel Seizure Case that this very sort of experience was bound to incline the Chief Justice toward the government's position. He had served three demanding years trying to manage difficult situations on behalf of the government, an experience that is bound to incline on toward a practical rather than a theoretical approach even to legal questions. It was easy to imagine him thinking that President Truman would not have seized the steel mills unless he had thought it absolutely necessary to maintain the production of these mills in the national interest, and that the courts therefore should bend over backward to uphold his "best effort" in this difficult situation.

To law clerks who didn't work for him, I think the Chief Justice appeared distant and old; a good deal older, for example, than did Frankfurter, who was in fact eight years his senior. Law clerks who did work for him spoke of his ready wit and fund of stories based on nearly thirty years' life in Washington. He, Tom Clark, and Sherman Minton managed to get out to a few of the Washington Senators baseball games in the spring of the year, and rumor had it that Vinson remained an intimate "crony" of the President and participated in regular poker games at the White House.

Hugo Lafayette Black was the senior associate justice on the Court. He had one of the most mellifluous voices and delightful accents that I, a northerner, had ever heard. Not for nothing had he been a renowned stump speaker in his two victorious campaigns to be elected United States senator from Alabama. I can still remember him beginning his announcement of a dissenting opinion in a rather technical and uninteresting case involving administrative law by saying that the case involved a fight between "large corporate truckers" and "little independent truckers"; the correct result, in Justice Black's eyes, seemed foreordained by that description of the parties.

After graduating from the University of Alabama Law School with honors, he moved to Birmingham to hang out his shingle and seek his fortune. In Birmingham he worked part time as a police-court judge trying defendants accused of minor crimes; for a while he served as prosecuting attorney for the county, and he served briefly stateside in the United States Army during the First World War. Upon his return from service he became a very successful private practitioner, representing some labor unions but specializing in plaintiffs' personal-injury claims. When he announced for the Democratic nomination for the United States Senate seat in 1926, he was regarded as an underdog to several of his opponents whose names were better known and who had been active in politics for a longer period of time. But Black tirelessly campaigned in every part of the state, running as a candidate of the "common man," and duly won the Democratic nomination, which was then tantamount to election. He was reelected to the seat by a large margin six years later in 1932. During his second term he was the principal author of a bill that later became the Fair Labor Standards Act: It was the first congressional prescription of national standards for minimum wages and maximum hours in American industry. He also chaired at least two Senate investigatory committees looking into various lobbying practices, during which he received considerable publicity. He developed a reputation as a strong New Dealer and supported President Franklin Roosevelt's program lock, stock, and barrel, including the latter's ill-fated Court-packing plan.

During the course of the debates on that plan Justice Willis Van Devanter, one of the nine old men, had announced his intention to retire, and therefore Roosevelt was able to appoint to a vacant seat on the Court even though his Court-packing bill was killed by the Senate. Less than a month after the Senate buried the Court-packing plan, Hugo Black was invited to the White House by Franklin D. Roosevelt. Black's biographer describes the encounter in these words:

> "Taking an appointment form from a desk drawer, [the President] said, "Hugo, this is a form for the nomination of a Supreme Court Justice. May I fill in your name?" Black replied, "Mr. President, are you sure that I'll be more useful in the Court than in the Senate?" The President replied, "Hugo, I wish you were twins because Barkley says he needs you in the

Senate; but I think you'll be more useful on the Court." On August 12, 1937, the President put his hardest-hitting New Dealer on the Supreme Court. [Frank, John P., "Hugo L. Black" in Friedman and Israel, Vol. III, p. 23]

The nomination was roundly criticized in establishment circles outside the South, but praised by the minority of the press strongly sympathetic to the New Deal. The Senate confirmed the nomination by a vote of 63 to 16, and Justice Black and his wife set out for a European vacation. While they were absent, in September 1937, the Pittsburgh *Post Gazette* ran a series of stories revealing that Black had been a member of the Ku Klux Klan during his days in Alabama politics. Black made a national radio address on his return to the country, admitted that he had been a member of the Klan for a short time, said he had resigned sometime ago, and had had nothing further to do with it. The matter then dropped from public notice.

On the Court Black, as expected, became a champion of "judicial restraint" when dealing with social and economic legislation of the kind he had actively fought for in the Senate—laws, for example, regulating the minimum wages and maximum hours of workers in interstate commerce, and laws regulating the relationship between management and labor. This came as a surprise to no one. But after he had been on the Court for a few years, he began to differentiate sharply between this kind of law on the one hand, and on the other hand, laws that tended to infringe rights he thought to be guaranteed in specific language by the Bill of Rights. He became a strong upholder of the constitutional rights of criminal defendants and political dissidents; as to them he was not an apostle of judicial restraint. He had dissented in both of the two recent cases written by Vinson upholding governmental authority to prosecute Communists and to require non-Communist affidavits.

On the thirtieth anniversary of Justice Black's appointment— in 1967, some fifteen years after my arrival at the Court as a law clerk—a distinguished student of United States constitutional law spoke of Black as the most influential of the many strong figures who have sat during the thirty years that have passed in his Justiceship. He has exhibited to a singular degree an intense moral commitment, concentrated through the focus of an unwavering vision, and brought to bear with immense prowess. One thinks of Justice Brandeis' confident formula for achievement: brains, rectitude, singleness of purpose, and time. [Frank, op. cit., quoting Professor Paul Freund]

One year after President Roosevelt appointed Black to the Court, Justice George Sutherland announced his retirement and to replace him the President chose Stanley Forman Reed of Kentucky. By the time I saw him when I was a law clerk, Justice Reed was in his late sixties and bald as an egg. To me he looked more like a doctor than a lawyer, although I cannot say why. His visage in the formal picture of the Court taken about that time makes him look quite avuncular, with broad shoulders and large ears.

He was thought of as the quintessential moderate. In the late 1940s, when there had been four liberals on the Court, he often provided them with a fifth vote to vindicate their views of constitutional law. But in recent years he had sided with Chief Justice Vinson in rejecting civil-liberties claims in cases such as *American Communications Association* v. *Douds,* and *Dennis* v. *United States,* 341 U.S. 494. What, if anything, I thought to myself, could be foretold about his vote in the Steel Seizure Case?

Reed had practiced in his native Kentucky until 1929 when he went to Washington to become a lawyer for the government. After serving as general counsel for two different government agencies, Reed was appointed by Franklin Roosevelt as solicitor general in 1935. This little-known office was very important at the time Reed occupied it and is, if anything, more important today. The solicitor general's ranking in the Department of Justice hierarchy varies from administration to administration, but his job does not: He is responsible for conducting all of the government's litigation in the Supreme Court of the United States, and also has considerable supervisory powers over the United States attorneys in the field who seek to appeal lower-court decisions adverse to the government. The solicitor general and his staff must not only write the briefs and orally argue cases to which the government is a party in the Supreme Court, but they must also decide which of the cases the government loses in the lower courts they will seek to have reviewed by the Supreme Court, and which they will let go. Understandably, the lawyers in the office of the solicitor general must be closely attuned to the current mood of the Court, and yet at the same time they must vigorously urge upon the Court the position adopted by the government.

Reed's nomination came at a time when the solicitor general was just beginning to catch the bleak winds blowing from the "marble palace" across the plaza from the U.S. Capitol. It generally takes a year or two for a challenge to a newly enacted law to wind its way through the court system to the point where it may be reviewed by the Supreme Court. In the next three years, Reed was to handle a number of vitally important government cases, losing some and winning others.

One year after Franklin Roosevelt appointed Stanley Reed to the Court, he filled the vacancy resulting from the death of Justice Cardozo by appointing his long-time adviser and confidant, Professor Felix Frankfurter of the Harvard Law School. Following his distinguished performance as a member of the Harvard Law School class of 1906, Frankfurter successively served a short time as an associate in a large Wall Street law firm, as an assistant to Henry L. Stimson when the latter was United States attorney for the Southern District of New York, and as Stimson's assistant when he became secretary of war under President William Howard Taft.

He returned to Harvard Law School in 1914, and except for a period of service on President Wilson's War Labor Mediation Board during the First World War, remained on the faculty of that institution until Roosevelt appointed him to the Court in January 1939.

Frankfurter was probably the preeminent academic student of the Supreme Court for much of the time he taught at Harvard Law School; he contributed major volumes analyzing its work, and significant articles dealing with various aspects of that work. He had been an adviser to Franklin Roosevelt when the latter was governor of New York from 1929 to 1933, and retained that role in a totally unofficial capacity when Roosevelt became President. Frankfurter delighted in his ability to place bright young law graduates in key spots in the many New Deal agencies that were created during Roosevelt's first term in office, and these bright young men were referred to as Felix's "happy hot dogs."

Frankfurter's participation in public affairs while on the Harvard law faculty had not been limited to scholarly articles. He served a role as public gadfly during the famous case of *Sacco and Vanzetti*, which was much in the public print during the 1920s; he argued a number of cases in the Supreme Court of the United States; he went to the Paris Peace Conference in 1919 to represent the interests of those who wished to see a permanent Jewish homeland established in what was then Palestine.

Frankfurter had been a forceful and vigorous critic of the "Old Court" and its propensity to declare unconstitutional state and federal legislation designed to improve the lot of working people by regulating business in one way or another. In this respect he was a disciple of Justice Brandeis, who retired from the Supreme Court after serving twenty-three years a month after Frankfurter's appointment. Frankfurter continued, after his appointment, to adhere to his broad view of governmental power to regulate economic and social matters.

But during the 1940s, the cutting edge of the debate over constitutional law shifted from the constitutional validity of economic and social regulation such as the Fair Labor Standards Act and the National Labor Relations Act to claims of civil liberties violations on behalf of various kinds of dissidents. Several of the Roosevelt appointees to the Court, led by Justices Black and William O. Douglas, drew a distinction between the constitutional limitation on the government's authority to regulate economic and social affairs, and its authority to regulate freedom of speech and of the press. They likewise were very receptive to claims by criminal defendants that the government had impinged on some constitutional right in the course of prosecuting them for the commission of a crime. But Frankfurter adhered to the belief that judicial restraint was required in one area as much as another, and therefore as the 1940s drew to a close he found himself allied with the conservative wing of the Court against its liberal wing. He had voted with the majority in the case of *American Communications Association* v. *Douds,* and had joined the Chief Justice's opinion in *Dennis* v. *United States* in 1951.

I must have met Felix Frankfurter on the first or second day after I went to work for Justice Jackson. He and Justice Jackson were in and out of each other's chambers often; they tended to agree on most legal issues, and enjoyed discussing them between themselves. One morning he simply "bounced" into the clerks' office where George and I were working, and said something to the effect that it looked like George had found someone to help him with all of the certiorari memos. Both of us stood up, and George introduced me to him.

In the argot of 1952, Felix Frankfurter would have been described as magnetic; in the argot of today, he would be described as charismatic. He could not have been more than five feet two or three inches tall, and he was possessed of bright eyes and a steady gaze. He immediately began talking to me about first one subject and then another, so that I was barely able to supply answers to his rapid-fire questions. We even managed to get into a lively argument about a recent opinion he had written for the Court, which I had the temerity to criticize. But unlike almost anyone else who had been a Supreme Court justice for fifteen years and before that a distinguished legal academician, he did not look askance at my temerity in venturing the criticism. He obviously welcomed it as an opportunity to engage in debate with the nearest person at hand who would defend a position with which he disagreed. In what seemed to me the middle of the debate, he quite suddenly left to talk to Justice Jackson, flinging over his shoulder to me the challenge that he bet I could not find a single case from any state supreme court that would support my proposition.

I must confess that I took some time off from my work for Justice Jackson that afternoon, and went up to the Supreme Court law library in search of the sort of cases Justice Frankfurter had assured me I would not find. I did find one that I thought filled the bill, took it over to his chambers, and left it with his secretary, assuming that this would be the last I would hear of it. But the next time I met him in the hall, he insisted that the case I had brought him was not the "white horse" case I had thought, and our debate briefly continued right there.

Obviously all of this made a great impression on me, two months out of a law school in the Far West which did not then have the national reputation it does today. I was tremendously drawn to him by his willingness to discuss and argue while asking no quarter by reason of his position or eminence. Although the Court was close to adjournment for the summer at the time it heard argument in the Steel Seizure Case, I would stay on next term as a law clerk for Justice Jackson and come to know Justice Frankfurter even better. I attended an elegant dinner at his Georgetown home with his law clerks and a few law clerks from other chambers, where the first course represented my first exposure to vichyssoise. I came within a hair of calling the maid's attention to the fact that my soup was cold and ought to be reheated. My good friend Alex Bickel, who clerked for Justice Frankfurter the following year, brought him to the party celebrating my engagement; in this group of typical Washington young people of the time, he played the role of the courtly Viennese to the hilt, kissing my fiancée's hand upon being introduced, and captivating the entire group.

When I was finally ready to leave my clerkship a year after the decision in the Steel Seizure Case, Justice Frankfurter one day asked me what I would be doing after I left. I told him that I was going to work for the firm of Evans, Hull, Kitchel, and Jenckes in Phoenix, and he nodded noncommittally. He asked me if I was going to get into politics, and urged me to do so, saying that conservatives as well as liberals ought to get active on the political scene.

A day or two later he and I were again talking about something when he asked me, out of a clear blue sky, so to speak, whether the Phoenix firm I was going with had at one time been called

Ellinwood and Ross. I told him that it had. He then responded that he thought that firm would suit me just fine. I had no idea what he was talking about at the time, and it was only after I arrived in Arizona and mentioned the incident that someone out there told me of Felix Frankfurter's experience during the First World War in Bisbee, Arizona, as a member of Wilson's War Labor Mediation Board. The Arizona copper industry was shut down by a bitter strike against the Phelps Dodge Company, and Frankfurter was one of the board members who came to Arizona to investigate the dispute. Sitting one morning having breakfast in the Copper Queen Hotel, Felix Frankfurter was approached by the sheriff of Cochise County, who told him in thinly veiled language that if he was not out of town by sunset, he would regret it. It was commonly thought that the firm of Ellinwood and Ross, which represented Phelps Dodge at that time, rendered not only legal advice but strategic advice to the company and its minions, among whom was more than one local official as well.

I doubt that my fondness for Justice Frankfurter was any different from that of any other law clerk or law student whom he first dazzled and then befriended. But it was brought home to me in that spring of 1952 that my reaction to him was by no means the universal one. My new landlord had a different opinion of him.

I had greatly enjoyed the hospitality of my great-aunt, and I thought that she probably enjoyed having me around, but after several weeks of staying with her I bestirred myself to find lodgings of my own. I answered a classified ad in the newspaper for a basement apartment on Kennedy Street N.W., a little bit east of Sixteenth Street. The lady of the house who showed me the basement apartment was a pleasant, middle-aged woman, and since the apartment met my principal wants I took it. Because my apartment had a separate entrance, I saw virtually nothing of her or her husband until my second rent payment was due, at which time I duly wrote out a check and knocked at their front door. The door was answered by the man of the house, who when he learned of my errand asked me to come in and sit down. I profered him a check in the correct amount which, perhaps with undue caution, I had made payable to both him and his wife.

When he noticed this fact, he told me that in the future the checks should be made out only to him, and explained that since his wife had no bank account there was no point in putting her name on the check. I thought briefly of explaining to him the knowledge acquired in my law-school course on bills and notes— that she needn't have a bank account in order to negotiate the check—but decided to let sleeping dogs lie. My landlord, who was long-faced with a sallow complexion and rather greasy hair pompadoured straight back from his forehead, then observed, "I understand you work for one of the Supreme Court justices."

I acknowledged with some pride that I worked for Justice Jackson.

"What's the story on this fellow Julius Frankfurter?" my landlord inquired. "I understand he's right in bed with the Communists."

I corrected him as to Justice Frankfurter's first name, and told him that quite contrary to his view, Justice Frankfurter had voted against the Communists in the *Dennis* case, and was one of the more conservative justices of the present Court. My landlord looked at me somewhat doubtfully, his expression suggesting not so much that I was trying to put something over on him, as that someone else, perhaps Justice Frankfurter, had put something over on me. He was obviously totally unconvinced by what I told him.

Perhaps his qualification to impartially judge the merits of those involved in the administration of justice might be thought questionable by reason of another incident that happened to me only a week or so later. My new location was nearly as far north of Capitol Hill as I had been at my aunt's house, but because I was now east of Rock Creek Park, I took a wholly new route to work, usually going by the Soldiers' Home en route. One morning when I was a little later getting started than I should have been, I was driving along Michigan Avenue going about forty miles an hour in a thirty-five-mile zone. Sure enough, a motorcycle policeman appeared in my rearview mirror with red light flashing, and I was given a ticket. I was offended by the officer's manner—I daresay most motorists who are stopped are quite critical of the officer's manner—and I was outraged by the fact that he said he had clocked me at forty-five miles per hour, a figure that he put on the ticket.

This encounter continued to rankle as I drove home from work that evening, and like a true lawyer I had managed to persuade myself not merely that the officer was wrong as to my speed but that I never should have been stopped at all. They always allow you five miles over the speed limit, I reasoned, and I was only going five miles over the speed limit; if the officer had correctly clocked my speed, he would have seen that I was only going five miles over the speed limit, and would never have stopped me.

In this frame of mind I parked my car in front of the Kennedy Street house and was walking toward the entrance to my apartment when my landlord, who was sitting on his glass-enclosed porch, waved to me and asked me to join him. I went up on the porch and sat down with him, declining his offer of a drink, and recounted to him my tale of woe about the traffic ticket. He nodded sympathetically during my account, and when I had finished he asked me if I had the traffic ticket with me. I said that I did, and he asked to see it. So far as I knew he had no connection with the Metropolitan Police Department, although I remember his wife having said that he worked for the government, but I handed it to him. He then said that he would see what could be done about it, and I should check with him tomorrow night. My better instincts told me that I should protest, but my sense of self-pity immediately overcame my better instincts. I managed to convince myself in the twinkling of an eye that the most he planned to do was to relate my account of things to someone who could perhaps right the injustice that had been inflicted upon me.

The next evening I looked for him up on the porch as I got out of my car, and sure enough he was there with a rather knowing smile on his face. I inquired of him whether he had had any success, and he assured me that he had, that the whole matter was taken care of. I thanked him profusely, and for a moment thought I would be spared any further inquiry into just how he had accomplished this feat. But as I turned to leave, he coughed slightly and told me that the officer who had "intervened" on my behalf wanted a fifth of whiskey. Momentarily I felt a sense of moral outrage—I had never agreed to anything like this! But then I quickly asked myself, "What did you agree to? That your traffic ticket would be fixed but that you would not pay the going rate?" I told my landlord that I would have the fifth of whiskey for him the next evening, and I did.

My landlord's idea of Justice Frankfurter might be set at naught because of his apparently cynical view of the justice system generally, but I am sure that a number of other people in the United States who paid very little attention to the Supreme Court or even to the major outlines of its decisions may have shared my landlord's view of Frankfurter. Foreign name, high priest of the New Deal, witness for the defendant in the Alger Hiss case; what more did one need to conclude that he was indeed "in bed with the Communists"?

I learned much later from members of the Court who had sat with Frankfurter that the latter in conference discussion with the other justices never fully relinquished his role as a very intellectually gifted professor of law lecturing to students some of whom might be a little slow to see the point. But this very manner assumed in conversation with law clerks endeared him to them; at least it made a warm admirer out of me.

The fourth Roosevelt appointment to the Supreme Court had come only a month after Frankfurter's, upon the retirement of Justice Brandeis. For this vacancy President Roosevelt selected William O. Douglas, who had grown up in the state of Washington. Douglas was only forty when he was appointed to the Court in April 1939, the youngest man to be appointed since Joseph Story had been chosen by President James Madison in 1811. When I first saw him in the spring of 1952, he was in his early fifties, spare and rangy, with sandy hair and a craggy face.

Douglas had grown up in Yakima, Washington, having to do a number of odd jobs even in high school to help his widowed mother support the family. He graduated from Whitman College in Walla Walla, Washington, and then taught school for a couple of years in that area. He lost his small amount of savings in a business venture that turned sour, and when he went across the country to enroll in Columbia Law School, he rode in a freight car in charge of a herd of sheep. He made a brilliant record at Columbia and upon graduation spent two years with the Cravath firm in New York as an associate. He then returned to Yakima to practice law, but was soon enticed back to the East Coast by the offer of a professorship at Columbia Law School. He shortly moved from Columbia to Yale Law School, where he became a recognized authority in the law of corporate finance.

Shortly after the coming of Franklin Roosevelt and the New Deal in 1933, Douglas left the Yale faculty to head up a division of the newly formed Securities and Exchange Commission. He was appointed a commissioner of that body in 1936, and was named its chairman a year later. He was an intimate of many prominent New Dealers, joining in the President's poker circle, which often met at the home of Harold Ickes in suburban Maryland. It was not at all unexpected that Douglas, despite his youth, would be chosen by Roosevelt to succeed Justice Brandeis in 1939.

On the Court, Douglas had joined with the other Roosevelt appointees to solidly establish the validity of both state and federal regulation of business. But when in the 1940s the split among the Roosevelt appointees occurred on civil-rights issues, Douglas along with Black championed the claims of civil-rights litigants who sought to impose constitutional limits upon governmental power in that area.

Justice Douglas maintained a number of outside interests while on the bench. He was a conservationist long before it became fashionable to be one, and his efforts were instrumental in bringing the C&O Canal into the National Park System. In 1952 he had begun traveling extensively during the summer, and the first of his many books, *Strange Lands and Friendly People*, had just been published.

He had been considered for the vice-presidential nomination of the Democratic party in both 1944 and 1948, and some thought that he might be available for the ticket in the November election of 1952. Due to a strange set of circumstances he had barely missed succeeding Franklin Roosevelt when the latter died in of-

fice in 1945. During Roosevelt's third term Henry A. Wallace was
the Vice-President, but while the Democratic National Convention meeting in Chicago in 1944 was willing to nominate Roosevelt for a fourth term as President, it was unwilling to nominate
Wallace for a second term as Vice-President. Roosevelt sent word
to the convention that he would prefer to see Wallace renomi-
nated as Vice-President, but that if it was not to be Wallace, he
would be happy to run on a ticket with either Bill Douglas or
Harry Truman. Douglas recounts that this message was relayed
through D.N.C. Chairman Robert Hannegan. When the message
came from Roosevelt it placed Douglas's name before Truman's,
but by the time it was read to the convention Truman's name was
in first position. Truman, of course, was nominated to run with
Roosevelt. Were it not for this quirk of fate, perhaps it might
have been President William O. Douglas, and not President
Harry S Truman, who seized the steel mills.

The most junior of the five Roosevelt appointees to the Court
at this time was my boss, Robert H. Jackson. He grew up in the
small town of Frewsburg in northwestern New York State, and
after graduating from high school, he attended Albany Law
School in the state capital where he did two years' work in one.
He then returned to western New York to continue reading law in
his cousin's law office. He passed the state bar exam and was
admitted to practice in 1913 at the age of twenty-one. He was the
last justice of the Supreme Court to have been admitted to practice law without having obtained a degree from a law school. For
the next twenty-one years he engaged in an increasingly successful law practice in western New York. During the depths of
the Depression, in the relatively small city of Jamestown, his
practice netted him an average of $30,000 per year.

In 1934 Henry Morgenthau, Roosevelt's fellow Hudson River
squire and secretary of the treasury, prevailed upon Jackson to
come to Washington as general counsel to what was then called
the Bureau of Internal Revenue. While in that position Jackson
was the principal government lawyer in the civil tax-fraud case
against Andrew Mellon, who had been Calvin Coolidge's secretary of the treasury. After nearly a year, the trial resulted in a

standoff between the government and Mellon. In 1936 Jackson was moved to the Justice Department as an assistant attorney general, and served successively as the head of the tax division and the head of the antitrust division. He was one of the principal spokesmen within the administration for President Roosevelt's Court-packing plan; although he did not fully agree with the plan, he felt that some sort of "reform" of the Court was necessary and that the plan proposed by the President was the only one with any chance of acceptance.

In 1938 he was promoted to the office of solicitor general and proved such an able advocate for the government that Justice Brandeis commented, "Jackson should be solicitor general for life." In 1940 he was named attorney general, and was at one time thought to be Franklin Roosevelt's choice to succeed him as President. In the event, however, it proved that Roosevelt did not want any candidate groomed to succeed him; he ran for a third term in 1940 and was elected by a large majority, and the following year he named Jackson to the Supreme Court. Jackson was viewed as an ardent New Dealer at the time of his nomination, but his votes proved to be a good deal less predictable than those of Justices Black and Douglas.

Remarks he made to me at various times gave me the impression that Justice Jackson by 1952 no longer believed very enthusiastically that the New Deal formula of governmental solutions for the country's major problems would work. I remember once when we were coming back from a very pleasant outing that he had arranged for Elsie Douglas, George Niebank, me, and himself on Chesapeake Bay right after the decision in the Steel Seizure Case. He had chartered a boat and we had gone fishing for rockfish out in the bay. Although I have never been any great shakes as a fisherman I greatly enjoyed this expedition. Driving back on the hot June day past some government buildings, the justice commented that he thought one of the great harms wrought by central air conditioning was that it had enabled the government in Washington to function during the summer, rather than closing up shop and leaving people alone the way it had formerly done. As we talked about this effect, I realized that his comment was only half in jest.

After serving five years on the Court, Jackson was named as chief prosecutor for the United States at the Nuremberg war-crimes trials which followed the Allied victory in the Second World War. I had not been paying much attention to public opinion about these trials at the time that they took place, but by 1952 I was aware of the fact that there had been a good deal of criticism of the trials themselves, and of Jackson's participation in them. There seemed to many to be an element of *ex post facto* lawmaking about them, and a good deal of vagueness about what constituted the crime of "waging an aggressive war." Both within the Court and without, there was feeling that Jackson should not have left his duties at the Court for a full year unless he resigned the office, and also a feeling that a sitting judge was not ideally cast in the role of a prosecutor. I was therefore quite loath to bring up the subject with Justice Jackson.

I had spent a year at the Harvard Graduate School of Arts and Sciences before going to law school, and one of my close friends from that time visited me in Washington shortly after I started working for Justice Jackson. He was working on a Ph.D. in international relations, and was very interested in the Nuremberg trials. One morning he drove in to work with me in order that he could see the Court building, and I was in the process of showing him around my office when Justice Jackson, as he did on occasion, popped his head in. I introduced my friend to him, and much to my chagrin the friend asked him point-blank how he felt now about the Nuremberg trials.

I was almost ready to hide my head under my desk in embarrassment, but Justice Jackson did not seem to find the question at all embarrassing. He proceeded with a very reasoned, often eloquent, defense of these prosecutions, and I told my friend afterward that I did not think he would ever hear an abler one.

Following his return from the Nuremberg prosecutions, and at a time when the Court was increasingly concerned with challenges to governmental actions that were claimed to infringe on civil liberties, rather than challenges to economic and social legislation, Jackson voted increasingly with the conservative wing of the Court. He agreed in part and disagreed in part with the result reached by the Court in the *Douds* case, and voted with the Chief

Justice in the *Dennis* case. Indeed, the opinion he had written in *Sacher* v. *United States*, which had been circulated the day I came to work for him, upheld the contempt citation against the lawyers who had defended the Communists in the *Dennis* trial.

Justice Jackson undoubtedly drove the snappiest car of any of the nine justices: it was a robin's-egg blue late-model Buick convertible, which he drove back and forth to his home at Hickory Hill in McLean. The only remotely close contender for this honor that I knew of was Stanley Reed's black Chrysler Imperial, a car that veritably cried out for a chauffeur but was piloted at a very deliberate pace by the justice himself. The Reeds had lived at the Mayflower Hotel since 1929, and would continue to live there until 1975—surely some sort of a record. Sherman Minton and his wife lived right across the street from the Supreme Court in an apartment in the Methodist Building; Felix Frankfurter walked part of the way from his Georgetown home with Secretary of State Dean Acheson most mornings, and then took a cab. He relied on his law clerks and their cars for the rest of his automotive transportation. Chief Justice Vinson and Justice Burton both lived at residential hotels: the Chief Justice and his wife at the Wardman Park and Justice Burton and his wife at the Dodge Hotel. The Burtons had a reputation of being habitués of embassy parties and other events on the Washington social circuit.

Franklin Roosevelt died suddenly in Warm Springs, Georgia, on April 12, 1945, having served but little over a month of the fourth term to which he had been elected the previous November. He was succeeded by his Vice-President, Harry S Truman, and Truman had been in office only a few months when the retirement of Justice Roberts gave him a vacancy to fill on the Supreme Court.

Considerable public sentiment was expressed that the new justice ought to be a Republican; Roberts was a Republican who had been appointed by Herbert Hoover, and the remaining eight justices had all been placed in their present positions by Franklin Roosevelt. Truman, moved by this sentiment, nominated Harold H. Burton, Republican senator from Ohio, and he was of course promptly confirmed by the Senate.

Burton had been born in Massachusetts in 1888, and attended Bowdoin College and Harvard Law School. Upon graduation from the latter institution in 1912, he moved first to Cleveland, Ohio, and then successively to Salt Lake City, Utah, and Boise, Idaho, where he did legal work for utility companies. He served overseas as a captain in the First World War, and was decorated with the Purple Heart and the Belgian Croix de Guerre. When he was mustered out he returned to Cleveland where he lived until his appointment to the Court some twenty-five years later. He was thrice reelected mayor of Cleveland, and was elected as a Republican senator in 1940. He was named as a minority member of the Senate War Production Committee chaired by none other than Senator Harry S Truman from Missouri. Burton and Truman developed a close working relationship on this committee, and Truman admired Burton's industriousness and fairness in dealing with committee matters.

Burton tended to side with the conservative wing of the Court in cases involving governmental power; he had joined the opinion of Chief Justice Vinson in both the *Douds* and *Dennis* cases. He was not thought to be either a brilliant lawyer or an interesting writer but he was greatly respected for the total detachment with which he approached the cases he was obliged to decide.

For four years after Burton's appointment, the Court functioned without any change of personnel. Then, quite suddenly, Justice Frank Murphy died in July 1949, and Justice Wiley Rutledge in September 1949. Appointed by Roosevelt, both had been staunch allies of Justices Black and Douglas in the liberal bloc on the Court, and their sudden departure had a marked effect on the Court's alignment. This was because President Truman, now in his second term, chose Tom C. Clark of Texas and Sherman Minton of Indiana to replace them.

Tom Clark was born in Dallas, Texas, in 1899, and received his law degree from the University of Texas in 1922. His father was a prosperous Dallas lawyer, and Clark practiced with his father's firm and then elsewhere very successfully in Dallas for fifteen years. He was active in Democratic party politics in the state, and in 1937 joined the Justice Department. He worked on

important assignments while there, and was made assistant attorney general in charge of the Criminal Division in 1943. As head
of the Criminal Division he prosecuted those who sought to de-
fraud the government, many of whom were uncovered in the first
instance by the investigative activities of the Truman committee.
He thus came to know Harry Truman, and when the latter became President in 1945 he appointed Clark his attorney general.
Clark was active in promoting the government's "loyalty program" during the beginning of the cold-war period, and was the
first compiler of the then famous "Attorney General's list" of sub-
versive organizations. He argued several cases before the Supreme Court during his tenure as attorney general, and his
nomination by Truman to the vacancy in 1949 came as no surprise. Clark's nomination was opposed in the Senate by liberals
who disliked his support of the government's loyalty program, but
he was confirmed with little difficulty. In the three years between
the time of his appointment and the decision in the Steel Seizure
Case, Clark had all but invariably voted with Chief Justice Vinson
in cases such as *Douds* and *Dennis*.

To fill the second of the two vacancies occurring in the fall of
1949, Truman named Sherman Minton, then a judge of the Court
of Appeals for the Seventh Circuit in Chicago, and before that,
United States senator from Indiana. Minton was born in
Georgetown, Indiana, directly across the Ohio River from
Louisville, Kentucky, in 1890, and graduated from Indiana Law
School first in his class. He was active in Democratic politics in
Indiana, and was elected to the Senate in 1934. He was one of the
dozen and a half senators who earned the accolade—if it be
that—"battalion of death" because even after all hope had been
lost for passage of Roosevelt's Court-packing bill, these loyalists
voted against recommitting the bill and thereby killing it.

Minton's entry into the Senate in 1934 coincided with that of
the freshman senator from Missouri, the newly elected Harry S
Truman. Minton had been considered for the vacancy to which
Roosevelt ultimately appointed Hugo Black, and with Truman's
penchant for appointing friends to high office it was quite natural
for him to name Minton to the High Court.

These, then, were the nine justices who were going to decide whether or not President Truman had acted lawfully when he seized the steel mills. The time they had allowed the parties and themselves to prepare for oral argument was remarkably short; on Saturday, May 3, the Court had entered its order granting certiorari, and only nine days later the case was set for oral argument. The Justice Department attorneys worked until midnight for five successive days and turned out a one-hundred-and-seventy-five-page brief. The steel-company attorneys undoubtedly put in the same sort of hours, and filed comprehensive briefs setting forth their reasons for upholding Judge Pine's decision. The Court set aside five hours for oral argument of the case, allowing two and a half hours to each side, as well as time to the steelworkers' union to argue as *amicus curiae,* a phrase that literally means "friend of the court"—someone who is not a party to the litigation, but who believes that the court's decision may affect its interests.

At twelve noon on Monday, May 12, every seat in the public section of the courtroom was filled, and the lawyers' section in front of the bar was populated on each side with attorneys for the respective parties. The law clerks all made sure that they were in their "pews," each of which contained several hard, uncomfortable chairs. The justices came on the bench, and after the announcement of two opinions, the Court was ready to hear the oral argument in the Steel Seizure Case. At this point two hundred additional people were allowed into the courtroom to stand around the walls and listen to the arguments, while hundreds more waited in line outside.

As I look back with the benefit of some thirty years' experience, it seems ironic to me that in the most celebrated case to have come before the Court since I became a justice, the Nixon Tapes Case, I was not even able to listen to the argument. I had disqualified myself from participating in the case, and as a result was given by my colleagues the task of assigning the seats within the courtroom for those who wished to hear the oral argument. As might be imagined, there were far more people wishing to hear the argument than could be accommodated, and some who thought they had good reasons for being present were undoubtedly annoyed at being turned down. Although I would like to have heard the arguments just as a matter of interest, I decided that there was no place I could possibly sit in the courtroom and hear them without giving rise to speculation that perhaps I was secretly participating in the case after all, and so I simply remained in my chambers during the argument. The irony, of course, is that when I was a law clerk I was able to hear the argument in the Steel Seizure Case, whereas when I was a justice I was unable to hear the argument in the Nixon-Tapes Case.

Shortly before 12:30 P.M., John W. Davis, who was to argue for the steel companies, rose to make what was his one hundred and twenty-eighth argument before the Supreme Court. Now nearing eighty, he had been successively a congressman from West Virginia, solicitor general in the administration of President Woodrow Wilson, founding partner of the firm of Davis, Polk, Sunderland, Ward, and Kiendl, Democratic candidate for president in 1924, and a Supreme Court advocate whose reputation was matched only by Charles Evans Hughes before he became chief justice in 1930.

Davis's argument was a polished performance, which I thought was masterful. Naturally the law clerks debated the merits of the various lawyers arguing the case, and some of them thought that he appeared over the hill. I did not. He sat down after about an hour and a half, and the solicitor general, Philip B. Perlman, addressed the Court on behalf of the government. There was little dispute among the law clerks that Perlman was not a particularly effective advocate. Justice Jackson complained after the argument that he treated the Court like a jury, and it seemed to me that there was much merit in this complaint. While the Court had appeared to be almost in awe of Davis, and asked him only one question during his ninety minutes of argument, Perlman was virtually peppered with questions from the justices.

The solicitor general relied heavily in his brief and also in his oral argument on the opinion that Justice Jackson had written when he was attorney general, affirming President Roosevelt's authority to seize the North American Aviation Plant shortly before Pearl Harbor. Jackson commented from the bench that he was afraid that a lot of the basis for the government's seizure was being laid at his doorstep, and Perlman agreed. Jackson then responded: "I claimed everything, of course, like every other Attorney General does. It was a custom that didn't leave the Department of Justice when I did."

Every law clerk likes to see his own boss look "sharp" on the bench, as if the justice's performance somehow reflected credit upon the law clerk. I virtually glowed with satisfaction at Justice Jackson's comment, not only because I thought it was both relevant and witty, but because it seemed to me to suggest that he did not agree with the government's position.

The Court rose at 4:30 on Monday, and at noon on Tuesday resumed with the solicitor general's argument. In closing, Perlman became somewhat hortatory, and insisted to the Court, "This is wartime." Both Jackson and Frankfurter questioned him sharply on this point, pointing out that Congress had indicated rather strongly that it did not regard the present situation in Korea as war. John W. Davis closed with a predictably rhetorical, but nonetheless effective, peroration, and the Court left the bench. The conference on the case was scheduled for noon on Friday, and speculation was intense on the part of the press, the legal community, and, needless to say, the law clerks, as to what the result would be.

George Niebank and I were both present and eager to learn the outcome when the justices went into conference. The custom of the Court is that a buzzer sounds in all the chambers and in the hallway of the first floor of the building five minutes before conference is to start, and another buzzer sounds when the conference is concluded. I can remember sitting at my desk, trying to work on certiorari petitions, but always keeping one ear cocked for the sound of the buzzer that would announce the conclusion of the conference and, I hoped, the return of Justice Jackson to his chambers. It came about four o'clock in the afternoon, and George and I hung around the door waiting for Justice Jackson to make his appearance. He told us to come into his chambers, as he usually did after conference, and we had no sooner sat down with our tongues all but hanging out when he looked at us and said, "Well, boys, the President got licked." We looked at his conference vote sheet, which he customarily showed us, and saw that six members of the Court had voted to affirm Judge Pine's ruling that the President's action was unconstitutional: Justices Black, Frankfurter, Douglas, Jackson, Burton, and Clark. Three of the justices had voted with the government: the Chief Justice, Justice Reed, and Justice Minton.

As I look back now, I wonder if a case cannot be made for some sort of "geographic determinism" so far as the votes of the dissenters are concerned. Fred Vinson, Stanley Reed, and Sherman Minton had all grown up in towns along the Ohio River not more than two hundred miles apart. Vinson and Reed were from Kentucky, Minton from Indiana. I don't know what this proves, but it nonetheless seems to me an interesting fact.

Justice Jackson told us that Justice Black, who was the senior justice, would assign the opinion to himself, but that probably several opinions would be written. I don't know whether the justices had set themselves any sort of tentative deadline for circulating opinions in the case, but in a space of less than three weeks seven separate opinions had been written. Justice Black wrote an opinion for the Court, which was joined by Justices Frankfurter, Douglas, Jackson, and Burton. Justice Clark wrote separately, because although he agreed that the President had acted unconstitutionally, he did not agree with the analysis in Justice Black's opinion. When one reads the separate opinions written by Justices Jackson, Frankfurter, Douglas, and Burton, it is apparent that they, too, did not fully subscribe to the view set forth in Justice Black's opinion, but they nonetheless joined it. There simply does not seem to have been enough time for the negotiation that often goes on in order to enable those who disagree with minor parts of a proposed Court opinion, but not with the result, to effect some sort of compromise that will enable them to join the principal opinion.

Justice Black's opinion dealt rather shortly—one is tempted to say almost summarily—with the equitable arguments upon which the government had relied in urging the Court not to reach the constitutional question of the President's power to seize the mills.

Black's opinion said that because the damages the mills might suffer if the seizure was invalid would be very difficult to calculate, they were entitled to an injunction against the seizure. At the time this seemed to me a fine example of cutting through a lot of red tape to get to the real issue in the case, but reflection in later years has made me think that there was a lot more to the government's arguments on these issues than the Court gave credit for. On the merits, Justice Black's opinion was quite logical, but also quite abstract. He reasoned that the Constitution has given the lawmaking power to Congress, and has given to the executive certain other powers, which do not include the lawmaking power. Since the seizure of the steel mills was an exercise of what Black described as the lawmaking power, it was beyond the president's authority unless Congress had authorized it.

This very neat analysis obviously bothered most of the justices who joined Black's opinion, and it certainly bothered Justice Jackson. He prepared an opinion that was really more like an essay than a standard judicial opinion, but it is an opinion that proved valuable to subsequent courts and lawyers in discussing the relationship between the president and the Congress. Jackson took the position, not surprisingly, that the president's powers are at their zenith when exercised to execute a law that Congress has enacted; here the legislative and executive powers are combined, and they are potent indeed. The president occupies a middle ground when he seeks to use the executive power to accomplish a goal in an area where Congress has not legislated, and therefore where Congress cannot be said to have either approved or disapproved of the use of presidential power for the purpose for which it is used. The president's authority is at its nadir when the president acts to accomplish a goal in an area where Congress has already legislated, and when the president's authority is exercised in such a manner as to be inconsistent with the legislation of Congress.

The shortness of time would have precluded much participation by the law clerks in the drafting of Justice Jackson's opinion in any event, but I am sure that this was the sort of opinion in which he felt no need for the help of law clerks. We were shown the opinion in draft form, and as I recall, asked to find citations for some of the propositions it contained, but that was about the extent of our participation.

When the Court convened at noon on June 2, the Chief Justice announced immediately that the admission of attorneys, which usually was the first order of business after the Court came on the bench, would be deferred so that the opinions in the Steel Seizure Case could be announced. Then, for a little more than two hours, each of the seven justices who had written an opinion read or paraphrased it from the bench. First came Justice Black, whose opinion was the opinion of the Court in the case because it had been joined by at least four other justices; then came each of the four justices who had written separately but had joined Justice Black's opinion. Then came Justice Clark, who concurred in the result. Finally the Chief Justice announced his dissent, which was joined by Justice Reed and Justice Minton, and which accused the Court of adopting a "messenger boy" concept of the presidency.

The Court recessed at 2:25 that afternoon, nearly half an hour after the time when the lunch break was usually taken. Now, less than two months after it began, the Steel Seizure Case was over, and the President of the United States had been told by the Supreme Court of the United States that he had acted beyond his constitutional authority. The President immediately wrote Secretary Sawyer directing him to return custody of the mills to the owners, and the secretary promptly did so. One is tempted to wonder in how many countries who loudly proclaim that they have written constitutions would a harassed chief executive have so promptly carried out the adverse mandate of the nation's high court.

I had been quite surprised when Justice Jackson told us, "Boys, the President got licked." I thought about the outcome of the Steel Seizure Case some at the time, and I have thought about it a good deal more while writing this book. The law on the equitable issues was clearly in favor of the government, and while the law on the constitutional question was more or less up for grabs, the whole trend of the Court's decisions in the preceding fifteen years leaned toward the government. Why, then, did six members of the Court vote against the government in this case? I think that this is one of those celebrated constitutional cases where what might be called the tide of public opinion suddenly began to run against the government, for a number of reasons, and that this tide of public opinion had a considerable influence on the Court.

This was a case that unfurled in the newspapers before the very eyes of the justices long before any papers were filed in the Supreme Court. The members of the Court began learning about it the morning after President Truman's announcement of his seizure of the mills, when the press reported that the steel companies' attorneys had gone to Judge Bastian's home late in the evening to attempt to secure a temporary restraining order against the government. From beginning to end, the facts of the case and its progress through the courts were very much of a local event in Washington, heavily covered by the Washington newspapers. At that time, neither *The Washington Post, The Washington Evening Star,* nor *The Washington Times Herald* had the sort of national coverage *The Washington Post* has today, and if the lawsuit had been brought in Chicago, New York, or San Francisco, only those justices who regularly read *The New York Times* would have known about its course in such great detail.

The manner in which the case proceeded in the district court before Judge Pine had a considerable influence on public opinion. The government's original arguments in the district court, to the effect that the president's power was plenary unless some provision of the Constitution expressly denied authority to him, was rightly regarded as an extraordinary argument. The newspapers and commentators denounced it, and it obviously played a part in Judge Pine's decision in favor of the steel companies. The government quickly sensed that it had made a mistake in making these arguments, and recanted them almost immediately; by the time the case was argued in the Supreme Court, the arguments made by Holmes Baldridge in the district court had been entirely abandoned, but speaking as one who was on the scene at the time, I don't think they could be erased from anyone's mind. The government's litigation strategy in the district court, reported blow by blow in the Washington newspapers, undoubtedly had an effect on how the case was finally decided by the Supreme Court.

But I also think another, more deep-seated factor played a part in the tides of public opinion that were running at this time. There was a profound ambivalence on the part of much of the public about the Korean War, which was the principal basis upon which President Truman justified his seizure of the steel mills. When North Korea invaded South Korea, President Truman and his top advisers deliberately refrained from asking Congress for a declaration of war, and the United States continued to refer to the Korean conflict as a "police action" under the aegis of the United Nations rather than as a war. But in fact it seemed indistinguishable to most people from a war, in which the fortunes of the United States contrasted rather sharply with the success of that country and its Allies in the Second World War. In the latter conflict the United States had been attacked by the Japanese at Pearl Harbor, the President had asked Congress to declare war, and the country had mobilized for what rightly was seen to be a long, hard battle against the Axis powers. Things looked very dark for the Allied powers at the time the United States first entered the war, but beginning with the Casablanca invasion in the European theater and the Guadalcanal landings in the Pacific theater, the Allies had gradually pushed back their enemies on both fronts in a series of hard-fought victories.

The Korean conflict was quite different. The initial momentum of the North Koreans carried them far into South Korean territory, but then General MacArthur's landing at Inchon had regained the initiative for the allies and they victoriously crossed back over the thirty-eighth parallel boundary. But then the Chinese entered the war, and the allies were forced back from their earlier gains at great cost in men and matériel. In the spring of 1952, the Korean conflict appeared to be pretty much of a stalemate; the result was an erosion of public willingness to sacrifice. We had a draft, we had price controls, we had rent controls, we had production controls, but these measures, which had been borne resolutely during the Second World War, were borne less resolutely and with considerably more grumbling during the Korean conflict. After President Truman forbade General MacArthur to authorize air strikes beyond the Yalu River, which separated North Korea from China, it seemed very difficult to figure out how the United States could "win" in Korea, and sacrifices that will be cheerfully borne when related to a clearly defined objective will not be so cheerfully borne when the objective seems confused and uncertain. I think that if the steel seizure had taken place during the Second World War, the government probably would have won the case under the constitutional grant to the president of the war power, but I also have the distinct feeling that if the American objectives and strategy in Korea had been less uncertain, the government probably would have fared better in the Supreme Court even without being able to resort to the president's war power.

Finally, although President Truman has today been accorded at least his just deserts by historians who have written since he left office, his standing in public opinion at the time of the Steel Seizure Case was at its nadir. When Truman first succeeded Roosevelt in 1945, Roosevelt loyalists were wont to say that the mistakes of the new administration never would have happened if Roosevelt were alive. Now political wags said that the Korean War would never have happened if Truman were alive; others coined the phrase "To err is Truman." The President himself had something of a tendency to put his foot in his mouth, with the result that his press secretary would be required to issue "clarification" of the President's public statements. His administration during the latter part of his second term was beset by influence-peddling scandals; none of them touched the President, but they nonetheless created an atmosphere referred to by his political opponents as "the mess in Washington." Though all but one of the justices of the Supreme Court had been allied with the Democratic party before their appointments, Democrats were often as critical of Truman as Republicans were; the former compared him frequently to Franklin Roosevelt, and all but invariably found him wanting.

These are the factors that I think played a considerable part in the way the Steel Seizure Case was decided. I was recently asked at a meeting with some people in Washington, who were spending a year studying various aspects of the government, whether the justices were able to isolate themselves from the tides of public opinion. My answer was that we are not able to do so, and it would probably be unwise to try. We read newspapers and magazines, we watch news on television, we talk to our friends about current events. No judge worthy of his salt would ever cast his vote in a particular case simply because he thought the majority of the public wanted him to vote that way, but that is quite a different thing from saying that no judge is ever influenced by the great tides of public opinion that run in a country such as ours. Judges are influenced by them, and I think that such influence played an appreciable part in causing the Steel Seizure Case to be decided the way it was.

4

MARBURY
V. MADISON

$\mathcal{T}$he Steel Seizure Case, decided in June 1952, is rightly regarded as one of the historic confrontations between the executive and the judicial branches of the United States government. But those who make no claim to be students of United States history in general or of the Supreme Court of the United States in particular are entitled to ask, "Why was the Supreme Court of the United States able to set at naught President Truman's order seizing the steel plants as it did?" This is a perfectly sensible question: One might certainly argue that the president takes an oath of office to be bound by the Constitution just as surely as do the justices of the Supreme Court, and why, therefore, should he, as head of the executive branch of the government, be bound to take the word of the Supreme Court, which is the head of the judicial branch of the government, as to whether or not his acts comply with the Constitution? For the answer to this question we must go back in United States history one hundred fifty years from the time of the decision of the Steel Seizure Case to the case of *Marbury* v. *Madison*.

One need understand very few of the cases that it has decided in order to understand the Supreme Court's role in our nation's history. But one must assuredly understand the case of *Marbury* v. *Madison*. This case established the authority of the federal courts to declare a law passed by Congress unconstitutional and therefore void. The vitally important legal principle of the case can be condensed into a sentence or two, and the justification for the doctrine espoused by Chief Justice John Marshall in his opinion for the Court can be comprehended in a page or two. But like so many abstractions standing alone, these tend to go in one ear and out the other when people have no regular need to repair to such doctrine. I think that a fuller understanding of the doctrine itself may be gained by a knowledge not only of the facts of the case but of the times in which it occurred and of the place at which it occurred.

Those who have seen the city of Washington in the latter part of the twentieth century, firmly ensconced as a metropolis of three million at the southern end of the eastern "urban corridor" of the United States, may have difficulty envisioning the city of Washington that existed in 1803, the year the Supreme Court decided the case of *Marbury* v. *Madison*. The Constitution adopted by the Philadelphia Convention in 1787 had provided for the creation of a "district" not exceeding ten miles square to become "the seat of the Government of the United States," but it had left the location of that district to Congress. Congress decided that the site of the government should be moved from New York to Philadelphia in December 1790, and ten years later that it should be moved again to the District of Columbia, a ten-mile square territory on either side of the Potomac River. Maryland ceded the necessary territory on the north side of the river, including the city of Georgetown, and Virginia ceded the necessary territory on the south side of the river, including the city of Alexandria.

It is easy today to think of Washington at the opening of the nineteenth century as a somewhat smaller version of the Philadelphia and New York of that time. But nothing could be further from the truth. There were two honest-to-goodness cities in the District—Georgetown in the northwestern part with a population of about three thousand, and Alexandria in the southern part with a population of about five thousand. But that part of the District of Columbia designated to be the federal city, and named after George Washington, was still largely a wilderness. The census of

1800 gave it a population of just over three thousand people. Philadelphia at this time had existed for more than a century, and had a population of more than forty thousand; New York had existed for a century and a half, and had a population of nearly eighty thousand.

The various departments of government began moving to Washington from Philadelphia during the year 1800, and John Adams was the first president to occupy the newly built President's House, as it was then called. His wife, Abigail, arriving there for the first time in November 1800, observed:

> I arrived about 1 o'clock at this place known by the name of the city, and the Name is all that you can call so. As I expected to find it a new country, with Houses scattered over a space of 10 miles, and trees and stumps and plenty with a castle of a house—so I found it—The President's House is in a beautiful situation in front of which is the Potomac with a view of Alexandria. The country around is romantic but wild, a wilderness at present. [Junior League of Washington, p. 81]

Albert Gallatin, designated by Thomas Jefferson to be secretary of treasury as soon as the former assumed the presidency on March 4, 1801, said upon his arrival in the city to take up the duties of his office:

> Our local situation is far from being pleasant or even convenient. Around the Capitol are 7 or 8 boarding houses, 1 tailor, 1 shoemaker, 1 printer, and washing woman, a grocery shop, a pamphlet and stationery shop, a small dry goods shop and an oyster house. This makes the whole of the federal city as connected with the Capitol. [Junior League, p. 87]

A contemporary traveler observed that "the entrances or avenues, as they are pompously called, which lead to the Am. seat of Gov't, are the worst roads I passed in the country. . . . Deep ruts, rocks, and stumps of trees every minute impede yr. progress and threaten yr. limbs with dislocation." [Junior League, p. 82]

Jenkins Hill, a prominent elevation roughly in the center of the District, had been chosen as the site for the Capitol building, but by the time of Jefferson's first inauguration in 1801, only the north, or Senate, wing had been completed. The south wing was a temporary brick structure known as the "oven" and occupied by the House of Representatives. A list of Washington buildings drawn up in November 1801 showed a total of 621 houses standing on private land.

On March 4, 1801, Jefferson simply walked from his nearby boardinghouse to the Senate chamber inside the Capitol building to take his oath from John Marshall, his distant cousin and the newly appointed Chief Justice of the United States. Marshall, who throughout his thirty-four years as Chief Justice lived with his colleagues in a boardinghouse near the Capitol during the time they were in Washington, probably walked from his own boardinghouse to administer the oath to Jefferson.

Just as it is difficult to imagine the Washington of 1801 on the basis of the Washington that exists today, it is also difficult to envision the way in which the Supreme Court was housed in 1801 on the basis of the "marble temple" in which it is housed today. Surely many of those who have seen the beautiful Supreme Court building located opposite the east plaza of the Capitol must have felt it was entirely fitting that each of the three independent branches of the federal government should be symbolized by a building—the president by the White House, the Congress by the Capitol building, and the Supreme Court by its building.

But such was not the case in 1801. It was not until January 20, 1801, that any notice was taken of the need to provide the Supreme Court with a place to conduct its term, which would begin the next month. At this time the District Commissioners recommended to Congress, "As no house has been provided for the Judiciary of the United States, we hope the Supreme Court may be accommodated with a room in the Capitol to hold its sessions until further provisions shall be made, an arrangement, however, which we would not presume to make without the approbation of Congress." Congress responded to this suggestion by designating a committee room on the first floor of the Capitol building as a "courtroom," and there the Court sat for seven years until more spacious quarters were afforded it. In the words of a leading student of the Court:

In this small and undignified chamber, only 24 feet wide, 30 feet long and 21 feet high, and rounded at the south end, the Chief Justice of the United States and his associates sat for eight years. [Warren, Vol. I, p. 171]

And what of the Chief Justice and his five associate justices?

John Marshall, universally referred to as "the great Chief Justice," was born in Fauquier County, Virginia, in 1755. He had commanded a line company in the Revolutionary War and had fought in the battles of Brandywine, Germantown, and Monmouth before he was twenty-five years of age. He served under George Washington at Valley Forge, from whom he acquired "a strong sense of nationalism and respect for discipline and authority." [Haskins and Johnson, p. 102] After independence was achieved, Marshall served first in the Virginia legislature and then in Congress. He was appointed one of the famous "XYZ" commissioners sent to deal with Talleyrand and the French Directory in 1798, and upon his return he served as secretary of state to John Adams in the closing days of the latter's administration.

At that time a vacancy occurred in the chief justiceship by reason of the resignation of the incumbent, Oliver Ellsworth, in December 1800. By then it already appeared that the election of 1800 had gone against the Federalists, and John Adams felt a strong need to put a dedicated Federalist on the bench before the government should come into the hands of Jefferson and the Republicans. He offered the position to John Jay, who had earlier occupied it before resigning to run for governor of New York, but Jay declined in early January. Adams then passed over two associate justices of the Court, William Cushing and William Paterson, whom he was thought to be considering, and "like a bolt out of the blue," nominated John Marshall.

From the portraits of John Marshall in existence today it seems to me that the most striking characteristics about the man are his piercing dark eyes. He looks like a man who has a good sense of humor and is mentally keen. In physical appearance he was tall, loose-jointed, and often negligently dressed. William Wirt wrote, "In his whole appearance, and demeanor; dress, attitudes, gestures; sitting, standing or walking; he is as far removed from the idolized graces of Lord Chesterfield, as any other gentleman on earth." [W. Wirt, *The Letters of the British Spy* (Baltimore, 1811), p. 95, quoted in Haskins and Johnson, p. 104]

His longtime colleague on the Court, Joseph Story, said of him: "I love his laugh—it is too hearty for an intriguer; and his good temper and unwearied patience are equally agreeable on the bench and in the study." [Junior League, p. 101] Andrew Oliver, in his interesting work *The Portraits of John Marshall,* makes this observation:

> [T]here is a remarkable consistency in the several types of his portraits, the only difference being due, undoubtedly, not so much to Marshall's change in appearance as he grew older but rather to the eye of the artist. . . . There is no difficulty in discovering in Inman's aged Chief Justice the young and handsome envoy to France as he appeared in 1797. Jefferson and the two Adams grew old, old and tired, tired and wearied looking. Marshall, aged 80, in the face of the dreaded operation for the stone only a day or two later, looks down on us from Inman's canvas as serene, as gentle, and yet as firm, as he appeared before his elevation to the Court 30 years before. And as he looked while on the bench throughout his career as Chief Justice.

The Court's senior associate justice, William Cushing, was a native of Massachusetts, appointed to the Court by George Washington in 1789. He was a solid, competent lawyer, although by 1801 he was apparently showing some of the infirmities of age. William Paterson, appointed by Washington in 1793, was a distinguished New Jersey lawyer and an important figure in the Constitutional Convention in Philadelphia. A majority of the Senate that confirmed Marshall as Chief Justice would have apparently much preferred to see President Adams nominate Paterson to that position.

Samuel Chase of Maryland, because of his brownish-red complexion known as "old bacon face," was an able lawyer, strongminded, and clear-thinking. But he was also "a man of violent opinions, overbearing manners, and fierce temper, he made en-

emies rapidly and easily, and he was always a center of controversy, in law as in politics." [Haskins and Johnson, p. 91] The
commencement of the Supreme Court's term, scheduled to begin
in August 1800, had to be delayed partly because Justice Chase
was speaking to political gatherings in Maryland on behalf of John
Adams's candidacy for the presidency. [Warren, Vol. I, p. 156]
Bushrod Washington of Virginia had been appointed to the Court
by John Adams in 1798. He was the nephew of George Washington, and was destined to serve thirty-one years as an associate
justice at the Court. He was regarded by his contemporaries as an
accomplished lawyer, but seems to have been primarily a legal
craftsman rather than anything like a broad-gauged statesman. He
was short in stature, boyish in appearance, and like Marshall, was
apparently a careless dresser.

The most junior justice of the Court in 1801 was Alfred
Moore, who had been appointed by President Adams two years
earlier. Since he was destined to serve only five years on the
Court, we know very little about him. He was a North Carolinian,
well thought of at the bar of that state. He apparently looked
much like a child, being only four and a half feet tall, and weighing between eighty and ninety pounds.

These, then, were the six men who comprised the Supreme
Court of the United States when the case of *Marbury* v. *Madison*
was commenced before it in December 1801.

William Marbury was one of the so-called "midnight judges,"
appointed justice of the peace in the District of Columbia by
President John Adams on the eve of his surrendering that high
office to his successor, Thomas Jefferson. But while Marbury had
been duly nominated by the President and confirmed by the Senate, because of a last minute mixup occasioned by the change of
administration on March 4, 1801, his commission executed by the
President had never been delivered to him by the secretary of
state. Jefferson, upon assuming office, issued commissions to a
majority of the some forty justices of the peace in Marbury's position, but declined to issue Marbury's. Marbury requested that
James Madison, newly appointed as Jefferson's secretary of state,
deliver him his commission, but Madison declined. Marbury then

sought a writ of mandamus from the Supreme Court of the United States, which would direct Madison to deliver him his commission. The proceedings were begun in December 1801; the Court heard final arguments in the case in February 1803, and handed down its opinion later that same month.

During the stormy presidency of John Adams, from 1797 to 1801, bitter divisions in public opinion between the Federalists and the anti-Federalists, or Republicans, had manifested themselves, divisions that were to affect history for a number of years. In 1798 Congress enacted the so-called Alien and Sedition Acts, consisting of four different laws. The first three dealt with aliens: They raised the waiting period for naturalization from five to fourteen years, permitted the detention of subjects of an enemy nation, and authorized the president to expel any alien considered by him to be dangerous. The fourth law was the Sedition Act, which outlawed the publishing of false or malicious writings against the government and the inciting of opposition to any act of Congress or of the president.

The Republicans with considerable reason claimed that all of these laws were directed at them. The French and Irish immigrants who were subject to the provisions of the alien laws had by and large allied themselves with Jefferson and his adherents. The Sedition Act was bitterly denounced as violative of the freedom of speech and freedom of the press guarantees of the First Amendment to the United States Constitution. Indictments were brought under one or the other of these acts and tried before several of the justices of the Supreme Court sitting as trial judges on circuit, and the Supreme Court justices in that capacity had upheld the constitutionality of these acts.

The crowning indignity, perhaps, in the eyes of the Republicans, was the enactment by Congress on February 13, 1801—less than three weeks before Jefferson would succeed Adams as President—of a law formally titled the Circuit Court Act and quickly dubbed the Midnight Judges Act by its opponents. There were legitimate reasons for enacting such a bill; under existing law, the justices of the Supreme Court were required to "ride circuit" and sit as trial judges in the various geographic areas of the new nation, and given the condition of transportation facilities in the country at the time, the judges fervently desired at least partial relief from these duties. In the words of one of the principal students of the times: "Had this measure been adopted at an earlier period and under less partisan auspices, there would have been strong arguments in its favor, for it brought about a reform long recognized as desirable." [Warren, Vol. I, p. 185.]

But coming as it did when Federalist control of the presidency and Congress was breathing its last gasp, it created an uproar. The bill relieved the Supreme Court justices of their circuit duty, reduced the number of judges from six to five, and established six new circuit courts with sixteen new judges to administer them. All sixteen of the new judges were, of course, appointed by John Adams, the lamest of lame-duck presidents.

Thomas Jefferson, in a private letter written later in the same year, described the Federalists in these words: "On their part, they have retired into the judiciary as a stronghold. There the remains of Federalism are to be preserved and fed from the Treasury, and from that battery all the works of Republicanism are to be beaten down and erased." [Malone, p. 458, note 5]

Jefferson was not the sort of president to take this threat lying down, and when the Republicans gained control of the presidency and the White House under his aegis in 1801, they promptly enacted a new judiciary bill, which repealed the obnoxious provisions of the Midnight Judges law. Congress at the same time passed a law abolishing the June and December terms of the Supreme Court, which had been created by the act of 1801, and restoring the old February term but *not* the old August term. By dint of this rather extraordinary measure, enacted with ill-disguised hostility toward the Supreme Court, an adjournment of that body was enforced for fourteen months—from December 1801 to February 1803.

It was in this atmosphere of bitter, divisive hostility between the two principal political parties in the country that a Supreme Court consisting entirely of Federalist appointees was called upon to judge the claim of another Federalist appointee, William Marbury, against a Republican secretary of state, James Madison.

The case was argued to the Supreme Court in early February 1803, and it was decided later in the same month. Chief Justice John Marshall delivered the opinion of the Court, an opinion in which all of the associate justices concurred. If the opinion be parsed for substance, rather than form, it deals with four successive questions: (1) Does Marbury have a legal right to the position of justice of the peace for the District of Columbia, and thence to the commission which is the badge of office? (2) If he has such a right, does the law give him a remedy? (3) Is a writ of mandamus a proper remedy in this case? (4) May such a writ of mandamus issue from the Supreme Court in this case?

Marshall, in answering the first of these questions, traces the president's appointing power as set forth in the Constitution and points out that the final step in this process is the president's affixing of his signature to the commission of office. The law then directs the secretary of state to deliver the commission to the appointee, after having affixed the great seal of the United States to it and recording it. But the actual "appointment" that enables the officeholder to occupy the office occurs when the president affixes his signature to the commission. At that point, Marbury was entitled to the office, and to the commission evidencing his appointment.

Marshall then turned his attention to whether, if Marbury had a right to the office under the commission, "do the laws of his country afford him a remedy?" The question, so put, is of course almost rhetorical, and Marshall answers the question with a rolling period: "The government of the United States has been emphatically termed a government of laws, and not of men. It will certainly cease to deserve this high appellation, if the laws furnish no remedy for the violation of a vested legal right."

Marshall then turns to the question of whether a writ of mandamus (a Latin word meaning "we command") is proper in this case. This question, rather than the final question of the power of courts to declare acts of Congress unconstitutional, was the more controversial in its time. Thomas Jefferson, James Madison, and the other Republicans who now controlled both the executive and legislative branches of the federal government, were understandably concerned that the judiciary might seize this opportunity to establish its authority to direct high officers of the executive branch how to discharge their official responsibilities. If the federal courts could order James Madison, secretary of state appointed by the President, to deliver a commission to a justice of the peace, what would they next be ordering a cabinet officer to do?

Marshall's opinion refers to cases decided by the English courts, which had approved the issuance of a writ of mandamus directing a particular action to a public official in England. He then notes that the "intimate political relation subsisting between the President of the United States and the heads of the departments, necessarily renders any legal investigation of the acts of one of those high officers peculiarly irksome, as well as delicate; and excites some hesitation with respect to the propriety of entering into such an investigation." But the opinion goes on to distinguish between executive responsibilities that involve a measure of discretion, which are not reviewable by the courts, and questions with respect to which the law imposes a duty to act upon a high official of the executive branch, which questions are subject to judicial control by a writ of mandamus.

Marshall in his opinion then turned to the fourth and final question before the Court: Could a writ of mandamus issue from the Supreme Court of the United States? The difficulty here arose from the fact that Marbury had originally filed his lawsuit not in a lower court but in the Supreme Court itself. Since the judicial article of the Constitution prescribes the jurisdiction of the Supreme Court and of such lower federal courts as Congress may create, these courts necessarily have only "limited" jurisdiction, and a person who wishes to file a suit in one of them must show that some provision of law authorizes him to bring his suit in that court.

Marbury relied for his right to sue in the Supreme Court on a section of the first law that Congress ever enacted dealing with United States courts—the Judiciary Act of 1789—which provided that the Supreme Court should have the power "to issue writs of mandamus in cases warranted by the principles and usages of law, to any courts appointed, or persons holding office, under the authority of the United States." Considered by itself, this provision supported Marbury's right to sue in the Supreme Court: He desired a writ of mandamus against the secretary of state, and the secretary of state was obviously a "person holding office under the authority of the United States." Marshall's opinion conceded as much, but then went on to decide that this section of the Judiciary Act of 1789 was unconstitutional.

His reasoning on this point begins, as it obviously had to, with the language of the Constitution itself. Article III of the Constitution, which deals with the federal judiciary, provides for one Supreme Court and such other federal courts as Congress may create. It then goes on to state that "the Supreme Court shall have original jurisdiction in all cases affecting ambassadors, other public ministers and consuls, and those in which a state shall be a party. In all other cases, the Supreme Court shall have appellate jurisdiction."

The traditional distinction between original jurisdiction and appellate jurisdiction is this: Original jurisdiction means the power to hear and decide a lawsuit in the first instance, while appellate jurisdiction means the authority to review the judgment of another court which has already heard the lawsuit in the first instance. Trial courts are courts that exercise original jurisdiction; courts of appeals and supreme courts generally exercise appellate jurisdiction. But, Marshall pointed out, the Constitution had not left this matter to speculation. In a few special cases Article III provided that the Supreme Court should exercise original jurisdiction, to wit: cases affecting foreign ambassadors and cases in which one of the states itself was a party. Thus, if the Constitution meant what it said, Marbury could not bring his lawsuit in the Supreme Court of the United States because he was asking the Supreme Court to grant him relief in the first instance, without his ever having gone to a lower court. But Article III said this could be done only in cases involving foreign ambassadors or in cases where one of the states was a party to the lawsuit.

It might have been urged on behalf of Marbury that this provision of the Constitution granting original jurisdiction to the Supreme Court was not meant to prevent Congress from changing the limits of that jurisdiction, but Marshall's opinion rejects this argument:

> If Congress remains at liberty to give this Court appellate jurisdiction, where the Constitution has declared their jurisdiction shall be original; and original jurisdiction where the Constitution has declared it shall be appellate; the distribution of jurisdiction, made in the Constitution, is form without substance.

There was probably more to this argument on behalf of Marbury than the Court suggests, but most students of the subject agree that the Court was correct as a matter of logic on this point. The result was that Congress in the Judiciary Act of 1789 had passed a law that granted the Supreme Court a kind of jurisdiction that Article III of the Constitution by negative inference said it could not have; what was the Court to do?

The Court decided without much hesitation that the Constitution, which had been ratified by assemblies representing all of the people of the United States, would have to prevail over an act of Congress, which was simply one branch of the federal government exercising powers delegated to it by the people through the Constitution. There have been countless refinements, discussions, and exegeses on the question of by what right one branch of the federal government, the judiciary, should take it upon itself to declare unconstitutional a law duly enacted by Congress and signed by the president, coordinate branches of that government. But Marshall was a first-rate expositor of doctrine, and the justification contained in his opinion for the Court in this case is worth setting forth verbatim:

> The question, whether an act, repugnant to the constitution, can become the law of the land, is a question deeply interesting to the United States; but, happily, not of an intricacy proportioned to its certain principles, supposed to have been long well established, to decide it.
>
> That the people have an original right to establish, for their

future government, such principles as, in their opinion, shall most conduce to their own happiness is the basis on which the whole American fabric has been erected. The exercise of this original right is a very great exertion; nor can it, nor ought it, to be frequently repeated. The principles, therefore, so established, are deemed fundamental. And as the authority from which they proceed is supreme, and can seldom act, they are designed to be permanent.

This original and supreme will organizes the government, and assigns to different departments their respective powers. It may either stop here, or establish certain limits not to be transcended by those departments.

The government of the United States is of the latter description. The powers of the legislature are defined and limited; and that those limits may not be mistaken, or forgotten, the constitution is written. To what purpose are powers limited, and to what purpose is that limitation committed to writing, if these limits may, at any time, be passed by those intended to be restrained? The distinction between a government with limited and unlimited powers is abolished, if those limits do not confine the persons on whom they are imposed, and if acts prohibited and acts allowed, are of equal obligation. It is a proposition too plain to be contested, that the constitution controls any legislative act repugnant to it; or, that the legislature may alter the constitution by an ordinary act.

Between these alternatives there is no middle ground. The constitution is either a superior paramount law, unchangeable by ordinary means, or it is on a level with ordinary legislative acts, and, like other acts, is alterable when the legislature shall please to alter it.

If the former part of the alternative be true, then a legislative act contrary to the constitution is not law: if the latter part be true, then written constitutions are absurd attempts, on the part of the people, to limit a power in its own nature illimitable.

Certainly all those who have framed written constitutions contemplate them as forming the fundamental and paramount law of the nation, and, consequently, the theory of every such government must be, that an act of the legislature, repugnant to the constitution, is void.

This theory is essentially attached to a written constitution, and is, consequently, to be considered, by this court, as one of the fundamental principles, of our society. It is not therefore to be lost sight of in the further consideration of this subject.

If an act of the legislature, repugnant to the constitution, is void, does it, notwithstanding its invalidity, bind the courts, and oblige them to give it effect? Or, in other words, though it be not law, does it constitute a rule as operative as if it was a law? This would be to overthrow in fact what was established in theory; and would seem, at first view, an absurdity too gross to be insisted on. It shall, however, receive a more attentive consideration.

It is emphatically the province and duty of the judicial department to say what the law is. Those who apply the rule to particular cases, must of necessity expound and interpret that rule. If two laws conflict with each other, the courts must decide on the operation of each.

So if a law be in opposition to the constitution; if both the law and the constitution apply to a particular case, so that the court must either decide that case conformably to the law, disregarding the constitution; or conformably to the constitution, disregarding the law; the court must determine which of these conflicting rules governs the case. This is of the very essence of judicial duty.

If, then, the courts are to regard the constitution, and the constitution is superior to any ordinary act of the legislature, the constitution, and not such ordinary act, must govern the case to which they both apply.

Those, then, who controvert the principle that the constitution is to be considered, in court, as a paramount law, are reduced to the necessity of maintaining that courts must close their eyes on the constitution, and see only the law.

This doctrine would subvert the very foundation of all written constitutions. It would declare that an act which, according to the principles and theory of our government, is entirely void, is yet, in practice, completely obligatory. It would declare that if the legislature shall do what is expressly forbidden, such act, notwithstanding the express prohibition, is in reality effectual. It would be giving to the legislature a practical and real omnipotence, with the same breath which professes to restrict their powers within narrow limits. It is prescribing limits, and declaring that those limits may be passed at pleasure.

John Marshall's opinion for the Court in this evoked less notice at the time than might have been expected. That part of the press that supported the Republicans devoted its principal criticism to the doctrine that an extraordinary writ such as mandamus could, in Marshall's view, be in some circumstances directed to a high official of the executive branch. But Marshall's opinion in this respect had been quite guarded, and the mischief anticipated by the Republicans did not materialize at that time. The proposition for which the case stands in United States constitutional law—that a federal court has the authority under the Constitution to declare an act of Congress unconstitutional—was not seriously challenged by contemporary observers, and has remained the linchpin of our constitutional law ever since *Marbury* v. *Madison* was handed down.

William Marbury never did get his commission as a justice of the peace for the District of Columbia. James Madison's eight years as secretary of state in the administration of President Thomas Jefferson gave way in 1809 to two terms as President in his own right. Madison, of course, would have been remembered equally well in American history as the father of the Constitution, drafter of the Bill of Rights, and two-term Republican President, even if he had delivered William Marbury's commission and thereby avoided the lawsuit of the latter. But William Marbury has been saved from historical obscurity only by the fact that he was the plaintiff in the most famous case ever decided by the United States Supreme Court.

5

THE
MARSHALL COURT

$\mathcal{T}$he Supreme Court of the United States decided the case of *Marbury* v. *Madison* when John Marshall had been Chief Justice only two years. He continued to serve as Chief Justice for another thirty-two years, until his death in July 1835. During this period of time cases brought to the Supreme Court established important ground rules as to just how much authority the Constitution had conferred upon the newly created national government, and how much it had curbed the previously completely sovereign authority of the states at the time they entered the Union. Everyone agreed that the national government—Congress, the president, and the federal judiciary—was a government of limited or delegated powers: That is, unless a power was granted to the national government in the Constitution, the national government did not possess that power. Conversely, the states were viewed as having all the normal powers of a sovereign government unless the Constitution by its language took away those powers. The question of how broadly the Supreme Court would construe the powers given to the national government would be of extraordinary importance in determining just how strong and effective that government would be.

The Constitution granted Congress no general power to "make laws"; instead, any law that Congress enacted had to be based upon one of the express grants of authority in the Constitution. Probably the most important of these powers granted to Congress was the so-called "commerce power," which provided that Congress should have the power "to regulate commerce with foreign nations, and among the several states. . . ."

The most important case to reach the Marshall Court under this clause was *Gibbons* v. *Ogden,* which involved steamboats traveling across the Hudson River between New York and New Jersey. A resident of New York by the name of Aaron Ogden took an assignment from Robert Fulton, one of the inventors of the steamboat, of the exclusive right granted to Fulton by the New York legislature to operate a steam ferry across the Hudson River between New York and Elizabethtown, New Jersey. Thomas Gibbons operated his steamboats on the same run, and he had obtained a license for plying the coastal trade under an act of Congress passed in 1793. Ogden sued in the New York courts to enjoin Gibbons from competing with him on the steam-ferry run from New York to Elizabethtown because the New York legislature's grant of the right to him was an exclusive monopoly. The New York courts ruled in favor of Ogden, and Gibbons appealed to the Supreme Court of the United States.

The Supreme Court, in an opinion written by Chief Justice Marshall, broadly defined the term "regulate" in the constitutional provision dealing with commerce as meaning the power "to prescribe the rule by which commerce is to be governed." Thus the activity of operating a ferry from New York to New Jersey was clearly subject to the commerce power of Congress, and the Court held that by enacting the licensing statute Congress had exercised its power to permit Gibbons to compete with Ogden. William Johnson, an associate justice of the Court, expressed his opinion separately in the same case that even if Congress had never granted a coasting license to Gibbons, the New York grant of monopoly would have been invalid simply because of the Constitution's grant to Congress of the power to regulate commerce among the several states.

The Constitution grants to Congress not only specific powers, such as the authority to regulate commerce, but also the authority "to make all Laws which shall be necessary and proper for carrying into execution the foregoing Powers." The meaning of this Necessary and Proper Clause came before the Supreme Court in the famous case of *McCulloch* v. *Maryland* in 1819. In 1791 Congress, adopting one of the major features of the fiscal policy urged upon it by Secretary of the Treasury Alexander Hamilton, chartered a corporation called the Bank of the United States. There was much debate in President Washington's Cabinet at the time the charter was pending as to whether Congress had the authority to charter a bank; Secretary of State Thomas Jefferson maintained that since the Constitution nowhere granted to Congress such power, it was beyond the competence of that body to charter a bank. Hamilton, however, in what must be regarded as one of the great state papers in our country's history, contended that the Necessary and Proper Clause allowed Congress to charter a bank if such action was reasonably adapted toward an end with respect to which Congress could legislate. Hamilton's views carried the day in Washington's Cabinet, and the President signed the bill chartering the bank. Congress later renewed the charter of the Bank of the United States, but the bank was extremely unpopular in some sections of the country.

Manifesting this hostility to the bank, the Maryland legislature in 1818 passed an act imposing a tax on all banks or bank branches operating in the state of Maryland that were not chartered by the Maryland legislature. The tax was computed at a percentage of the value of the notes issued by the bank, and of course placed the banks subject to such a tax at a marked disadvantage in competing with banks chartered by the Maryland legislature. James McCulloch, the cashier of the Baltimore branch of the Bank of United States, issued notes of that bank on which no state tax had been paid, and the state of Maryland sued in the state courts to enforce the provisions of its bank-note tax law. The Maryland courts ruled in favor of the state, and McCulloch appealed to the Supreme Court.

The state of Maryland argued in the Supreme Court that Congress had not been granted by the Constitution any authority to charter a bank, and therefore that the Bank of the United States was not a true instrumentality of the federal government. But the Court rejected this contention, again in an opinion by John Marshall, which was handed down by the Court only three days after the last day of argument in the case. The Court held that although the national government was limited to those powers delegated to it by Congress, when it acted within those powers the Constitution had expressly made such actions "the supreme Law of the Land; and the Judges in every state shall be bound thereby, any Thing in the Constitution or Laws of any State to the Contrary notwithstanding." So if the chartering of a bank was within the powers granted to Congress, a state could not impose a tax on the bank without violating the Supremacy Clause. Marshall went on to hold that the incorporation of a bank was a "necessary and proper" means for carrying out the powers expressly delegated to Congress of raising and collecting taxes. In this connection Marshall said in his opinion: "Let the end be legitimate, let it be within the scope of the Constitution, and all means which are appropriate, which are plainly adapted to that end, which are not prohibited, but consistent with the letter and spirit of the Constitution, are constitutional. . . ."

The Marshall Court was less hospitable to claims of state authority than it was to claims of authority on the part of the national government. The Constitution specifically prohibited certain actions by the states, and one of these prohibitions was against a state law "impairing the Obligation of Contracts." The meaning of this clause was interpreted by the Supreme Court in the famous *Dartmouth College* case.

Dartmouth College, in Hanover, New Hampshire, had received a royal charter from the Crown before the American Revolution. The charter provided for twelve trustees to govern the college and authorized them to fill vacancies occurring among their own number. The trustees had exercised their authority to turn the president of the college out of office, only to see his cause becoming a burning political issue in the state. In 1818, the New Hampshire legislature converted Dartmouth College into Dartmouth University, raised the number of trustees from twelve to twenty-one, and made other changes in the governance of the institution. The majority of the old trustees refused to accept the amendment to the charter, and sued in the state court claiming that the changes "impaired the obligation of contract" in violation of the United States Constitution.

When the case was carried to the Supreme Court of the United States, that Court in an opinion by Chief Justice Marshall decided that the royal charter was a "contract" between the donors, the trustees, and the Crown (to whose rights and obligations New Hampshire had succeeded). The opinion went on to hold that the changes in the governance of the institution made by the New Hampshire legislature in 1816 "impaired" the obligation of this contract. By this time, concurrences and even dissents were making their appearance on the Marshall Court. A dissenting opinion is a statement by one of the members of the Court of the reasons why he disagrees with the result reached by the majority of the Court. A concurring opinion is a statement by one of the members of the Court of reasons different from that adopted by the Court for reaching the same result as the Court does. Justice Story wrote a separate concurrence in the *Dartmouth College* case, elaborating on Marshall's reasoning and marshaling numerous common-law authorities supporting the result reached by the Court. Justice Washington also wrote a separate concurring opinion, and Justice Duvall, who in his more than twenty years as a justice of the Court wrote almost nothing, dissented without opinion. And so Dartmouth University went back to being Dartmouth College, governed by twelve trustees appointed in the manner prescribed by the royal charter granted by King George III in 1769.

For all his leadership of the Court, Chief Justice John Marshall found himself in dissent in 1827 when the majority of the Court gave a narrower construction to the Commerce Clause of the Constitution than he did. But he continued to preside over the Court until his death in July 1835, after having served as Chief Justice for thirty-four years. When he was appointed in 1801, he found the Supreme Court functioning much like the highest court in England, supervising a judicial system designed to resolve disputes between individual litigants. He left the Court a genuinely co-equal branch of a tripartite national government, having added to its normal function of a court of last resort the awesome responsibility of being the final arbiter of the meaning of the United States Constitution. He found the national government with its fate as yet undetermined by any binding judicial interpretation as to the extent of its powers. He left it a limited but strong central government equal to the large tasks that would confront it.

One of Marshall's major innovations in judicial procedure was in the manner in which the Supreme Court delivered its opinions. The tradition for the delivery of oral opinions in those English courts that consisted of more than one judge had been for each judge to deliver his own opinion on the matter, a practice called the delivery of opinions seriatim. Marshall, in what his biographer calls "an act of audacity," changed this tradition in the Supreme Court of the United States so that an opinion for the Court was delivered by only one of the justices, and in virtually every important case during his tenure that one turned out to be the Chief Justice. There apparently was doubt during the very early days of this new practice whether a dissent was permissible; Justice William Johnson, appointed by President Jefferson, wrote to Jefferson that when he first disagreed with the reasoning of one of Marshall's opinions for the Court and wrote a separate concurrence, he "heard nothing but lectures on the indecency of judges cutting at each other" for the rest of the term (ZoBell, *Division of Opinion in the Supreme Court*, 44 Cornell L.Q. 186, 192–196 [1959].

Yet at the time of Marshall's appointment by President Adams, though he was recognized as one of the ablest members of the Federalist party in Virginia, he was not regarded as among the very top flight of lawyers even there. How then did he achieve his mastery?

Marshall's dominance of his colleagues cannot be explained simply on the grounds of political allegiance: John Adams, who appointed him, was the last Federalist to be elected president of the United States. After him, for twenty-four years the Virginia dynasty of Republican presidents held sway: Thomas Jefferson, James Madison, and James Monroe. These presidents dearly wanted their appointees to the Court to challenge Marshall, but it simply didn't work out that way. Joseph Story, the ablest member of the Marshall Court next to the Chief Justice, was a Republican, albeit something of a renegade, at the time he was appointed by Madison. But Story became Marshall's right-hand man on the Court. Marshall stood for broad construction of the powers granted to Congress and the president by the Constitution, and for corresponding limitations on the powers of the states; Story stood shoulder to shoulder with him in virtually every important case that came before the Court.

It is tempting to explain Marshall's preeminence on the basis that he was, so to speak, "present at the creation," and that any able person serving as chief justice when he did would have been able to leave a similar mark. But of course Marshall was not the first chief justice; he was either the third or the fourth, depending on whether one counts John Rutledge of South Carolina who received a recess appointment from President Washington but was denied confirmation by the Senate. Marshall's predecessors were probably both better-known men in the young republic at the time of their respective appointments than Marshall was in 1801, but neither appeared to see any opportunity in the post in which they served. John Jay, the first Chief Justice, while serving in that capacity, accepted appointment by President Washington as envoy to England to negotiate what became the Jay Treaty, and is far better remembered in history for that effort than for the six years he spent as Chief Justice. He resigned in 1795 to run for governor of New York, where he apparently felt the action was a that time. His successor, Oliver Ellsworth of Connecticut, fell ill and died while in France after having served six years as Chief Justice.

But what Jay and Ellsworth failed to see in the office of chief justice, Marshall saw almost immediately. And the fact that he acted, in a case such as *Marbury* v. *Madison*, to make the Court a genuine co-equal branch of the government, undoubtedly appealed to some of his colleagues who, though they lacked the vision to lead, were quite willing to follow. Most people appointed to be officers of an institution would prefer to have it assume an important role than an unimportant one.

Of course, the Court could have fully asserted its right to declare invalid such acts of Congress as it thought unconstitutional and still have relegated the new national government very much to the backseat in the affairs of the nation. But Marshall not only had an opinion as to the position of the Court in the new government, he also had strongly held views that inclined him to give considerable scope to the powers granted to the national government. Later he would say that his experiences as a commander of line infantry in the Revolutionary War confirmed him in the habit of "considering America as my country and Congress as my government" before the Constitution was even adopted.

But Marshall had more than simply the desire to make the Court the institution he thought the Constitution intended it to be; he also possessed the ability to explain clearly and forcefully why the Court reached the conclusions it did. His colleague Story once observed that "in the law, the power of clear statement is everything." Marshall had the power of clear statement in spades, and his opinions reflect it. At a time when the English and American legal systems were still bogged down in the forms of action and the niceties of pleading, his opinions are a breath of fresh air.

Finally, there must have been a strong measure of the ability to persuade his colleagues in Marshall. Obviously Marshall's one month of law studies before his admission to the bar did not give him the tools to overawe his colleagues with learning, but perhaps his experience in dealing with his fellow human beings in such positions as the command of an artillery company during the winter at Valley Forge was a more than adequate substitute for book learning. The conviviality of the boardinghouse life to which he and his colleagues submitted themselves during the short time each year they were in Washington seems to have been made for someone who could capitalize on his abilities as "team leader." Marshall apparently did just that. Even in his own lifetime his accomplishments as Chief Justice made such a public impression that John Adams in his retirement would say, "John Marshall was my gift to the American people."

6

THE
TANEY COURT

*W*hen John Marshall died in 1835, times were considerably different from those in which he had been appointed. Andrew Jackson, a Tennessean representing that part of the nation west of the Appalachian Mountains, was President of the United States. Jackson appointed his secretary of the treasury and one-time attorney general Roger B. Taney to succeed Marshall as Chief Justice, and the latter was confirmed by the Senate in 1836. Taney had had an active political life, and was a strong political partisan of the Jacksonian Democratic stripe, just as Marshall had been of the Federalist stripe. Roger Taney was born to a family of the southern Maryland tobacco-planting aristocracy in March 1777. His family was Roman Catholic, and he remained a communicant of that faith throughout his life. He was a younger son, and thus had to fend for himself as far as inheritance was concerned because under the Maryland law at that time his older brother would inherit the family estate.

Taney was not robust in health, but this did not prevent him from leaving home at age fifteen in 1792 to attend Dickinson College at Carlisle, Pennsylvania, in what was then the frontier country of that state. He graduated from Dickinson in 1795, and the following year began to read law in Annapolis, the state capital. He was admitted to the bar in 1799 at the age of twenty-two.

He moved from southern Maryland to Frederick in 1801 to take advantage of the retirement of two elderly lawyers there. He lived in Frederick and practiced law for twenty some years, developing a statewide practice based on his considerable abilities as a lawyer. He married Ann Key, the sister of Francis Scott Key, in 1806; they had six daughters, but Mrs. Taney was not Catholic and the daughters were raised in her Protestant faith.

In 1823 Taney moved to Baltimore to better accommodate his flourishing practice. He supported Andrew Jackson in his unsuccessful bid for the presidency in 1824, and again in his successful effort in 1828. But Jackson was besieged by office seekers; Taney expected no Cabinet position and was initially offered none. Indeed, his entrance into the Jackson Cabinet in 1831 came only after Jackson had determined to reconstitute this body after the Peggy Eaton Affair.

When he made up his Cabinet in 1829, Jackson chose as secretary of war his Tennessee friend John H. Eaton. Eaton's wife had a tarnished reputation because of gossip about her conduct while she was living at a Washington boardinghouse operated by her mother. Although her husband was in the navy, or perhaps because of that fact, her name was linked to more than one lonesome legislator, including Senator Eaton. After the death of her husband, Eaton married Peggy Timberlake, formerly Peggy O'Neale, and his appointment to the Cabinet necessarily brought his wife into Cabinet society.

The wives of several members of the Cabinet, including Attorney General John Berrien of Georgia, refused to recognize Mrs. Eaton socially. Indeed, even the wife of Jackson's nephew, Andrew J. Donelson, who served as his private secretary, eventually declined further social intercourse. All of this exasperated Old Hickory, who regarded all of the clamor as being caused by others seeking Eaton's Cabinet position and by gossips.

He wrote to a friend:

If I had a tit for every one of these pigs to suck at they would still be my friends. They view the appointment of Eaton as a bar to them from office, and have tried here, with all the tools of Clay helping them on, to alarm and prevent me from appointing him. . . . I did not come here to make a cabinet for the ladies of this place, but for the nation. [Swisher, *Taney*, p. 135]

Goaded on by his protégé, Martin Van Buren, whom he had appointed secretary of state, Jackson conceived the idea of reorganizing his Cabinet because of the factionalism within it. Van Buren, who as a widower was able to make his own decisions about whether or not to socialize with Mrs. Eaton, submitted his resignation with a public lament over the friction within the Cabinet, and Eaton likewise resigned in April 1831. Jackson then suggested to the opposing faction in the Cabinet, including Attorney General Berrien, that he would be grateful for their resignations. In due course they complied, and Jackson appointed Roger Taney as attorney general in June 1831. Thus the Peggy Eaton affair not only gave the nation the song "Peggy O'Neal" but gave it Roger Taney as attorney general.

In those days, the attorney general was allowed to maintain a private practice on the side, and Taney, although moving to Washington, continued to practice law privately as well. In the Jackson Cabinet he was caught up in the battle between the President and the Bank of the United States. He alone of the Cabinet members urged the President to veto a bill passed by Congress rechartering the Bank in 1832, and Jackson followed his advice. After Jackson was reelected President in 1832, he directed Louis McLane, his secretary of the treasury, to withdraw United States funds from the Bank of the United States. McLane refused; Jackson removed McLane and appointed Taney as secretary of the treasury. Taney then carried out the President's instructions to remove the funds from the bank. This move aroused bitter hostility in the Senate, and because Taney was serving as secretary of the treasury under a recess appointment, his name had to be submitted to the Senate before the close of the following session. In June 1834, Jackson submitted Taney's name to the Senate, but his nomination was rejected by a vote of 22 to 18. He thereupon returned to his law practice in Maryland. In January 1835, Jackson nominated Taney to be an associate justice of the Supreme Court, but the same bitter hostility to him in the lame-duck Senate prevented the nomination from ever coming to a vote. In December 1835, Jackson nominated Taney to be Chief Justice of the United States to succeed John Marshall, and a Senate in which the anti-bank Democrats had increased their representation by reason of the 1834 election confirmed this nomination by a vote of 29 to 15. Thus the third time proved to be the charm.

Taney was fifty-nine years old when he took his seat in the center chair of the Supreme Court. He would serve as Chief Justice for twenty-eight years. During a period of more than sixty-three years, in which there were fifteen presidents of the United States, there were only two chief justices: John Marshall and Roger Taney.

During the first part of this period, the Court had occupied the one room previously described in the basement of the Capitol. In 1818, it moved to somewhat more commodious quarters in the lower level of the Capitol, where it remained until 1860. A reporter for the *New York Tribune* described the courtroom in these words:

You discover a narrow passage, lighted with a dim lamp. You enter and crowding between two walls of old deal boxes, see a distant glass door. As you approach, it seems to be guarded by a personage with a visage just dark enough to correspond with the general gloom around him. . . . Before you have time to knock him down for stopping up the way, he profoundly inclines his head, gently swings the door, and, descending two or three steps, you are ushered into a queer room of small dimensions, shaped over head like a quarter section of a pumpkin shell, the upper and broader rim crowning three windows, and the lower and narrower coming down garret-like to the floor; the windows being of ground glass, and the light trickling through them into the apartment. That which most arrests your attention is a long pew, just in front of these windows, slightly elevated above the floor, along which are ranged in a straight line nine ancient persons, clad in black silk gowns. . . . A man stands in the pit, in front of them, shaking

a roll of manuscript convulsively in the face of the central figure of the group . . . and blazing away at the whole nine like
Mose at a fire. Half a dozen persons are lounging on chairs, or
idling about the room. . . . [*New York Tribune*, March 26,
1859, quoted in Swisher, *The Taney Period*]

This courtroom has been restored to its original condition and
was opened to the public in 1974.

As might be expected, the Supreme Court during the time
that Roger Taney was Chief Justice did not decide all of its cases
in the same way that the Marshall Court would have decided
them. This is not merely because Roger Taney had a different
judicial philosophy from John Marshall's, but because the associate justices who sat with each of them differed from one another
in their views.

Observers of the Court commonly refer to a particular period
in the Court's history by the name of the Chief Justice of that
time, e.g., the Marshall Court, or the Taney Court. But it is
worth noting that this shorthand carries a good deal different implication than references to a particular period in national history
as the "administration of Andrew Jackson" or the "administration
of Grover Cleveland." When a president comes into office, he
brings with him his own nominees for the Cabinet departments
and other executive positions, so that there is usually a genuine
housecleaning of high-level positions in the executive branch with
each change in the presidency. But that is not at all true in the
case of the Supreme Court; John Marshall, for example, when he
was appointed Chief Justice, brought no associate justices with
him; the institution is set up in such a way that an incoming chief
justice must take, for better or for worse, the associate justices
already sitting on the Court. Thus, while it may be a convenient
form of shorthand to refer to a particular epoch in the Court's
history as, for example, the Taney Court, the limited connotation
of the phrase should be borne in mind.

The Taney Court did gradually come to differ more and more
from the Marshall Court, but this was largely attributable to the
fact that Taney served twenty-eight years as Chief Justice, and

during this time death and resignation inevitably took their toll of the associate justices who had served with Marshall but continued to serve under Taney. From 1832 until 1860 Democratic presidents were in power for twenty out of the twenty-eight years, and as might be expected, this fact was reflected in the composition of the Supreme Court just as it was in other aspects of the policy of the national government. Andrew Jackson did not appoint to the Court justices who would have shared the views of those appointed to the Court by George Washington or John Adams.

Within one year after Taney's appointment as Chief Justice, the Court heard reargument in the celebrated *Charles River Bridge* case. For those familiar with the present Court's rules, which allow counsel for each side to argue for only one half hour in a case, the time taken for the argument in the *Bridge* case will come as a surprise. Four lawyers, two on a side, and including those giants of the bar Daniel Webster and Simon Greenleaf, argued the case for five full days with the Court sitting four hours each day: January 19, 21, 23, 24, and 26 of 1837.

The case arose out of the fact that in 1785 the Massachusetts legislature had granted to the Charles River Bridge Company the right to construct a bridge across the Charles River from Boston to Charlestown, and to charge tolls of those who used it. The bridge was built, and in 1792 its charter was extended to 1856, after which time it would belong to the Commonwealth of Massachusetts. All went swimmingly with the Charles River Bridge and its owners until 1828, when the Massachusetts legislature granted to the upstart Warren Bridge Company the right to build another bridge over the Charles River only a couple of hundred feet from the Charles River Bridge. The Warren charter provided that as soon as the expenses of the proprietors had been reimbursed through the collection of tolls, the bridge would revert to the state and be a free bridge.

The owners of the Charles River Bridge claimed that this act of the Massachusetts legislature chartering the Warren Bridge impaired the obligation contained in the commonwealth's previous charter to them. They relied, of course, on the Contract Clause of the United States Constitution, construed by the Supreme Court in the *Dartmouth College* case. But there was crucial difference between their charter and the Dartmouth charter; the latter dealt in express terms with the power of the trustees, but the former said nothing about whether or not the state might grant another charter to another bridge company. The owners of the Charles River Bridge, therefore, had to argue that the charter granted to them not only the rights stated in the instrument, but by implication a promise by the legislature not to charter another competing bridge.

The Supreme Court by a divided vote ruled against the proprietors of the Charles River Bridge. Chief Justice Taney wrote the opinion for the Court, and rejected the argument of the Charles River Bridge proprietors that the grant to them of the right to collect tolls from their bridge implied an undertaking by the state not to charter a free bridge so close to the location of the Charles River Bridge. The Court said it was unwilling to read into a state charter promises by the state that had not been made in so many words in the charter itself. Chief Justice Taney's opinion reflects a very sensible concern with the consequences that would flow from a contrary decision:

> Let it once be understood, that such charters carry with them these implied contracts, and give this unknown and undefined property in a line of traveling; and you will soon find the old turnpike corporations awakening from their sleep, and calling upon this Court to put down the improvements which have taken their place. The millions of property which have been invested in railroads and canals, upon lines of travel which had been before occupied by turnpike corporations, will be put in jeopardy. We shall be thrown back to the improvements of the last century, and obliged to stand still, until the claims of the old turnpike corporations shall be satisfied; and they shall consent to permit these states to avail themselves of the lights of modern science, and to partake of the benefit of those improvements which are now adding to the wealth and prosperity, and the convenience and comfort, of every other part of the civilized world (11 Peters 551).

Justice Joseph Story, who had been Marshall's good right hand during the days of the latter's chief justiceship, dissented, and in a long opinion expressed the view that the Contract Clause and the Dartmouth College Case required a result opposite to that reached by the Court. Story thought that the investors in the Charles River Bridge must have relied on an implied promise on the part of the Massachusetts legislature that it would not authorize any new bridge whose operation would cut into the traffic on, and therefore the profits from, the Charles River Bridge. If the legislature regretted its grant of a monopoly to the Charles River Bridge Company, it must condemn the franchise under the power of eminent domain and pay fair value to the investors for the right taken. Justice Smith Thompson joined in this dissent.

Story himself was to set a longevity record in service upon the Supreme Court, serving a few months longer than John Marshall's thirty-four years and four months. He was in essence a bridge between the Marshall Court and the Taney Court. Appointed in 1811 by James Madison, he served under Marshall for twenty-four years and under Taney for nearly ten years until his death in September 1845. He had been born in 1779 at Marblehead, Massachusetts, and graduated from Harvard with honors in 1798. He returned to Marblehead to study law, and was admitted to the Massachusetts bar. He was from the start, in 1801, a successful practicing lawyer in Salem and, more unusual in that part of Massachusetts, a Jeffersonian Republican. He was elected both to the Massachusetts legislature and to the United States House of Representatives while he was still in his twenties, and at the time of his appointment as an associate justice was only thirty-two years old.

Joseph Story was by far the most learned in the law of any of the early members of the Supreme Court. During his lifetime he wrote numbers of treatises on various branches of the law, many of which were considered by large sections of the American bar to be definitive treatments of their subject. When it is realized that most of this work was done while he was a justice of the Supreme Court, with circuit-riding duties in New England as well as attendance on the Court in Washington, one must regard him as having been possessed of extraordinary energy. But scholarly treatises were not the only extracurricular activities in which he engaged. He was made president of the Merchants Bank in Salem in 1815, a member of the Board of Overseers of Harvard College in 1819, a member of the Harvard Corporation in 1825, and in 1829 he was made a professor of law at Harvard Law School. On the side he wrote speeches for Daniel Webster, drafted bills for Congress on judicial questions, and unsuccessfully ran for the presidency of the Massachusetts Constitutional Convention in 1820.

In 1816 Story wrote the opinion for the Supreme Court in the case of *Martin* v. *Hunter's Lessee*, which announced the important rule that the Supreme Court had authority under the applicable law to review final judgments of state courts where those judgments had decided federal constitutional questions. One of his last opinions for the Court, in the 1845 case of *Swift* v. *Tyson*, established an important rule of decision in cases brought to federal courts by reason of the diversity of citizenship of the parties, a rule that endured for ninety-three years. Had Story served at a time when less dominant figures than Marshall or Taney presided over the Court, he would probably be remembered for more notable opinions and constitutional doctrine than he now is.

Not long after Story's death, the Taney Court decided the case of *Cooley* v. *Board of Wardens of the Port of Philadelphia*, 12 How. 299. There the Court qualified the broad implications of the Marshall Court's decision in *Gibbons* v. *Ogden*. Pennsylvania had enacted a law in 1803 requiring every ship bound to or from a foreign port, and every ship of a burden of seventy-five tons or more bound to or from a port not within the Delaware River, to take on a pilot before it could enter the port of Philadelphia. The master of any ship that failed to take on a pilot was required to pay to an official of the state a sum equal to half of the pilotage fee thus avoided. The master of a vessel so charged sued to recover the fee, claiming that the Pennsylvania law violated the provision of the United States Constitution granting Congress the power to regulate interstate and foreign commerce.

The Supreme Court held that merely because Congress had been granted the authority to regulate all aspects of interstate and foreign commerce did not mean that by the very fact of that grant the states were disempowered from regulating any aspect of such commerce. Where Congress had not exercised the authority given to it by the Constitution, laws of the states regulating pilotage into busy harbors were sufficiently local in nature so as to be permissible in the absence of legislation by Congress on the subject. Justice John McLean dissented because he thought that Congress had to affirmatively approve such a state law before it could be valid; Justice Peter Daniel, one hundred and eighty degrees on the other side of the question, dissented because he thought such a state law was valid whether Congress approved it or disapproved it.

During the same term the Supreme Court decided another important commercial case, but it dealt not with the Authority of Congress under the commerce *power* but with the *power* of Congress to regulate the "admiralty" jurisdiction of federal courts. The judicial article of the Constitution provided that the judicial power of the United States should extend "to all cases of admiralty and maritime jurisdiction," and further provided that Congress might create courts inferior to the Supreme Court to exercise this jurisdiction.

The term "admiralty and maritime jurisdiction" had a rather well-defined meaning in the English law; in England there were separate courts of admiralty dealing with contracts and torts affecting ships. But in England the jurisdiction of these courts had always been restricted to areas within the ebb and flow of the ocean tide, and in 1825 the Supreme Court of the United States had unanimously decided that the same rule should be applied in this country. But in 1845 Congress enacted a law extending the admiralty jurisdiction of the federal courts to cases "upon the Lakes and navigable waters leading into or connecting the same." Justice Story, regarded as an expert in admiralty law, apparently played a large part in drafting the bill.

The act of 1845 came before the Court in the case known as *The Propeller Genesee Chief*, 12 How. 443. The schooner *Cuba* laden with nearly six thousand bushels of wheat and bound from Sandusky, Ohio, to Oswego, New York, had collided with the propeller ship *Genesee Chief* about forty miles below Niagara on Lake Ontario, and had sunk with her cargo. Her owners brought suit in federal court to recover the value of the cargo. But since federal courts were courts of limited jurisdiction, the only basis upon which the owners could bring their suit in federal court was if the admiralty jurisdiction granted by the Constitution had been properly extended to the Great Lakes by the act of 1845.

Chief Justice Taney wrote the opinion for the Supreme Court holding that the act of Congress was a permissible extension of admiralty jurisdiction. His opinion noted that the traditional rule in the English admiralty courts, defining their jurisdiction by the ebb and flow of the tide, was suitable to that country because there was in England no navigable stream beyond the ebb and flow of the tide. But in the United States conditions were quite different, and there was no reason why Congress could not extend admiralty jurisdiction to any public water used for commercial purposes in domestic or foreign trade. The Great Lakes obviously fell within this definition.

These examples of the way in which the Taney Court dealt with commercial matters show that Court at its best. It left in place the principal precedents of the Marshall Court, but qualified them in favor of the need for state regulation when common sense seemed to require such qualification. But this Court, which was so sound and sensible in the commercial area, went totally awry when it jumped into the heated dispute over slavery which gripped the country in the year shortly before the Civil War. The occasion was the ill-starred case of *Dred Scott* v. *Sandford*, which the Court decided in 1857 and in which Chief Justice Taney wrote an opinion for the Court holding an act of Congress unconstitutional for the first time since the decision in *Marbury* v. *Madison*.

The *Dred Scott* case was in one sense a classic "test case," designed originally to answer the legal question of whether a slave who was taken by his owner first to a free state, and then to a free territory, but then returned to the slave state from whence he had come, was emancipated by virtue of his stay in the free state or territory. Actually the facts of the case suggest that there may have been less altruistic motives involved. Dred Scott was born a slave in Virginia in 1795, whence he was taken to St. Louis and sold to one John Emerson. Emerson was an army surgeon, and took Scott with him first to Rock Island, Illinois, and then to Fort Snelling, in what was then Wisconsin territory, during the 1830s. After Emerson's death Scott became the property of the surgeon's widow and her brother, John Sanford, who still lived in St. Louis. (The spelling *Sandford* in the usual citation of the case is the result of a clerk's error.) As he grew older, he apparently proved to be more of a liability than an asset, and so the suit that he brought in the Missouri state courts against his owner, Mrs. Emerson, may have been commenced with mixed motives. In the state-court suit, the Supreme Court of Missouri ultimately ruled that Dred Scott's sojourn in free territory and in a free state did not elevate him from his status as a slave when he had returned to Missouri.

The litigation in the Missouri state courts decided an important question of Missouri law, but was scarcely of earthshaking consequences. After the conclusion of this state lawsuit, Dred Scott brought suit in federal court against John Sanford, Mrs. Emerson's brother, claiming the right to be in federal court by reason of "diversity of citizenship." The circuit court in St. Louis decided the case against Scott, holding that the law of Missouri controlled and that under the law of Missouri a journey by a slave and his owner to free territory did not emancipate the slave. Since Scott was still a slave, he could not be a "citizen" of any state for purposes of federal jurisdiction. It was this ruling that Dred Scott appealed to the Supreme Court.

But now another wrinkle appeared in the case. Part of Scott's claim was based on his residence in Wisconsin territory, where the status of slavery was governed by the Missouri Compromise that Congress had enacted in 1820. The Missouri Compromise provided that slavery was forever prohibited in the United States territories north of the parallel that formed the southern boundary of the state of Missouri. If the Supreme Court should deem it desirable, it could make the case not a relatively simple one turning on the law of Missouri, but a very complicated and important one involving the authority of Congress to prohibit slavery in the territories that had not yet been admitted to the Union as states.

One cannot place the *Dred Scott* decision in its proper context without having some understanding of its historical setting in the controversy over slavery. The Founding Fathers who met in Philadelphia in 1787 to draft the United States Constitution were precise and exact in some of the language they used, deliberately vague and general in their choice of other language. But the subject of slavery, though it was obviously in the minds of the delegates, was never expressly mentioned in the Constitution. The provisions of the Constitution dealing with slavery—and there are several—are all couched in euphemism.

Article I, providing for representation in the House of Representatives, directs that representatives shall be apportioned among the several states according to their respective numbers, "which shall be determined by adding to the whole of the number of free persons, including those bound to service for a term of years, and excluding Indians not taxed, three fifths of all other persons." Article IV provides that "no person held to service or labour in one state, under the laws thereof, escaping into another, shall, in consequence of any law or regulation therein, be discharged from such service or labour, but shall be delivered up on claim of the party to whom such service or labour may be due." Article I provides that "the migration or importation of such persons as any of the states now existing shall think proper to admit, shall not be prohibited by the Congress prior to the year 1808. . . ."

The Founding Fathers had to deal with the practicalities of slavery, but they did not want to talk about it; they were apparently content to hope that the institution would die a natural death, which it then appeared to be on the way to doing. But only a few years after the adoption of the Constitution, Eli Whitney's invention of the cotton gin suddenly made cotton a valuable cash crop, which could be raised throughout most of the South with the labor of slaves.

The northern states, which did not countenance slavery, and the southern states, which did, recognized that they were different from one another on this issue, and were at some pains to assure that each time a northern state was admitted to the Union, a southern state should also be admitted, and vice versa. In 1820,

Maine was admitted as a free state, and Missouri as a slave state; and as a part of the act admitting these states, known as the Missouri Compromise, Congress prohibited slavery thereafter from any part of the United States territories north of the parallel that constituted the southern boundary of the state of Missouri. By now it was apparent that slavery would not soon die a natural death, and its continued existence and extension was a cause of increasing concern in the North. In New England those who demanded immediate abolition of the institution throughout the nation came to be known as abolitionists, and their principal spokesman was William Lloyd Garrison. Garrison regarded the United States Constitution as a "convenant with hell," because of its ambiguity on the question of slavery, but his views calling for immediate abolition of that institution were shared by only a tiny minority even in the North. Nonetheless, serious concern about the South's peculiar institution continued to increase, both in the North and in the South.

By the early 1840s, antislavery groups were submitting to Congress more and more petitions opposing slavery and requesting its curtailment or abolition. John Quincy Adams, who after retiring from the presidency in 1825 was elected to the House of Representatives, became a principal spokesman for the right of these people to have their petitions considered in some way by Congress. For many years he was unsuccessful, but finally the petitions were at least referred to a committee, where they nonetheless died. Meanwhile the inexorable westward movement of the nation from the Atlantic to the Pacific created new aspects to the slavery question.

That part of Mexico known as Texas was settled principally by United States settlers from the slave states, and when those settlers revolted against Mexico and established the Lone Star Republic in 1836, they recognized the institution of slavery. Texas was anxious to be annexed to the United States, but while this request was sympathetically received by the southern states, the northern states were hostile because the admission of Texas would mean at least one more slave state. In 1845, just as President Tyler was leaving office, Congress finally approved the annexation of Texas, and the following year the United States and Mexico commenced hostilities over the location of the boundary between Texas and Mexico. The Mexican War that followed resulted in the annexation to the United States of a large part of the present southwest known as the Mexican Cession, and no sooner had the territory been acquired than Congress sought another compromise by which parts of it could be admitted to the Union. After much debate Congress enacted the Compromise of 1850, whereby California was admitted as a free state, a more stringent fugitive-slave law was adopted, and other provisions were made for the governance of the newly acquired territory.

Voices on both sides of the Mason-Dixon Line spoke out in favor of accepting the Compromise of 1850, of putting the slavery question behind them and going about the nation's business. But the slavery issue would not die. It was made to burn far brighter by the "popular-sovereignty doctrine" enunciated by Stephen A. Douglas, a young senator from Illinois. In 1854 Douglas introduced his Kansas-Nebraska Bill, which applied that doctrine to the territories of Kansas and Nebraska: The settlers in those territories should decide for themselves whether or not they should have slavery; the provision of the Missouri Compromise that would have forbidden slavery in these territories was repealed.

The Kansas-Nebraska Act, although passed in Congress by large majorities, inflamed the North. Bonfires burned, orators spoke, and a new party—the Republican party—was formed in Michigan and Wisconsin. Since the administrations of John Quincy Adams and Andrew Jackson had dissolved the "era of good feeling" engendered by President James Monroe, the two dominant political parties had been the Whigs and the Democrats. Both of these parties prided themselves on being national parties, embracing both northerners and southerners, but they were able to maintain this position only by being equivocal on the slavery issue. Because of this fact, as concern over slavery increased in the North, splinter parties such as the Free Soil and Liberty parties formed. These splinter parties did not take the extreme view of Garrison that slavery should be abolished forthwith, but that the institution should be limited geographically to where it then existed in hopes that it would ultimately disappear. The Republican party grew rapidly in a very few years, bringing in members from the antislavery splinter parties, from the Whigs, and from the northern Democrats. But the Republican party was of necessity a sectional party, because one of the principal planks in its platform was resolute opposition to the extension of slavery in the territories.

Thus the issue of whether Congress had authority to ban slavery from a part of the United States territories, as it had done in the Missouri Compromise, was a much different kind of question from whether Congress had constitutional authority to enlarge the "original" jurisdiction of the Supreme Court. Few people understood, and even fewer cared, how the latter question was resolved in the case of *Marbury* v. *Madison*. But after the Kansas-Nebraska Act in 1854, the evils of slavery and its extension were debated in town meetings and at firesides in every state north of the Mason-Dixon Line. What if the Supreme Court were to say that Congress had no authority to ban slavery in the territories?

By now the Supreme Court consisted of nine members, because Congress created new circuits as new states were admitted to the Union, and practice dictated that there should be a Supreme Court justice assigned to each circuit. The members of the Court at this time were Chief Justice Taney from Maryland, Justice James M. Wayne from Georgia, Justice John McLean from Ohio, Justice John Catron from Tennessee, Justice Robert Grier from Pennsylvania, Justice Samuel Nelson from New York, Justice John Campbell from Alabama, and Justice Benjamin Curtis from Massachusetts. Five of the nine justices—Taney, Wayne, Daniel, Catron, and Campbell—were from slaveholding states. These states were at a steadily increasing disadvantage in the House of Representatives as the population of the nation had increased, because the population growth in the North far exceeded the population growth in the South and representatives were allocated to the states on the basis of population. But because of the peculiar arrangement of the circuits to which each of the justices of the Supreme Court was assigned, this disadvantage was reversed on the Supreme Court. At this time in the history of the

Court, considerations of geography in appointments were a matter of much greater concern than they are in the present day. Part of this concern was due to sectional rivalries, but part of it was also due to the fact that each Supreme Court justice was required to spend part of the year sitting as a trial judge in the various lower federal courts located within his geographical circuit. Because so much of the business of these lower federal courts required a knowledge of the law of the state in which the court sat, it was considered essential that the Supreme Court justice for that circuit have a familiarity with the law of at least one of the states in the circuit, the sort of familiarity that could have been acquired only by practicing law in that state.

It should be noted parenthetically that this sort of geographic rigor in Supreme Court appointments has long since disappeared, the last logical reason for it having gone out with the repeal of the circuit-riding duties of the Supreme Court justices many years ago. Today it could be said that the Supreme Court has two justices from Arizona—Justice O'Connor and me—although my pedigree is doubtful; my commission as associate justice showed me as being from Arizona, but my commission as Chief Justice shows me as being from Virginia, where I have resided for the last eighteen years. At the time of the Steel Seizure Case Chief Justice Vinson and Justice Reed were both from Kentucky, and for the six years from 1932 to 1938 there were three New Yorkers on the Supreme Court: Chief Justice Hughes, Justice Stone, and Justice Cardozo.

But because of the requirement for geographic identification that obtained in the nineteenth century, it would have been inconceivable to appoint a justice who had not resided and practiced law in the circuit for which he would become circuit justice. The most recent change by Congress in the establishment of the circuits at the time of the *Dred Scott* case created nine judicial circuits, to each of which a Supreme Court justice was assigned. But because the circuits were created at least in part for geographic convenience, in order that a justice might get around his circuit within a reasonable period of time, the factors of area and distance from Washington played a much greater part than population in deciding how the circuits should be constituted. In 1857 they were constituted, and had a white population, as follows:

1st (Maine, N.H., Mass., R.I.) 2,028,594
2nd (N.Y., Conn., Vt.) 3,724,826
3rd (Pa., N.J.) 2,723,669
4th (Del., Md., Va.) 1,383,912
5th (Ala., La.) 682,005
6th (N.C., S.C., Ga.) 1,394,163
7th (Ohio, Ind., Ill., Mich.) 4,173,309
8th (Ky., Tenn., Mo.) 2,110,253
9th (Miss., Ark.) 457,907

It was this peculiar history of the circuit-riding duties of the Supreme Court justices that resulted in the southern majority on the Supreme Court at the time of the *Dred Scott* case.

The case was argued to the Court in the spring of 1856, but no decision was reached during that term and the case was set for re-argument in December 1856, a month after the 1856 presidential campaign. After re-argument, the case was not taken up at conference until February 15, 1857, and it was then apparently agreed among a majority of the justices that there was no need to decide whether or not the Missouri Compromise was constitutional. They need decide only that Missouri law governed the question of whether Dred Scott remained a slave, and Missouri law held that he did. All the justices agreed that a slave was not a "citizen" entitled to sue in the federal courts on the grounds of diversity of citizenship.

But when it became apparent that two of the justices, McLean and Curtis, would dissent on the question of whether or not Scott was still a slave, and thereby necessarily treat the constitutionality of the Missouri Compromise and uphold it, the other members of the Court had second thoughts. Justice Wayne persuaded Chief Justice Taney and Justices Campbell, Daniel, and Catron to go whole hog and decide the issue of the constitutionality of the Missouri Compromise. But Justice Grier, a Pennsylvanian, was adamant that the Court ought not to reach the latter issue.

At this point the Court made what must be judged to be a serious error by the standards of judicial conduct today, and to me seems inexcusable by even the somewhat laxer standards of that day. Justice John Catron, who did not cease dabbling in Democratic politics at the time he was appointed an associate justice by Andrew Jackson, decided that perhaps Grier's fellow Pennsylvanian, newly elected President James Buchanan, might be able to bring Grier around to agreeing that the Missouri Compromise was unconstitutional. It is also interesting to note parenthetically that Grier and Buchanan, like Taney, were alumni of Dickinson College. With the knowledge of Chief Justice Taney, Catron wrote Buchanan and urged the latter to write to Grier as to the desirability of the latter's joining with the majority on this question. Buchanan apparently did so, and Grier's response to Buchanan gives a full chronology of the case within the Court to that date, and indicates that Grier had now been persuaded to join the majority.

Buchanan, apparently basking in this foreknowledge at the time of his inaugural address, included in it a paraphrase of a statement Justice Catron had written for him, saying that the authority of Congress over slavery in the territories was "a judicial question, which legitimately belongs to the Supreme Court of the United States, before whom it is now pending, and will, it is understood, be speedily and finally settled. To their decision, in common with all good citizens, I shall cheerfully submit, whatever this may be."

This portion of Buchanan's inaugural address received attention from more than one antislavery newspaper, the *New York Tribune* saying:

You may "cheerfully submit"—of course you will to whatever the five slaveholders and two or three dough faces on the bench of the Supreme Court may be ready to utter on this subject; but not one man who really desires the triumph of freedom over slavery in the territories will do so. We may be constrained to obey as law whatever that tribunal shall put forth; but, happily, this is a country in which the people make both laws and judges, and they will try their strength on the issues here presented (*New York Tribune*, March 5, 1857).

Two days later, on March 6, 1857, the Court assembled for the reading of the opinions in the *Dred Scott* case. The delivery of the opinion of the Chief Justice himself, now more than eighty years old, with his voice low and feeble, took two hours. That opinion declared first that Negroes, whether or not they were slaves, had been regarded as persons of an inferior order at the time when the Constitution was adopted, and therefore could not be citizens within the meaning of the act of Congress that allowed suits in which the plaintiff and the defendant were citizens of different states to be brought in federal court. The opinion then went on to say that there was another reason why Dred Scott was not a citizen within the meaning of that act, and that was because he remained a slave even though his former master had taken him into the Northwest Territory where slavery had been forbidden by the Missouri Compromise. The circuit court in St. Louis had reached this same conclusion, but based it on the fact that under Missouri law a journey by a slave with his master into a free state did not emancipate the slave when he returned to Missouri. But Taney's opinion placed the result upon the ground that the Missouri Compromise, in which Congress had sought to ban slavery from all United States territory north of the southern boundary of Missouri, exceeded the power of Congress over the territories. Although the Compromise of 1850 had repealed the Missouri Compromise, Dred Scott's travels in free states and territories had occurred before 1850, and so the validity of the Missouri Compromise was necessarily involved in the decision of his case. Taney's opinion said that Congress was obligated to let citizens of all states of the Union take their property with them when they migrated to a territory, and this included southerners who wished to bring with them slaves regarded as "property" under the laws of the southern states.

Only Justices Wayne and Daniel joined the part of the Chief Justice's opinion dealing with whether or not Negroes could be citizens. The rest of the Chief Justice's opinion was joined not only by Wayne and Daniel, but by Justices Catron, Campbell, and Grier. Justice Nelson adhered to his view that the only point that need be decided was whether Dred Scott was emancipated by his trip to the Northwest Territory, and if the law of Missouri where his former master resided said that he was not so emancipated, the Supreme Court would follow the law of Missouri. Justices John McLean from Ohio and Benjamin Curtis of Massachusetts read their dissenting opinions the following day, taking five hours to do so. They disagreed with all three of the points made by Chief Justice Taney in his opinion.

Northern opinion was outraged. Horace Greeley's *New York Tribune* said: "The long trumpeted decision . . . having been held over from last year in order not too flagrantly to alarm and exasperate the Free States on the eve of an important Presidential election . . . is entitled to just so much moral weight as would be the judgment of a majority of those congregated in any Washington bar-room." [Quoted in Warren, Vol. III, p. 27]

William Cullen Bryant joined Greeley's *Tribune* in denouncing the decision. Bryant wrote in the *New York Evening Post:* "Are we to accept, without question, these new readings of the Constitution—to sit down contentedly under this disgrace—to admit that the Constitution was never before rightly understood, even by those who framed it—to consent that hereafter it shall be the slaveholders' instead of the free men's Constitution? Never! Never!" [Quoted in Nevins, *The Emergence of Lincoln*, p. 96]

Needless to say, while the *Dred Scott* decision may have "settled" the question of congressional authority to exclude slavery from the territories in the strictly legal sense, it exacerbated rather than ameliorated the clash of opinion over slavery. The decision cast a pall over the Supreme Court in the eyes of the increasingly ascendant antislavery forces in the nation. It was, in the well-chosen words of Charles Evans Hughes, a "self-inflicted wound" from which it took the Court at least a generation to recover.

Much learning has been devoted to the question of whether it was proper for Chief Justice Taney's opinion to advance not merely one but several reasons for the result it reached; some of this discussion is couched in terms of pleading and appeal procedures that were long ago superseded and are of only historical interest today. But quite apart from these niceties of practice, the Court's opinion in the *Dred Scott* case violated at least one and probably two canons of sensible constitutional interpretation.

From the time of John Marshall, the Court has said that the authority to declare an act of Congress unconstitutional is the most awesome responsibility that any court could possess, and the authority to do so must be exercised with extraordinary circumspection. The first canon violated by the *Dred Scott* decision is based on this view, and it holds that the Court will never decide a question of constitutional law unless the decision of that question is absolutely essential to dispose of the case before it. Whether or not the issues canvassed in the Taney opinion were properly before the Court in the technical legal sense, no one disputes that Justice Nelson's opinion would have provided a perfectly adequate basis for deciding the case. His opinion depended on the proposition that a slave could not be a citizen of any state for purposes of federal court jurisdiction—a proposition that all nine members of the Court agreed with—and beyond that it simply held that in a case coming from Missouri the Court would follow Missouri law on such a question. The question of whether Congress had authority to exclude slavery from the territories was not touched upon.

The second canon is one for which I can cite no specific authority, and yet I think it makes very good sense. The Court undoubtedly has the power to declare an act of Congress unconstitutional because that act conflicts with some provision in the Constitution. Judges will disagree with one another as to how the Constitution should be read in a particular case, and some may find a particular law unconstitutional while others will not. But it seems to me that even given the milieu in which the Court operated in 1857, where the South regarded slavery either as an established fact or even as a positive good, and antislavery leaders such as Abraham Lincoln wished only to confine it to where it at that time existed, the *Dred Scott* opinion falls short of that minimum degree of plausibility that should be required before a court declares any act of Congress unconstitutional. The Constitution expressly gave to Congress the authority to make rules and regulations for the territories of the United States, and Taney's opinion relies on no provision in the Constitution that would even arguably make the Missouri Compromise fall outside this general grant of power. The opinion is based almost entirely on the sense of the unfairness to southerners of preventing them from bringing with them their peculiar institution when northerners were allowed to bring property of all descriptions. But a sense that a law is unfair, however deeply felt, ought not to be itself a ground for declaring an act of Congress void.

Not only did the *Dred Scott* decision not settle the question of slavery in the territories in any larger sense, but ironically and in a somewhat roundabout way it helped to bring about the election of Abraham Lincoln. In 1858, the year following the Court's decision, Lincoln, a Republican little known outside of Illinois, challenged Stephen A. Douglas for one of that state's seats in the United States Senate. The candidates conducted a famous series of debates during the course of their campaign at various places in Illinois; during these debates Lincoln demanded of Douglas what remedies were left to those northerners who wanted to restrict the spread of slavery after the Supreme Court's decision in the *Dred Scott* case. Douglas, in a speech at Freeport, Illinois, replied that slavery was the sort of institution that needed positive law to support it, and while Congress or territorial legislatures could not prohibit the importation of slaves by their masters, such bodies, by refusing to enact protective legislation for the slaveholder, could in effect prevent the institution from taking root in their states.

The southern "fireaters" in Congress—the extremist faction of the proslavery group—saw the truth of Douglas's Freeport Doctrine, and demanded that Congress enact a federal slave code to support the institution of slavery in the territories. Douglas and other northern Democrats, who thought they had gone a long way to propitiate the slaveholding interests, balked at this extraordinary demand. Douglas in 1860 was probably the leading candidate for the Democratic nomination for the presidency, but one of the long-standing rules of the Democratic Convention was that a candidate must receive not merely a majority of the votes in order to be nominated, but two thirds of them. Douglas, with the support of almost all the northern Democrats, received a majority of the votes at the convention in Charleston, South Carolina, but because of the opposition of the southern wing of the party, to whom his Freeport Doctrine was anathema, he was unable to muster the necessary two thirds to obtain the nomination at that time. The convention adjourned until later in the spring in Baltimore, at which time Douglas received the Democratic nomination but in such a form that it would prove worthless to him. The southerners walked out of the Baltimore convention, or never sent delegates at all, and nominated their own proslavery ticket for the presidency. A group composed principally of old-line Whigs nominated a ticket called the Constitutional Union Party, and the Republicans in Chicago nominated Abraham Lincoln. With four presidential tickets competing with one another throughout various sections of the country, the United States elected Abraham Lincoln President in November 1860, with a majority of the electoral vote but only a minority of the popular vote.

Chief Justice Taney administered the oath of office to Abraham Lincoln on March 4, 1861, and listened on the platform to one of the most memorable inaugural addresses ever given by a president. Although then nearly eighty-four years old, the Chief Justice was destined to preside over the Court for another three and a half years. Indeed, Senator Ben Wade of Ohio during that time made the rather unkind comment that "no man had prayed harder than he did that Roger Taney would outlive the administration of James Buchanan, but now he was afraid he had overdone it."

But Roger Taney saw what had up until then been the Taney Court disappear before his very eyes in these last years. Justice Peter V. Daniel had died in 1860, Justice McLean died in the spring of 1861, and a few weeks later Justice Campbell resigned from the Court to follow his state of Alabama into the Confederacy. Abraham Lincoln appointed Republicans Noah Swayne, Samuel F. Miller, and David Davis, respectively, to fill these vacancies. When Congress created a tenth circuit and a tenth seat on the Court in 1863, Lincoln appointed War Democrat Stephen J. Field to the position. Thus the makeup of the Taney Court changed dramatically in the last three years of the Chief Justice's life.

One last burst of notable judicial activity was reserved for Taney in his eighty-fifth year. His duties as Chief Justice required him not only to preside over the Supreme Court when it was in session but to sit as a circuit judge in places such as Baltimore. After the fall of Fort Sumter in April 1861, northern troops began moving to Washington in response to President Lincoln's call for 75,000 volunteers. The natural route these troops would follow from the northeast to Washington led through the city of Baltimore, which was at that time a hotbed of secessionist sympathy. Troops moving through the city were stoned, bridges along the Baltimore and Ohio Railroad were destroyed, and for a while troops were shipped by sea to Annapolis and then proceeded overland to Washington, in order to avoid Baltimore. On April 27, 1861, Lincoln directed General Winfield Scott to suspend the writ of habeas corpus if it should prove necessary to preserve the public safety. Congress was not in session at the time, and therefore could not authorize or ratify the suspension of the writ. Article I of the Constitution, dealing with the powers of Congress, provided that the writ of habeas corpus should not be suspended "unless when in cases of rebellion or invasion the public safety may require it." From its place in the text of the Constitution, a strong inference might be drawn that Congress alone—or, more accurately, Congress and the president together enacting a law— could suspend the writ.

In May 1861, the general who had been ordered to put a stop to interference with troop movements between Philadelphia and Baltimore caused the arrest of one John Merryman, the president of the state agriculture society and an active secessionist in Maryland. He was confined in Fort McHenry, and on the day of his arrest he petitioned the federal circuit court in Baltimore for a writ of habeas corpus. The following day Chief Justice Taney, sitting in the circuit court in Baltimore, issued what is called "an order to show cause" directing that the custodian of the prisoner seeking habeas corpus make a return before the court so that the legality of the imprisonment may be determined.

Taney's writ was directed to General George Cadwalader, the commander of Fort McHenry, and on the following day Cadwalader sent his aide-de-camp, Colonel Lee, to read a statement to the court calling its attention to the President's order for the suspension of the writ, and requesting the postponement of the case until the President could be consulted.

Taney was incensed by the conduct of the military, and directed that an attachment be issued against the general returnable at noon on the following day. A crowd of several thousand people assembled the next day to witness the outcome of this test of strength. Taney asked the marshal for his return on the writ of attachment, and the marshal replied in writing that he had not been allowed to enter Fort McHenry to serve the writ. Taney then declared his opinion that the suspension of the writ of habeas corpus by the President alone was unconstitutional. He declared that he would write out his opinion and send a copy to the President of the United States, since it was impossible for him to enforce the process of the court against the superior military force arrayed against him. In due course he did so, and Lincoln apparently received a copy of the letter. Lincoln never acknowledged its receipt in so many words, but in his July Fourth message to a special session of Congress, he stated that the legality of authorizing the suspension of the writ had been questioned. He said that he had been called upon to "take care that the laws be faithfully executed" and not himself violate the laws. He responded that all the laws were being resisted and nearly one third of the states had attempted to secede. He then went on to say:

> Must [the laws] be allowed to finally fail of execution even had it been perfectly clear that by the use of the means necessary to their execution some single law, made in such extreme tenderness of the citizen's liberty that practically it relieves more of the guilty than of the innocent, should to a very limited extent be violated? To state the question more directly, are all the laws *but one* to go unexecuted, and the government itself go to pieces lest that one be violated?

Lincoln also defended the merits of his action under the Constitution, and left a more elaborate defense to an official opinion prepared by Attorney General Edward Bates.

As might be expected, Taney was denounced as furiously for his decision in *Ex parte Merryman* as he had been for his opinion in the *Dred Scott* case by much of the northern press. "Too feeble to wield the sword against the Constitution, too old and palsied and weak to march in the ranks of rebellion and fight against the Union, he uses the powers of his office to serve the cause of the traitors." [Quoted in Warren, Vol. III, p. 92] But by now Taney must have become used to such abusive condemnation, and he continued to perform his duties as Chief Justice though his health rapidly deteriorated. A contemporary resident of Washington described Taney in his last years thus:

> There was no sadder figure to be seen in Washington during the years of the Civil War than that of the aged Chief Justice. His form was bent by the weight of years, and his thin, nervous, and deeply-furrowed face was shaded by long, gray locks, and lighted up by large, melancholy eyes that looked wearily out from under shaggy brows, which gave him a weird, wizard-like expression. He had outlived his epoch, and was shunned and hated by the men of the new time of storm and struggle for the principles of freedom and nationality. [Mrs. J. A. Logan, *Thirty Years in Washington*, p. 413, quoted in Swisher, *Taney*, p. 575]

Roger Taney died in October 1864 at the age of eighty-eight, having served twenty-eight years as Chief Justice. The last seven years of his life, from the time of the delivery of the *Dred Scott* opinion until his death, must have been bitter ones. So great was northern dislike for him that when in 1865 it was proposed in the Senate that funds be appropriated for a marble bust of Taney— just as funds had been appropriated for busts of all previous chief justices—Senator Charles Sumner successfully opposed the measure, saying that "Taney will be hooted down the pages of history." Sumner's radical counterpart in the House, Representative Thaddeus Stevens from Pennsylvania, responded to proposals that would have allowed the whites to govern the reconstructed South with the statement, "Sir, this doctrine of a white man's government is as atrocious as the infamous sentiment that damned the late Chief Justice to everlasting fame and I fear everlasting fire." [Quoted in Bowers] When Chief Justice Salmon P. Chase died seven years later, Congress without objection appropriated funds for busts of both Taney and Chase to be placed in the Supreme Court chamber.

The dust of controversy has long since had time to settle, and a calmer appraisal is obviously in order. Taney had a first-rate legal mind, and was a clear, forceful writer. Like Marshall, he was not overly wrapped up in legal learning for its own sake, and realized that constitutional law required vision and common sense as well as careful legal analysis. His willingness to find in the United States Constitution the necessary authority for states to solve their own problems was a welcome addition to the nationalist constitutional jurisprudence of the Marshall Court. His opinion in the *Dred Scott* case was a serious mistake for the reasons I have earlier suggested, but that opinion should not be allowed to blot out the very constructive work otherwise done in a career that spanned twenty-eight years. Charles Evans Hughes, shortly after he himself had been appointed Chief Justice of the United States, observed at a ceremony dedicating a bust of Taney in Frederick, Maryland, in 1931 that "the arduous service nobly rendered by Roger Brooke Taney has received its fitting recognition. He bore his wounds with the fortitude of an invincible spirit. He was a great Chief Justice."

Personally Taney appears to have been a warm, almost gentle person, not the "man's man" Marshall was, but equally cherished by his colleagues. Samuel Freeman Miller, appointed to the Court by President Lincoln in 1862, who served with Taney two and a half years, had this to say about the Chief Justice:

> When I came to Washington, I had never looked upon the face of Judge Taney, but I knew of him. I remembered that he had attempted to throttle the Bank of the United States, and I hated him for it. I remembered that he took his seat

upon the bench, as I believed, in reward for what he had done in that connection, and I hated him for that. He had been the Chief Spokesman of the Court on the *Dred Scott* case, and I hated him for that. But from my first acquaintance with him, I realized that these feelings toward him were but the suggestions of the worst elements of our nature, for before the first Term of my service in the Court had passed, I more than liked him; I loved him. And after all that has been said of that great, good man, I stand always ready to say that conscience was his guide and sense of duty his principle. [Quoted in Fairman, *Mr. Justice Miller,* p. 52]

7

JUSTICES
MILLER AND FIELD

$\mathcal{W}$ith the passing of Chief Justice Taney, the Supreme Court of the United States evolved into a significantly different institution. The dominance of Marshall and Taney during most of their sixty-three-year hegemony had largely eclipsed the numerous associate justices with whom they served. But for more than half a century following the Civil War, the four chief justices fell sufficiently short of the stature of Marshall and Taney so as to permit, if not require, the emergence of associate justices in leadership roles. Two of these associate justices were appointed by Abraham Lincoln: Samuel F. Miller of Iowa and Stephen J. Field of California.

Samuel Freeman Miller was born in Richmond, Kentucky, in 1816. Richmond is a county seat some twenty miles southeast of Lexington in the bluegrass country. He attended the medical department of Transylvania University between 1835 and 1838, and in the latter received a medical degree. He then settled in Barbourville, in the eastern part of the state on the Cumberland River, and practiced medicine there until 1847. But in 1845, apparently tiring of his work as a doctor, he began two years of the study of law while continuing to practice medicine. In 1847 he was admitted to the practice of law in Barbourville.

Three years later, at the age of thirty-five, he moved from

Kentucky to Keokuk, Iowa, largely because he wanted to live in a free state rather than in a slave state. Keokuk, located in the southeastern tip of Iowa that sticks down like a peninsula between Illinois and Missouri, was then at the head of deepwater navigation on the Mississippi River. At this time, Keokuk had a population of a little more than three thousand. Miller was widowed in 1854, but remarried the widow of his law partner in 1857.

While in Keokuk Miller opposed the repeal of the Missouri Compromise in 1854, and became an early member of the Republican party. He was head of the party county organization during the 1850s, and in 1860 was a member of the party's state central committee, which played an active part in securing Iowa's votes for the Republican nominee, Abraham Lincoln.

Almost immediately upon taking office President Lincoln found he had three vacancies on the Supreme Court to fill, but he postponed his court appointments while Congress tinkered with the allocation of justices to the geographic circuits in the various parts of the country. Because familiarity with local law was an important attribute of a circuit justice, it was regarded as essential that the Supreme Court nominee have practiced in the particular circuit to which he was assigned. Therefore, it was not only considerations of judicial administration that were involved in the impending congressional decision on this question. The chances of the various candidates for the vacancies would be helped or hurt by the determination as to which states would be included in which circuits.

The situation that confronted Congress at this time was one that cried out for correction. Eight states, Wisconsin, Minnesota, Iowa, Kansas, California, Oregon, Texas, and Florida (some admitted to the Union as long as fifteen years previously), were not within any of the nine established circuits. Sentiment in Congress held that it was simply not feasible to continue to create new circuits in order to increase the number of justices. A reshuffle was therefore inevitable.

It was decided that three circuits should be created out of what were then regarded as the "western states," and how these states were to be grouped in the circuits would affect who would be named to vacancies in the Court. The Iowa bar, governor, legislature, and congressional delegation all united to push Miller for one of the Supreme Court vacancies, but his chances would be vastly improved if Iowa was aligned in a new circuit with other states that had no leading candidates of their own. Thus the Iowa delegation, and the Miller forces, wanted to group the four trans-Mississippi states—Iowa, Minnesota, Missouri, and Kansas—in one circuit, leaving the remaining midwestern states to be grouped in two circuits east of the Mississippi and north of the Ohio rivers. A contrary result—for instance, if Iowa were grouped with Illinois, its neighbor to the east—could prove disastrous to Miller's chances, since there were several Illinois aspirants to the High Court who had the sort of personal claims upon Lincoln that Miller did not have.

After six months in and out of committee and on the floor of both houses, the Miller supporters were successful in getting the circuit realignment that would favor their candidate's chances, and in early 1862, Lincoln appointed Miller to the Supreme Court. Miller was the first Supreme Court justice to have been born west of the Appalachian Mountains, and the first one to have been appointed from a state west of the Mississippi River.

Stephen J. Field was born in Haddam, Connecticut, in 1816. In 1819 his family removed to Stockbridge, Massachusetts, where he grew up as one of nine children, four of whom were to achieve fame. Field entered Williams College in September 1832, and was valedictorian of his class there. He then studied law in the New York office of his older brother David Dudley Field, and was admitted to practice before the New York bar in 1841. He practiced with his brother until 1845, and then removed his offices to another place in New York City, where he continued to practice until 1849. In that year, attracted by the lure of the California gold rush, he sailed for California by way of the Isthmus of Panama. He landed in San Francisco after a six weeks' journey, and after a very short stay in San Francisco took passage on a boat sailing up the Sacramento River to Marysville, a frontier town located above Sacramento on the river.

Things were definitely primitive in Marysville; Field was elected Alcalde or magistrate after he had been there only three days,
defeating another candidate who had arrived only the day before.
In 1850 he was elected to the California legislature, and there
played a major part in enacting a modified version of the Field
code—named for David Dudley Field, who had procured the
adoption of a similar code in New York—in California. He engaged in a successful law practice in Marysville during the 1850s
until in 1857 he was elected to the Supreme Court of California
and gave up his law practice. He was apparently earning an income of $40,000 a year at this time, and exchanged it for a salary
of $6,000 a year. At that time the chief justice of the Supreme
Court of California was David Terry, a hot-blooded southerner
with whom Field would have more than one confrontation later in
his life. In 1859 Terry resigned from the court and shortly afterward killed California Senator David Broderick in a duel.

In 1863 Congress created a tenth circuit to accommodate the
Pacific Coast states and Lincoln appointed Field, who had become an active War Democrat—a member of the Democratic
party who nonetheless supported Lincoln—to fill the newly created position. Some inkling as to Field's determination may be
gained from a case involving ownership of land where title was
based upon a Mexican land grant just beyond the borders of the
city of San Francisco. The United States Board of Land Commissioners charged with determining these titles had refused to confirm title in these lands to the city because of what it regarded as a
flaw in the Mexican title, but the city had appealed to the district
court. The district court, however, refused to hear the case, apparently because the district judge was interested in the claims
himself. Field determined that the matter should be settled, and
proceeded to draft a bill providing that when a district judge was
interested in land claims pending before him, the district court
should order the case transferred to the circuit court—in this case,
the court presided over by newly appointed Justice Field when on
circuit duty. Senator Conness from California sponsored the bill,
and it was passed by Congress.

The case was then argued before Field alone, sitting as circuit judge in California, and he decided that the city of San Francisco had good title to the property in question. But after Field had left San Francisco to go to Washington and sit with the Supreme Court, the city and the private claimants both sought appeals to the Supreme Court, which allowed them over Field's dissent. Before the cases could be heard on the merits, Field drafted a bill to confirm San Francisco title to the land, and the bill, shepherded through Congress by members of the California delegation, was duly passed. The result was that the Supreme Court could not hear the case on the merits, and the title to the land was awarded in the same manner as Field had ruled in the circuit court.

Shortly before Field and Miller took their seats on the Court, it moved from its rather cramped quarters in the basement of the Capitol to the chamber occupied by the Senate until 1860. A contemporary observer described the setting in these words:

The hall is small but one of the handsomest in the Capitol. It is semicircular in form, is seventy-five feet long, and forty-five feet high, and forty-five feet wide in the centre, which is the widest part. A row of handsome green pillars of Potomac marble extends across the eastern, or rear side of the hall, and the wall which sweeps round the western side, is ornamented with pilasters of the same material. The ceiling is in the form of a dome, is very beautiful, and is ornamented with square caissons of stucco. A large skylight in the centre of the room lights the chamber.

A handsome white marble clock is placed over the main door which is on the western side. Opposite, from the eastern wall, a large gilded eagle spreads his wings above a raised platform, railed in, and tastefully draped, along which are arranged the comfortable armchairs of the Chief Justice and his associates, the former being in the centre. Above them is still the old "eastern gallery of the Senate," so famous in the history of the country. The desks and seats of the lawyers are ranged in front of the Court, and enclosed by a tasteful railing. The floor is covered with soft, heavy carpets; cushioned benches for spectators are placed along the semicircular wall, and busts of John Jay, John Rutledge, Oliver Ellsworth and John Marshall, former Chief Justices, adorn the hall.

Coming from either the House or the Senate, you seem to have entered another world. Everything is so calm and peaceful, so thoroughly removed from the noise and confusion of political strife going on in the other parts of the Capitol, that the change is indeed delightful. [J. B. Ellis, *Sights and Secrets of the National Capitol*, 1869, pp. 253–54, quoted in Swisher, *Stephen J. Field*, pp. 126–127]

Just as the Court's quarters were changed about the time of the Civil War, so too were the legal issues coming before it. The Supreme Court as now constituted would first have to deal with important issues arising out of the conduct of the war, with the result that it handed down shortly after the end of hostilities its first decisions in favor of "civil liberties." Also, immediately after the Civil War Congress proposed, and the necessary number of states ratified, three amendments to the Constitution that would in due time present other new and important questions for the Court's decision. Finally, the economic expansion that had been going on apace before the Civil War was accelerated; America's phenomenal industrial and commercial growth would bring still added problems to the Court.

In time of war the government requires the necessary authority to conduct military operations successfully, and a concomitant of this fact is that individual freedom is accordingly circumscribed. The Civil War was no exception to this principle. A little more than a year and a half after Robert E. Lee surrendered to Ulysses S. Grant at Appomattox, the Supreme Court decided an important case involving the authority of the president to substitute trial by court-martial for trial by jury during time of war. The five justices whom President Lincoln had appointed to the Court—Salmon P. Chase, Noah H. Swayne, Samuel Miller, David Davis, and Stephen Field—found themselves only partly in agreement on the issues that the Court decided.

The majority of Democrats in the North supported the Union war effort during the Civil War, but a small minority simply wished to allow the southern states to leave the Union in peace. They were called Peace Democrats. In Indiana and Illinois the Peace Democrats formed a secret society called the Sons of Liberty. This organization actually planned efforts to forcibly release Confederate prisoners held in the Midwest, and for a seizure of government stores at Louisville, Kentucky. In October 1864, one Lambdin P. Milligan and other members of the society were tried for conspiracy against the government, affording aid to rebels, inciting insurrection, and related offenses. Each of the acts charged constituted a violation of United States law and the defendants could have been criminally charged in the federal courts, but Governor Oliver P. Morton of Indiana and Secretary of War Edwin M. Stanton decided on more draconic procedures. Milligan and his cohorts were tried before a military commission in Indianapolis in the fall of 1864, found guilty on all charges, and sentenced to be hanged. A few months later, lawyers for Milligan sought a writ of habeas corpus from the federal circuit court in Indianapolis, claiming that the United States Constitution forbade Milligan's trial by a court-martial under these circumstances. The two judges of the court differed in opinion, and so under the law as it then existed the case was certified to the Supreme Court on legal questions.

The lawyers for Milligan had a very good argument that did not depend on the United States Constitution at all, but on a law passed by Congress in 1863. That law authorized the president to suspend the writ of habeas corpus during time of rebellion, but it also required the secretaries of state and war to furnish to the judges of the circuit and district courts lists of all persons who were citizens of states loyal to the Union but held as political prisoners; where a grand jury had met and adjourned without finding an indictment against such persons, they would be entitled to their discharge upon taking an oath of allegiance. Milligan's lawyers argued that Congress when it passed this law clearly authorized the president to detain and hold political prisoners, but he could hold them only pending trial in the civil courts. Why else would Congress provide that if such prisoners had not been indicted by a grand jury, they would be entitled to their release?

Milligan's lawyers also argued that even if the act of Congress did not mean what they said it meant, the government might not try persons such as Milligan before a court-martial when the civil courts were open and functioning, as they were in Indiana.

The government's response to these arguments in the Supreme Court was made by James P. Speed of Kentucky, surely one of the nation's least-gifted attorneys general. In arguments that cannot fail to remind one of the government's argument before Judge Pine in the Steel Seizure Case some eighty years later, Speed argued that in time of war the president was "the sole judge of the exigencies, necessities, and duties of the occasion. . . . During the war his power must be without limit. . . ." Insofar as the guarantees of the Bill of Rights, such as the right to jury trial, "these, in truth, are all peace provisions of the Constitution, and . . . are silence amidst arms. . . ." [Quoted in Fairman, *History of the Supreme Court*, p. 201.]

The Court was as little inclined to accept this sort of argument in 1866 as it was in 1952. Justice David Davis wrote an opinion for a five-man majority of the Court, holding that Milligan could not be constitutionally tried by a court-martial and opining in dicta that this result would obtain even if Congress had expressly authorized his trial by a court-martial. Four of the justices joined a separate opinion by Chief Justice Chase which criticized the majority for expressing an entirely gratuitous opinion on the authority of Congress, when no one contended that Congress had authorized the trial of Milligan by a military court. Justice Field joined the opinion of Justice Davis for the majority, while Justice Swayne and Justice Miller joined the opinion of the Chief Justice. Justice Davis in his opinion for the Court responded to the government's argument to the effect that the Constitution did not apply in time of war with this memorable passage:

The Constitution of the United States is a law for the rulers and people, equally in war and in peace, and covers with the shield of its protection all classes of men, at all times, and under all circumstances. No doctrine, involving more pernicious consequences, was ever invented by the wit of man than that any of its provisions can be suspended during any of the great exigencies of government (*Ex parte Milligan*, 4 Wall. 2, 71 U.S. 281, 295 [1866]).

All nine members of the Court agreed that the President, acting on his own authority and without authorization from Congress, could not compel Milligan, a civilian residing away from any theater of war in Indiana, to be tried by a military court. They differed as to whether Congress might authorize such a trial. Here, again, as in the *Dred Scott* case, the opinion for the Court felt obliged to opine on a question not before it: If Congress had authorized trial of Milligan by a military court, would such a trial have been constitutional? The minority of the Court, which joined Chief Justice Chase's opinion, probably in reaction to the comments in the Court opinion, treated the question also and concluded that Congress *could* have authorized such a trial. But the only question presented by the facts of Milligan's case was whether a president, acting *without* authorization from Congress, could authorize trial by a military court in this situation. It is indeed regrettable that both opinions rendered felt a need to discourse on an issue not presented by the case.

Less than a month later, the Court decided two cases involving test oaths imposed upon citizens during and after the Civil War in order for them to hold office, vote, or practice a particular vocation. *Ex Parte Garland* dealt with a former Confederate senator from Arkansas, and *Ex Parte Cummings* with a Catholic priest from Missouri. In 1862, in the second year of the Civil War when Union fortunes were at a low ebb, Congress enacted a law requiring that any holder of federal office other than the president should be required to take an "ironclad" oath addressing not merely his present loyalty to the Union but his past conduct in that regard. James Wilson, a Republican congressman from Iowa, who introduced the measure into the House, stated as to its purpose: "[T]he sole object of this bill is to keep out of office under the Government of the United States men who have taken up arms against the United States, and who have endeavored to destroy the Government under which we live." [Quoted in Beltz]

During its debates over reconstruction of the seceded states in 1864, Congress debated the extent to which such an oath should be required from potential voters or officeholders in those states, but President Lincoln pocket-vetoed the Wade-Davis Bill, which would have imposed such a requirement. In 1865, rather casually, at the suggestion of Senator Charles Sumner of Massachusetts, Congress extended the provisions of the act of 1862 to anyone seeking to practice before a federal court. Soon afterward Augustus H. Garland, until recently a Confederate senator from Arkansas, and later to be governor of that state, petitioned for leave to resume his practice before the Supreme Court without taking the loyalty oath thus required.

Arkansas's neighbor, Missouri, had enacted an even more stringent and more sweeping test-oath requirement, applicable not merely to officeholders and attorneys, but to voters and, of all things, to clergymen. One John A. Cummings was a Catholic priest who refused to take the elaborate oath; he was tried, convicted, and fined for acting as a priest without having taken the oath.

Few parts of the Union were tranquil during the Civil War, but the experience of Missouri was particularly grim. It was one of the three border states that President Lincoln desperately wanted to keep in the Union after the Confederacy was established, and because of its location, it became during the Civil War the same sort of "dark and bloody ground" that Kentucky had been earlier.

Missouri recognized the institution of slavery, and emigrants from Missouri had participated extensively in the affairs of "Bleeding Kansas" in the late 1850s. In the election of 1860, Missouri's electoral votes had gone to Stephen A. Douglas, but the "Little Giant" had received only a minority of the popular vote, which was split among four candidates. The slaveholding population of the state was primarily along the Missouri River, which roughly bisects the state from west to east. The area around St. Louis contained a substantial number of Union supporters, including a large number of recent German emigrants. Lincoln had chosen Edward Bates from Missouri as his attorney general, and Frank Blair, the congressman from that district, was a close confidant of the President.

At the time of the outbreak of the Civil War in April 1861, Claiborne Jackson, the governor, and the state assembly favored secession, but a convention called to consider the question turned out to be dominated by a majority of Unionists. This convention ultimately deposed Jackson as governor, and the latter fled to Lexington, Missouri, fifty miles east of Kansas City on the Missouri River, where he set up a sort of Confederate headquarters. In July 1861, John Charles Fremont, the "Pathfinder," who had been the Republican nominee for president in 1856, was appointed by Lincoln as military commander of the Department of the West with his headquarters in St. Louis. As a military commander, Fremont was more show than substance, lacking both the military experience and the tact to discharge his responsibilities effectively. After minor successful engagements with the rebels in Missouri, Fremont issued an emancipation proclamation granting freedom to all slaves within the rebel lines in his district. Lincoln, desperately wishing to keep the border states in the Union and not yet ready to commit himself to emancipation as a war aim, directed Fremont to revoke the proclamation. Fremont, in an extraordinary act of insubordination, refused to do so, and his charismatic wife, Jessie Benton Fremont, journeyed to Washington to plead with Lincoln to change his mind. Lincoln refused, the order was revoked, and Fremont was eventually removed as the commander in the west.

In August 1861, Sterling Price, who earlier in the year had presided over the state convention to decide secession but was now a general in the Confederate Army, defeated a Union Army at Wilson's Creek in southwestern Missouri, thereby assuring that even though the state was nominally under Union control, there would be Confederate raids and guerrilla activities there for the duration of the war. Storybook characters such as Governor Jim Lane of Kansas on the Union side and William C. Quantrill for the Confederates vied with one another in the bushwhacking activities of their forces. Quantrill took his raiders to Lawrence, Kansas, where they brutally fell upon a number of civilians and killed them in cold blood. "Kill every man big enough to carry a gun," Quantrill had ordered, and so they did, with the loss of only one of their force.

Four days after the sack of Lawrence, General Thomas Ewing, who had succeeded Fremont, issued his drastic Order Number 11. That order required all residents of four counties in the vicinity of Kansas City to leave their homes. The grief and suffering of those exiled called forth a well-known painting by George Caleb Bingham entitled *Order Number Eleven.* Ewing's justification for this order is stated by one of the historians of this period in these words:

> The civilian population of the border counties encompassed some thousands of persons who were eager to fight for the Confederacy. Although they did not, ordinarily, wear uniforms and fight in regular military units, many were bold and re-sourceful; and they were skilled in taking advantage of the credulity and the weaknesses of officers who were given the job of keeping them in order. Without sufficient cavalry to police the country roads and backwoods communities, unable to descend suddenly upon remote places that were used for refuge by the Bushwhackers, the commander could not bring the District under control as long as Southern sympathizers lived unmolested in their homes and worked secretly with the guerrilla bands. [McReynolds]

The Union triumph in the Civil War brought a bittersweet reaction in Missouri. If one lived in Vermont or Wisconsin, the enemy had been hundreds of miles away: citizens of the same nation, but not physically close. But in Missouri, whether one was a Confederate supporter or a Union supporter, the enemy might have been one's next-door neighbor. It is thus understandable, if not justifiable, that when the Radical Republicans gained control of the Missouri legislature in 1864, and of a constitutional con-vention called by the legislature in 1865, some of the measures they enacted were draconic indeed. One of them was the ironclad oath challenged in the Supreme Court by the Catholic priest John Cummings. It is interesting to note that the constitution of 1865, containing this oath, and voted on by an electorate limited to those who could qualify under the oath, was adopted by a majority of fewer than two thousand votes out of the nearly eighty-five thousand cast.

The federal oath required the customary statement that the affiant "will support and defend the Constitution of the United States against all enemies, foreign and domestic, and will bear true faith and allegiance to the same," and this portion of the oath was of course not challenged. But there were four additional declarations required which pertained to past conduct and from which the oath derived its appellation "ironclad." Augustus Garland, the Confederate senator, would have had to swear that he had never voluntarily borne arms against the United States since he had been a citizen thereof, that he had not voluntarily given aid or encouragement to persons engaged in armed hostility to the United States, that he had never held office under any authority hostile to the United States, and that he had not voluntarily supported any governmental authority within the United States which was hostile to it. Obviously Garland could not truthfully take this oath.

The Missouri oath was even more ironclad, requiring more than thirty disavowals. John Cummings, the priest, would have had to deny that he had ever been in armed hostility to the United States, that he had ever "by act or word" manifested his adherence to enemies of the United States, or his desire for their triumph over the arms of the United States; that he had never harbored or aided any person engaged in guerrilla warfare against the loyal inhabitants of the United States, and that he had never entered or left the state of Missouri for the purpose of avoiding enrollment or draft in the military service of the United States. Finally, he would have had to deny that he had ever indicated in any terms "his disaffection to the Government of the United States in its contest with the rebellion."

If the Missouri case arose today, rather than one hundred twenty years ago, it would be disposed of quite simply under either the religion clauses of the First Amendment to the United States Constitution or under the Free Speech Clause of that Amendment. Governmental licensing of priests would be a clear affront to the religion clauses, and a requirement that forbade the expression of any disaffection with the North in the Civil War would abridge freedom of speech. But the cases arose in 1866, and everybody involved agreed that the First Amendment applied only to Congress and the federal government, not to the states and their legislatures.

The Supreme Court decided by a vote of 5 to 4 that each of the oaths was unconstitutional because it constituted a "bill of attainder" and an "*ex post facto* law." The United States Constitution prohibited both the state and the national governments from enacting either of these things, so the question before the Court was whether the act of Congress or the Missouri statute came within the definition of the prohibited acts. These clauses of the Constitution are not of the broad, general nature of the Due Process Clause, but refer to rather precise legal terms which had a meaning under English law at the time the Constitution was adopted. A bill of attainder was a legislative act that singled out one or more persons and imposed punishment on them, without benefit of trial. Such actions were regarded as odious by the framers of the Constitution because it was the traditional role of a court, judging an individual case, to impose punishment. An *ex post facto* law was a law that punished for conduct that had occurred before its enactment. An early case from the Court, *Calder v. Bull*, had rather strongly intimated that this provision applied only to criminal laws.

Justice Field wrote the majority opinion for the Court in each case, and probably did as good a job as could have been done in trying to show that both acts were within the prohibitions against bills of attainder and *ex post facto* laws. In spite of his straining and stretching of the materials available to him, he really succeeded in showing only that the acts in question had some of the same effects of bills of attainder and *ex post facto* laws, and this was apparently good enough for the five-man majority of the Court. Field was joined in his opinion by Justices Wayne, Catron, and Grier, who had also joined Chief Justice Taney's opinion in the *Dred Scott* case, and by Justice Nelson, who had concurred in the result in the *Dred Scott* case. Justice Miller, writing for himself, Chief Justice Chase, and Justices Swayne and Davis, viewed the acts as being obviously distasteful but as not being within the traditional meaning of either an *ex post facto* law or a bill of attainder.

These three cases—*Milligan, Garland,* and *Cummings*—are the first batch of decisions from the Supreme Court upholding claims of "civil liberties" under the United States Constitution. A civil liberty is a claim that an individual has against the government, and in these cases Lambdin Milligan and Augustus Garland prevailed in their constitutional claims against the United States, and John Cummings prevailed in his constitutional claim against the state of Missouri. In the test-oath cases, four of the Lincoln appointees dissented, while the fifth combined with the four pre-Civil War Democratic appointees to make up a majority of the Court. In the Milligan case, one of the latter—Justice Wayne—joined Justices Swayne and Miller in the Chief Justice's concurrence, while Justice Field joined three of the Democratic appointees in Justice Davis's opinion for the Court. Cases dealing with test oaths and martial law burned brightly on the judicial griddle immediately after the Civil War, but they almost immediately gave way to the lawsuits generated by America's economic and industrial expansion.

If any one aspect of industrial expansion in the United States in the middle of the nineteenth century typified the rest, it was the building of the railroads. Railroad building in the United States began in earnest about the time that Andrew Jackson was elected president. The first "railroads"—that is, systems of transportation that combined the use of rails with the idea of a steam locomotive pulling cars on them—appeared in the United States about 1830. In New England the Boston and Lowell, the Boston and Worcester, and the Boston and Providence all began operating during the 1830s. At about the same time in New Jersey the Camden and Amboy connected the Delaware River Valley to New York Harbor. In Maryland the Baltimore and Ohio began to build west from Baltimore toward the Potomac Valley. In South Carolina, the Charleston and Hamburg Railroad connected those two cities. In the eighteen years between 1830 and 1848, some six thousand miles of track were laid, but in the next eight years nearly three times that much—seventeen thousand miles—were laid. During the 1850s the four trunk lines that came to link the Eastern Seaboard with Chicago each laid tracks over or through the Appalachian barrier from the East Coast to the flatlands of the Ohio Valley and Great Lakes. The railroad that ultimately became the New York Central ran up the Hudson River Valley from New York to Albany, and then west along the route of the Erie Canal from Albany to Buffalo on Lake Erie. The Erie Railroad ran from a point on the Hudson River near New York City across New York's southern-tier counties to Dunkirk on Lake Erie. The Pennsylvania Railroad laid track from Philadelphia to Pittsburgh, negotiating its way through the Allegheny Mountains by means of the famous Horseshoe Curve. The Baltimore and Ohio tracks began in Baltimore, Maryland, and followed the Potomac Valley through Harpers Ferry and on to Wheeling, both then in Virginia, on the Ohio River. By 1860 through connections on each of these routes existed to Chicago.

With the settlement of the upper Midwest—Iowa, Minnesota, and Wisconsin, it became virtually foreordained that Chicago would be a great railroad center. One need only look at a map of the United States and see the three-hundred-mile water barrier Lake Michigan creates between these states and the Northeast to understand why Chicago, located as it was at the foot of Lake Michigan, would become a great transportation hub.

The coming of the railroad had a dramatic effect on farmers' choice of transportation for their products. In 1850 there was not a mile of railroad in Chicago, but by 1855 there were twenty-two hundred miles of track coming into the city, and one hundred trains departing and arriving each day. It was very likely the largest grain market in the world, and farmers in Iowa, Wisconsin, and Illinois who had previously shipped their grain to market by means of Mississippi River boats and barges now found it cheaper to get their product to market by means of railroad transportation to Chicago or other lesser centers. By 1858, Chicago had eclipsed St. Louis as a center of the grain trade, with twice as much of that commodity being shipped through the former as through the latter.

Beyond Chicago, the first railroad track reached the Mississippi River in 1854, and the Missouri River in 1859. But development beyond the Mississippi River to the Pacific Coast was obviously going to require support from the national government because of the extremely sparse settlement in most of the area through which such a Pacific railroad would go. The idea of such a railroad had been first broached in the 1840s, but sectional rivalries between the North and the South over whether the road should have its terminus in New Orleans, Memphis, St. Louis, Chicago, or St. Paul prevented Congress from settling on any one plan. One of James Buchanan's last acts before leaving the presidency was to veto a Pacific Railroad bill passed by both houses of Congress, and although President Lincoln signed a similar bill two years later, it was not until 1869 and the driving of the "golden spike" at Promontory Point, Utah, that the railroad linking the Pacific Coast with the rest of the nation became a reality. Even in 1865, there was only a little over three thousand miles of railroad track west of the Mississippi as compared with thirty-five thousand miles east of it. [Hawgood]

Obviously all of this trackage was not devoted to trunk lines, and not only sizable cities but virtually every small town was soon anxious to have its railroad connection. This was not merely a matter of local pride, but of economic survival:

> The pride or ambition of every community was a shining track and the lively whistle of a well-laden train, with the accompanying statistics of crops hauled, mills built, and values enhanced. What does the railway do for farmers? asked the Athens (Tenn.) *Post* in 1855. Before the railroad reached eastern Tennessee, it answered, the three counties of Bradley, McMinn and Monroe grew less than twenty-five thousand bushels of wheat, and sold it for less than fifty cents a bushel. But the fall of 1855 found them growing four hundred thousand bushels, and selling it for a dollar. [Nevins, *Ordeal of the Union*, pp. 194-195]

While many farmers had originally opposed the construction of railroads for fear that their market for horses and hay would be thereby ruined, the experience of the farmers in the Tennessee counties was duplicated in other parts of the nation, and showed just how important it was for every locality to have a railroad connection. What had previously been a local or at best a regional market for farmers' produce was thereby converted into a national and even an international market.

In 1851 Massachusetts held a railroad jubilee attended by state, national, and foreign notables. Within twenty years there had been completed in Massachusetts seven main lines of railroad track covering one thousand miles, and not a single town of five thousand population was without railroad transportation.

Obviously the availability of railroad transportation made a tremendous difference to farmers in the great breadbasket area of the upper Midwest, and the demand of each hamlet for access to the route of the iron horse was heard throughout that part of the country as well as elsewhere. But as with most other great economic developments in our country's history, the satisfaction of this great demand brought with it important and difficult legal questions. One of them was the situation that arose from the frequent practice of cities and counties borrowing money in order to pay a railroad company to extend the company's trackage into its area. As with most such enterprises, there were good, well-managed railroad companies and poorly managed railroad companies; there were legitimate entrepreneurs, but on the fringes were a host of speculators. When the counties or cities had second thoughts about the wisdom of the money advanced to the railroads, legal questions arose which worked their way to the Supreme Court of the United States in the era immediately after the Civil War. In the early stages of railroad building, some states either built railroads themselves or undertook to fund the building of railroads within the state. But the states were generally concerned with the location of trunk lines, and left it to cities and counties to worry about branch lines. The construction of these branch lines became a major concern to many cities and counties.

In 1856 the people of Mansfield, Ohio, applied to the Atlantic & Great Western for terms upon which the road would be extended through their town. The directors decreed that a subscription of $100,000 dollars for railway stock, and a right-of-way and station site at fair prices payable in stock, would be the terms. The town accepted, and the road was built.

If the Atlantic & Great Western may seem greedy for this request, its avarice was mild compared to that of the Northern Pacific which, in 1880, responded to a request for an extension of its lines into the city of Superior, Wisconsin, by requesting that the town give the railroad "one third of the 'lands, premises and real estate' in the city." This offer, too, was accepted. Agreements such as these were duplicated throughout the nation, and in state after state millions of dollars were put up by counties, cities, and even small towns to induce the railroads to run their lines in a particular way. Many of the arrangements undoubtedly proved beneficial to all concerned, but human nature being what it is, there was bound to be discontent on the part of local taxpayers who found their property-tax bills increased for many years after the railroad line had been completed in order to pay off the local bonds that had been issued to raise money to pay the railroads.

Generally speaking, if a private corporation issues a bond for which a purchaser pays good money, there is little or no doubt that the corporation is liable to the purchaser even though there may have been some minor defect in complying with the corporation's articles or bylaws in deciding to authorize the issuance of the bonds. But the law has traditionally been different in the case of municipal corporations such as counties and cities, which are viewed as mere creatures of the state and their powers limited to such as may be allowed by the Constitution and laws of the state in which they are located. Because of this difference, purchasers of bonds issued by municipal corporations usually take pains to assure themselves that the city or county issuing the bond is authorized by law to do so.

So it was in 1857 when the city of Dubuque, Iowa, undertook to issue $250,000 worth of city bonds to help with the construction of the Dubuque, St. Peter and St. Paul Railroad Company. The people of the city of Dubuque in a referendum voted favorably to the issuance of the bonds, and the Iowa legislature passed a special act authorizing Dubuque to issue these particular bonds, and to levy a special tax to meet the principal and interest of the bonds if such was required. Bonds were issued on July 1, 1857, the principal payable in twenty years to an agent in New York, and interest payable semiannually. Whether because of the effects of the Panic of 1857, the failure of the railroad to measure up to expectations, or whatever, the city defaulted upon its bonds. A decision of the Supreme Court of Iowa at the time the bonds were issued had held that there was no prohibition against their issuance in the Iowa constitution, but after the bonds were issued the Supreme Court of Iowa overruled this case and held that a particular provision of the Iowa constitution made their issuance invalid even though both the city council, the people, and the legislature had authorized their issuance.

One Mr. Gelpcke had paid out money for the bonds and sued the city in the federal district court in Iowa when it failed to pay the interest on the bonds when due. The federal district court, and ultimately the Supreme Court of the United States, were confronted with an intriguing legal problem.

On the one hand, there was no doubt that Gelpcke had paid good money for the bonds, and no doubt that had a lawyer minutely and meticulously examined the question in 1857, he would have concluded that the city was authorized by state statute and city ordinance to pledge its credit in this manner, and that there was nothing in the Iowa constitution that forbade such a pledge of credit by the city.

On the other hand, the question of the meaning of the Iowa constitution is preeminently a question to be decided by the Supreme Court of Iowa, and not by some other court. If that court is finally to conclude that the Iowa constitution forbids a city to issue this sort of bond, logic would indicate that its view should prevail unless there is some provision in the federal constitution that prohibits such a result.

The Gelpcke case was in the federal court only because of "diversity of citizenship"—Gelpcke was a citizen of a state other than Iowa, of which the city of Dubuque was a "citizen," and Congress in the Judiciary Act of 1789 had told the federal courts to apply state law where applicable to cases such as this. But the

Supreme Court of the United States, obviously feeling considerable sympathy for the bondholders who had paid good money for the bonds issued by the city, refused to follow the decision of the Supreme Court of Iowa. The case was decided by the Supreme Court in 1864, before any of the Civil War amendments went into effect, and the Supreme Court did not say that the Iowa court had violated the federal Constitution by reversing itself on an issue of state law, but it nonetheless held for the bondholders. It undertook to interpret the Iowa constitution for itself, and decided that the earlier decisions of the Iowa Supreme Court, which had upheld the constitutionality of such bonds, were "better reasoned" than the more recent decision. In a concluding bit of rhetoric, Justice Swayne's opinion said, "We shall never immolate truth, justice, and the law, because a State tribunal has erected the altar and decreed the sacrifice" (*Gelpcke* v. *Dubuque*, 1 Wall. 175, 206–207 [1864]).

Justice Field joined the majority in this case; Justice Miller disagreed with the rest of his colleagues, and in his dissent he said:

> [The majority of the Court] have said to the Federal court sitting in Iowa, "you shall disregard this decision of the highest court of the state on this question. Although you are sitting in the state of Iowa, and administering her laws, and construing her constitution, you shall not follow the latest, though it be the soundest, exposition of its constitution by the Supreme Court of that state, but you shall decide directly to the contrary; and where that court has said that a statute is unconstitutional, you shall say that it is constitutional. When it says bonds are void, issued in that state, because they violate its constitution, you shall say they are valid, because they do *not* violate the constitution."
>
> Thus we are to have two courts, sitting within the same jurisdiction, deciding upon the same rights, arising out of the same statute, yet always arriving at opposite results, with no common arbiter of their differences. . . ."

Thus the majority of the Supreme Court of the United States, without expressly holding Dubuque's actions in repudiating its bonds violative of the federal Constitution, accomplished the same result by simply refusing to follow the decisions of the Iowa courts when a case involving Iowa law was brought in federal court because of diversity of citizenship.

Reflecting the temper of the times, the Supreme Court of Pennsylvania in a case involving a similar fact situation in 1860 said:

> We know the history of these municipal and county bonds— how the legislature, yielding to popular excitements about rail- roads, authorized their issue; how grand juries, and county commissioners, and city officers, were molded to the purposes of speculators; how recklessly railroad officers abused the over- wrought confidence of the public, and what burdens of debt and taxation have resulted to the people. A monied security was created and thrown upon the market by this paroxysm of the public mind, and the question is now, how shall the judi- cial mind regard it?

At least so far as the Supreme Court of the United States was concerned, the "judicial mind" regarded the interests of the bondholders who had invested their money in these securities as weighing far more heavily in the scales of justice than the limita- tions state constitutions placed on the power of their cities and counties to donate money to the railroads. If the Supreme Court of the United States were a common-law court, with a general authority to lay down rules of law that best served its concept of justice in the cases coming before it, a decision such as that in *Gelpcke* v. *Dubuque* would be entirely defensible. Not only were bondholders totally unaware of any defect in the power of the city to issue its bonds, but if each bondholder had employed a compe- tent attorney at the time of his purchase and requested an opinion as to the authority of the city of Dubuque to issue the bonds, surely the attorney would have concluded that there was virtually no question but that the state constitution did not prohibit their issuance, and that a state law had by its express terms authorized their issuance. The later decision of the Supreme Court of Iowa overruling its earlier decision smacks a good deal of trying to get cities and counties, which had improvidently pledged their money to induce the railroads to construct lines to them, off the hook.

But viewed in the perspective of the American constitutional system, where the Supreme Court has no generalized mandate to "do justice," but is simply required to decide whether lawsuits dependent on state law raise any federal constitutional question, the answer must be considerably different. Save as restricted by the United States Constitution, the states are themselves sovereign entities with their own systems of laws and courts, and the supreme court of a state is concededly the final authority in construing the meaning of its own constitution and laws. The decision of the Supreme Court of Iowa overruling its earlier cases may have been improvident and ill-considered in the extreme, but these facts alone did not warrant the Supreme Court of the United States for simply setting the Iowa decision at naught. The Supreme Court simply relied on the accidental presence of diversity jurisdiction to totally disregard the decision of the Supreme Court of Iowa, and really had no better reason for doing it than that it thought the decisions were unfair to bondholders who had invested their money in reliance on the validity of the bonds.

The railroad-bond cases were very much a staple of the Court's business during the 1860s and 1870s, but like so many other legal questions they had all but disappeared by the latter part of the nineteenth century. But the Protean efforts of the railroads to link all but the smallest village and hamlet into the giant railroad grid soon produced popular reaction in many states which led to another and more far-reaching problem for the Supreme Court.

Railroads in the United States were organized in the corporate form, and capitalized through the sale of stock to largely private investors. Sometimes units of government bought stock, other times they may have contributed money or land to aid in the building of the railroad, but none of this changed the essentially private nature of the typical railroad corporation. The directors and the stockholders of these corporations, at least at first, regarded the operation of a railroad from Philadelphia to Pittsburgh as being little different from the operation of a general store in either of these two cities. The store owner bought or rented the land on which his store was located, and paid his suppliers for the goods which he in turn sold to his customers. The railroads paid for the right-of-way over which their tracks ran, bought the material necessary to construct the roads, hired the crews to build the lines, stations, and other necessary facilities. The Pennsylvania storekeeper could open his store when he chose in the morning, close it when he chose in the evening, and charge whatever he wished for the goods he sold to his customers. If the customers thought he was not open at convenient hours of the day, that he charged too much for his goods, or that his goods were of an inferior quality, they would presumably take their business elsewhere.

The railroad magnates viewed the operation of a railroad in much the same light. They had acquired every bit of property and equipment necessary to run their operation, from rights-of-way to rolling stock, and now they proposed to offer their services to the general public on such terms as they saw fit. But the people dependent on the service of a railroad line reacted quite differently to unfair pricing, inconvenient scheduling, and inferior service when offered by the railroad from the way they did to similar faults in a corner store. There were presumably other corner stores in the neighborhood to which they could repair if dissatisfied with the one at which they had been trading, but with railroad lines this was generally not the case. Unless one was located at a large railroad hub, he was usually dependent upon one particular railroad line for both freight and passenger service in and out of his town. And if the person in the town was a businessman trying to ship products to market, or a farmer trying to ship produce to market, the rates charged and the service afforded by the railroad could be a matter of life or death to the business.

Farmers were vitally affected by railroad practices. American farmers had generally prospered during the Civil War, but the latter third of the nineteenth century saw a period of sustained farm depression in the United States. The causes were manifold, but the farmers were convinced with good reason that a principal one was the large profits made by the railroads and middlemen in the transportation of farm goods to market. This attitude is typified by a paragraph in a North Carolina farm journal that appeared in the spring of 1887:

> There is something radically wrong in our industrial system. There is a screw loose. The wheels have dropped out of balance. The railroads have never been so prosperous and yet agriculture languishes. The banks have never done a better or more profitable business, and yet agriculture languishes. Manufacturing enterprises never made more money or were in a more flourishing condition, and yet agriculture languishes. Towns and cities flourish and "boom," and yet agriculture languishes. Salaries and fees were never so temptingly high and desirable, and yet agriculture languishes. [*Progressive Farmer* (Raleigh), April 18, 1887, quoted in Hicks]

Until roughly the time of the Civil War, a large majority of the people in the United States believed in a system of laissez-faire capitalism, in which each individual should be free to pursue his own best interests with little restraint from the government. But the plight of the farmers after the Civil War gradually converted that body of otherwise thoroughly independent souls to believers in governmental intervention in economic affairs. Railroads in most instances charged what the traffic would bear for shipment of farm products to market and also charged much higher rates per mile on local shipments than on long-distance shipments. Thus rates on wheat from Fargo to Duluth—a distance of a little over two hundred miles—were nearly twice as much as those from Fargo to Chicago, a distance of more than four hundred miles. The railroads replied that the large shipments on long runs with a steadier volume of traffic cost them less, and in addition, of course, on the long runs between principal cities there was very often competition between railroads. But whatever the merits of these justifications, they did not make the high local freight rates any more palatable to the farmer.

In those parts of the upper Midwest where grains were the principal crop, farmers also had cause to complain of the way the owners of grain elevators dealt with them. Since the grain elevators existed basically for the purpose of storing and then shipping grain, it was essential that they be built along railroad rights-of-way, and therefore, even if the elevators were not owned by the railroads, there was often a close tie between the interests of the elevator owner and the interests of the railroad. Though the grain-elevator owners were required by law in many states to serve all comers, most elevator operators were not merely in the storage business, but primarily in the business of buying grains from the farmer and selling them to the miller. Thus they had little incentive for encouraging farmers to use their facilities simply for storage in order to sell grain in competition with the elevator owner. The often monopolistic position of the grain-elevator owner in a particular locality enabled him to charge unreasonably high or arbitrarily discriminatory rates, and more than one elevator owner took advantage of such an opportunity.

When the farmers immediately after the Civil War turned to their state legislatures for help in dealing with the railroads, they found that the railroads effectively controlled many of the midwestern state legislatures. Often a single railroad was the dominant factor, such as the Sante Fe Railroad in Kansas, but sometimes two railroads shared control, as did the Burlington and the Union Pacific in Nebraska. One of the most pervasive methods by which the railroads exercised this control was the issuance of free passes to all sorts of government officials, passes that enabled them to ride without charge over the lines of the railroad. It was said at one point that in the Midwest the only people who didn't have passes were those who couldn't afford to pay their own fare. Faced with this sort of opposition, the farmers saw the necessity for organizing themselves.

The first national farm organization was begun shortly after the Civil War: Its full title was the National Grange of the Patrons of Husbandry, but it quickly became known as the Grange. It played a prominent role in many state political battles in the 1870s, but was gradually succeeded by the various Farmers' Alliances in the different parts of the nation. The Farmers' Alliances, like the Grange, eschewed the idea of forming a third party, and sought merely to influence the policies of the Democratic and Republican parties. But finally they became dissatisfied with the results of this course. One of the Minnesota farm leaders, Ignatius Donnelly, typified their conclusion when he said that the creation of a nonpolitical organization was like making a gun "that will do everything but shoot." [Ignatius Donnelly, Facts for the Granges, 18, quoted in Hicks, p. 206.]

The Farmers' Alliances joined together with other splinter factions to put the Populist party on a national basis in 1892. The party had a cast of characters the like of which has been seldom seen on the American political horizon: In addition to Donnelly, there was "Pitchfork Ben" Tillman from South Carolina, and "Sockless Jerry" Simpson and Mary Ellen Lease from Kansas. Mrs. Lease was noted for her exhortation to the farmers that they should "raise less corn and more hell."

The Populist party nominated James Weaver of Iowa for president in 1892, and in the election he received one million popular votes and twenty-two electoral votes. Four years later the Populist party fused with the Democratic party when it gave its own nomination to the Democratic nominee, William Jennings Bryan of Nebraska.

These political activities on the part of the farmers during the last third of the nineteenth century resulted in multitudes of state and local laws designed to redress the balance between the individual farmer and small businessman, on the one hand, and the railroads and their ilk on the other. The farmers worked through the legislatures and through the elective process, but when the railroads were unable to block legislation inimical to their interests in the legislatures, they often took to the courts to challenge the laws passed as violative of some provision of the United States Constitution. This sort of case became more and more abundant as the nation moved toward the twentieth century, and the Court upon which Samuel Miller and Stephen Field sat heard and decided a great number of them.

States began establishing primitive railroad commissions around the time of the Civil War, but the first important one is considered to be the Massachusetts commission established in

1869. The commission's role was primarily investigatory: It was charged with gathering information, recommending laws to the legislature, and making annual reports on the railroad industry. At this time there were sixty-two separate railroad corporations operating in Massachusetts—a state whose area was about one-fifth the area of midwestern states such as Wisconsin and Iowa, and there were no fewer than eight trunk lines operating in the state. The midwestern states, largely in response to the Granger movement, in the early seventies created what were called "strong" railroad commissions, and enacted laws that themselves prescribed to some extent the rates that might be charged by railroads and the schedules that should be maintained.

While the railroads were perfectly willing to live with a regulatory commission such as that in Massachusetts, which merely recommended legislation, they soon challenged many of the provisions of the midwestern Granger laws which regulated not only railroads but the prices that might be charged by grain elevators and other publicly used facilities. By now the railroads had available to them the provisions of the Fourteenth Amendment, one of the three Civil War amendments to the United States Constitution, which enacted a vaguely worded prohibition against state action that should "deprive any person of life, liberty, or property without process of law," that should "deny to any person the equal protection of the laws," or that should "abridge the privileges and immunities of citizens of the United States." It would be an unimaginative lawyer indeed who could not make a plausible claim that almost any state action ran afoul of one of these fuzzy generalities. And the lawyers for businesses that were being subjected to regulation were not unimaginative.

The first case requiring the Court to construe the language of the Fourteenth Amendment came from Louisiana and was decided in 1873. At this time the state was still undergoing Reconstruction, and the legislature passed a statute ostensibly to protect the health of the people of New Orleans but in fact granting to one slaughterhouse company for twenty-five years the exclusive privilege of operating abattoirs within the city. All other competing butchers had to come to the favored premises to slaughter their cattle. Some of the latter sued the favored monopolist in state court, claiming among other things that the state's granting of a monopoly to one competitor violated the newly enacted Fourteenth Amendment. The state courts upheld the Louisiana law, and the Supreme Court of the United States by a narrow margin agreed that Louisiana's rather blatant favoritism among its citizens did not violate the Fourteenth Amendment.

Justice Miller, who wrote the opinion for the majority of the Court, said that the "privileges and immunities" the amendment was talking about were ones that were given by the national government, not by the state governments, and that the right to engage in the slaughterhouse business was not of the former description. He went on to say that the principal beneficiaries of the amendment were the newly emancipated slaves, and that it was not meant to dramatically shift the balance between state and federal power in other areas.

Justice Field, writing for himself and three other dissenters, protested that if the Fourteenth Amendment meant no more than Miller said it did, it was all but meaningless—in Field's words, "A vain and idle enactment, which quite unnecessarily disturbed the people and the Congress."

Three years later the Court decided the famous Granger cases, the leading one of which is known as *Munn* v. *Illinois*. There the Illinois legislature, responding to popular discontent with what were felt to be exorbitant rates charged by privately owned grain warehouses, had set out to establish maximum rates above which the owner of a warehouse could not charge a farmer for the storage of his grain. This law, too, was challenged on the grounds that it violated the recently enacted Fourteenth Amendment— that it deprived the owner of the grain elevator of "property" "without due process of law." The Supreme Court, in an opinion by Chief Justice Morrison R. Waite, upheld the Illinois law. The Court said that even though the grain elevators were privately owned, their use was offered to the public generally and they were therefore subject to being regulated in the public interest. The Court recognized that this legislative "police power" to regulate privately owned property in the public interest was subject to abuse, but in a memorable phrase by Chief Justice Waite (who was not much of a phrase maker) it said that for protection against this abuse "the people must resort to the polls, not to the courts" (94 U.S. 113, 118 [1876]).

Thus the Court in its first dealings with the Fourteenth Amendment took a fairly restricted view of its coverage, and tended to sustain state regulation even of a kind that it might not feel was wise or fair. But regulated businesses continued to claim that one or another aspect of state regulation of their affairs denied them "due process of law," or abridged their "privileges and immunities," and over a period of time the Court began to succumb to these repeated challenges. The just-quoted language in *Munn* v. *Illinois* suggested that there were no exceptions to the rule; that if the police power of the state used to regulate business was abused, there was no judicial remedy for that abuse. But within ten years the Court had said that the power of regulation was not without constitutional limit, and that under pretense of regulating fares and freights the state could not require a railroad company to carry people or freight without any return (*Railroad Commission Cases*, 116 U.S. 307 [1886]). Finally, in the case of *Chicago, Milwaukee and St. Paul Railway Company* v. *Minnesota*, 134 U.S. 418 (1890), the Court held that a Minnesota statute that made final a rate determination by a commission without the opportunity to have the rate judicially reviewed in court was unconstitutional. The way had now been opened for two generations of battling over the constitutional limitations on what state railroad and utility commissions might do in the way of regulating rates.

At about the same time, the Supreme Court very sensibly decided that an Illinois statute forbidding discrimination between "long hauls" and "short hauls" could not be applied to interstate shipments that took place partly outside Illinois. With the consolidation and building of self-contained railroad systems during the last decades of the nineteenth century, most shipments by railroad were interstate, and after this decision in *Wabash, St. Louis and Pacific Railway Company* v. *Illinois*, 118 U.S. 557 (1886), state regulatory commissions were limited to regulating only the aspects of railroad transportation that occurred within the state in which they exercised their jurisdiction.

The necessary result of the *Wabash* case was to create a no-man's-land where states could not regulate but where Congress had made no effort to regulate, and therefore the shipping practice was subject to neither state nor federal control.

This led to the creation by Congress in 1887 of the first of what were to be a long series of independent regulatory commissions: the Interstate Commerce Commission. The Interstate Commerce Commission was first given a modest jurisdiction to prohibit unfair practices in railroad rate making, but the procedures it was obliged to follow were so cumbersome that at first it had little effect. But a series of amendments to the act in the early part of the twentieth century made the commission a major force in the regulation of interstate rail transportation.

Three years after it created the Interstate Commerce Commission, Congress in 1890 passed the Sherman Antitrust Act, which forbade monopolization of commerce and conspiracy to restrain trade. A few years earlier the major culprit in the world of big business had seemed to be the railroads, but now the trusts were coming in for their share of public scrutiny and criticism. Congress was getting into the business of economic regulation on a nationwide basis.

But for Field and Miller, the sun was setting on their judicial careers. Each had served first under Chief Justice Taney, then under Chief Justice Salmon P. Chase from 1864 to 1873, under Chief Justice Waite from 1874 to 1888, and then under Chief Justice Melville W. Fuller from 1888 on. In October 1890, Justice Miller held his last circuit court in St. Louis during the summer, and upon his return to Washington died after a short illness on October 13, 1890.

Justice Field's exit was less graceful. He survived Miller by several years, but became increasingly lame and often seemed lethargic to his colleagues. During the winter of 1896–97 his condition worsened, and his questions in the courtroom indicated that he had no idea of the issues being presented by counsel. His colleagues then devised a plan, which was later told by the first Justice Harlan to Chief Justice Charles Evans Hughes:

I heard Justice Harlan tell of the anxiety which the Court had felt because of the condition of Justice Field. It occurred to other members of the Court that Justice Field had served on a committee which waited upon Justice Grier to suggest his retirement and it was thought that recalling the incident to his memory might aid him to decide to retire. Justice Harlan was deputed to make the suggestion. He went over to Justice Field, who was sitting alone on a settee in the Robing Room apparently oblivious of his surroundings, and after arousing him gradually approached the question, asking if he did not recall how anxious the Court had been with respect to Justice Grier's condition and the feeling of the other Justices that in his own interest and in that of the Court he should give up his work. Justice Harlan asked if Justice Field did not remember what had been said to Justice Grier on that occasion. The old man listened, gradually became alert and finally, with his eyes blazing with the old fire of youth, he burst out:

"Yes! And a dirtier day's work I never did in my life!"

That was the end of that effort of the Brethren of the Court to induce Justice Field's retirement. . . . [Hughes, pp. 75–76.]

But a few months later, Justice Field sent to President McKinley his letter of resignation, to take effect December 1, 1897, and thereby bring to a close the longest term ever served on the bench of the Supreme Court up until that time: thirty-four years and nearly nine months.

To my mind, Samuel F. Miller and Stephen J. Field must rank at the very top of the associate justices who served the Court during the nineteenth century, and yet for quite different reasons. Miller's legal education was limited, almost perfunctory, and his practice in Iowa before his appointment to the Court, while substantial, is difficult to distinguish from that of hundreds of other successful lawyers of his time. It does not disparage Barbourville, Kentucky, or Keokuk, Iowa, to say that the opportunities, and therefore the challenges, found for a lawyer in cities of this size are simply not as great as those presented in larger cities with larger and more varied forms of commercial endeavor. But Miller, even if he was aware of these limitations in his legal background, gave no indication that he felt them a handicap in dealing with the business of the Supreme Court of the United States. Within two years of taking his position on that Court he had filed his dissenting opinion in the case of *Gelpcke* v. *Dubuque,* where he alone among his nine colleagues took the view that was ultimately vindicated by the Court itself many years later and must surely be regarded as the more sophisticated and broad-gauged one.

Miller's great gift, a gift not so fully vouchsafed to some of his more learned colleagues, was that of common sense. It may seem odd in a profession that now requires four years of college and three years of law school even to qualify to attempt to pass a bar examination and gain admission, that common sense should be rated so highly as an attribute of a judge. But it has been well said that legal education sharpens a person's mind by narrowing it, and in the battle of opposing counsel, each of whom seeks to deduce an opposite conclusion from the same premise, a good judge must at every moment be willing to call a halt and say to the advocate: "Your argument is perfectly logical, but the result for which you contend seems to me absurd." In an era when the weight of already decided cases had a good deal more authority than it does now, Miller never hesitated to ask this question. He was able to emancipate himself from currently fashionable intellectual dogma, which possessed much of his profession and many of his colleagues, and thereby to establish his reputation as one of the great justices who has served upon the Court.

Stephen F. Field was an outstanding associate justice almost in spite of himself. If one were to list the character traits that make up what most people would consider a "judicial temperament," Field possessed scarcely any of them. He was combative, he was often dogmatic, and one senses from his actions in the case of the *San Francisco Land Titles* that he conceived the role of a judge to be little different from that of any other public official—do your best to see that the matter is settled in the way you believe is correct.

As a single judge in a trial court, these attributes would be bound to place Field below the first rank of those judges, notwithstanding his keen mind and outstanding grasp of legal principles. But as one of nine members of a collegiate court, his dogmatism could be diffused by his eight colleagues, while they in turn were influenced by his own very trenchant arguments in favor of his own views. He was blessed with a lucid style of writing—far less common in his time among appellate judges than in our own—and with it he coupled an indomitable will to persevere in declaring what he thought was correct legal doctrine. A justice possessed of these attributes and permitted by Providence to serve thirty-four years on the Court is bound to have a significant impact on the institution. It was Field's view of the Fourteenth Amendment, not Miller's, that ultimately prevailed with the Court upon which they both sat.

Chief Justice Charles Evans Hughes
on his daily walk, April 12, 1939.

Collection of the Supreme Court of the United States

Justice Oliver Wendell Holmes, 1909.
Photograph by Harris and Ewing.

Collection of the Supreme Court of the United States

Justice Louis Brandeis, circa 1936.

Collection of the Supreme Court of the United States

Justice Stephen Field, circa 1895.
Engraving by Max Rosenthal.

Justice Samuel Miller, 1876.
Photograph by Fassett.

Collection of the Supreme Court of the United States

Chief Justice John Marshall, circa 1834.
Painting by John B. Martin.

Collection of the Supreme Court of the United States

Chief Justice Roger Brooke Taney, 1858.
Painting by George P. A. Healy.

The Vinson Court, 1949–1953.
Photograph by Bachrach.

Collection of the Supreme Court of the United States

The Supreme Court Exterior, circa 1935.
Photograph by Theodor Horydczak.

Collection of the Supreme Court of the United States

The Old Senate Chamber
(Home of the Supreme Court, 1860–1935).

Collection of the Supreme Court of the United States

The Old Supreme Court Chamber
(Home of the Supreme Court, 1810–1860).
Photograph by The Architect of the Capitol.

8

JUSTICES PECKHAM, HOLMES, AND BRANDEIS

With the deaths of Miller and Field, the Supreme Court along with the rest of the United States turned to face the twentieth century. The country had changed dramatically indeed from the time during the Civil War when each of these justices had been appointed to the supreme bench by Abraham Lincoln.

In 1860, the population of the United States was slightly more than 31 million people. By 1900 it had reached 76 million, and in another ten years it would reach 92 million. Some of this was natural increase, but a good deal of it resulted from emigration. In the forty years between 1860 and 1900, 14 million people had emigrated to the United States from foreign countries, primarily England, Ireland, Germany, and Scandinavia. In the first fifteen years of the twentieth century, 14.5 million more would emigrate, but more than half of these new emigrants would come from southern and eastern Europe: Italians, Slavs, and Jews fleeing the threat of persecution in Russian and Austria-Hungary.

In 1860, thirty-three states had been admitted to the Union. With the exception of Texas, California, and Oregon, the rest of the states lay in a contiguous area extending from the Atlantic coast westward to the band of states lying on the west bank of the

Mississippi River. The area between the western boundaries of these states and the Sierra Nevada mountains consisted entirely of territories. By 1900, all of the "lower 48" states except Arizona, New Mexico, and Oklahoma had been admitted to the Union. The noted historian Frederick Jackson Turner, writing in the last decade of the nineteenth century, had proclaimed the disappearance of the western frontier in America.

At the same time that emigrants and other settlers were populating the territories in the West, many other emigrants were settling in the large cities of the East and Midwest. At the close of the nineteenth century, the census statistics showed a notable trend of migration within the country from rural areas to urban areas. Suburbs began springing up around the core areas of large cities. Within the cities themselves various groups of emigrants jousted with native Americans and with other groups of emigrants for economic and political power.

From 1900 to 1914, the national income grew from $16 billion to $31 billion. Gross farm income more than doubled in the ten years between 1900 and 1910. While the real wages of laborers increased slowly but steadily during this period, the income of individual farmers rose dramatically. United States wheat was replacing Russian wheat in the European market, and the rise of prices in wheat boosted the income of many farmers. Naturally enough, the rise in farm income sharply increased the value of farmland, and tenant farming became increasingly common as the century progressed. But the general result of agricultural improvement was that the agrarian discontent, which had played such a prominent part in the Granger movement and in the Populist movement, subsided.

In 1898 the United States burst upon the international scene not just as a continental power but as a world power by reason of the Spanish-American War. Following the defeat of Spain in that conflict, the United States by the Treaty of Paris took possession of Cuba and Puerto Rico in the Caribbean Sea and of the Philippine Islands half a world away. In 1900 the United States joined with other Western European powers in suppressing the Boxer Rebellion in China and insisting on an open-door policy in that country. In the same year William Jennings Bryan had sought to make "imperialism" the principal issue of the presidential campaign when he and McKinley squared off for a repeat performance of their 1896 contest, but McKinley had won handily.

Theodore Roosevelt, who succeeded McKinley following the latter's assassination in September 1901, described his foreign policy as being to "speak softly, but carry a big stick." In 1903 Roosevelt encouraged what would later become the Republic of Panama to revolt against Colombia, and set up as an independent nation under the protection of the United States in order that the Panama Canal might be built. In 1905 Roosevelt invited the belligerents in the Russo-Japanese War to come to a peace conference in Portsmouth, New Hampshire, and the resulting Treaty of Portsmouth ended that war.

Domestically the nation witnessed a rapid acceleration of the trend to economic concentration that had begun after the Civil War. In the last third of the nineteenth century the corporation emerged as the dominant form of industrial organization in the United States, so that by 1890 65 percent of the goods manufactured in the country were turned out by corporations, and by 1900 79 percent were. At the same time that the percentage of corporate producers was thus increasing, the stock of many large corporations became publicly held and the ownership so dispersed that no one stockholder had much of a say in how the corporation was operated. The result of this phenomenon was that a class of corporate managers grew up: While they were legally responsible to the stockholders, that latter body was so numerous that many important corporate decisions were made by the managers themselves without any thought of obtaining advance authorization from the stockholders.

After the Panic of 1893, with its numerous railroad bankruptcies, prominent investment bankers such as J. P. Morgan & Co. and Kuhn Loeb & Co. set about reorganizing and consolidating the numerous bankrupt railroad properties. They were so successful that when they had accomplished this task they turned their sights on other industries with a view toward consolidation. As a result of Morgan's efforts, 60 percent of the steel production in the United States was represented by the companies merged together in 1901 under the name United States Steel Company. During the latter part of the nineteenth century, for a brief period of time the "trust" form of organization, rather than the corporate form of organization, was in vogue as a vehicle for consolidating, manufacturing, and fixing prices, and the "sugar trust" and the "tobacco trust" were glaring examples of this tendency. But state corporation laws, first in New Jersey and then in Delaware, were revised to allow one corporation to hold stock in another corporation, and thereby corporate "holding companies," such as Standard Oil, were made possible.

All of the activity directed toward consolidation required sale and purchase of shares of stock and obtaining large lines of credit, for which tasks the ever-present investment bankers were always available. After effecting a consolidation or creating a holding company, a house such as Morgan would retain seats on the board of directors of the consolidated corporation, would continue to underwrite new securities issues, and virtually controlled the sources of credit available to many corporations. Indeed, so rampant was consolidation in the field of banking that most major banking interests in the United States were soon allied either with the house of Morgan in New York or with the Rockefeller interests in the same city.

As previously noted, the real wages of labor had increased modestly at a rate of about 1 percent every two years from 1897 to 1914, but if laborers had made no substantial economic gains in terms of rates of pay, full employment nevertheless prevailed during this period of time. But the working conditions of the laborer left much to be desired. The average hours worked throughout industry in the United States fell from fifty-nine per week in 1897 to fifty-five in 1914. But there was a great difference between the hours worked in unionized industries, such as the building trades, which fell from roughly fifty-three hours per week to forty-nine hours during this period, and the hours worked in nonunion industries, which fell from sixty-two hours only to fifty-eight hours during the same period of time. Safety was also a concern of workmen on many jobs, because workers were killed, crippled, or seriously injured at a rate that was shocking by today's standards.

It was at about this time in our nation's history that organized labor began to take a more active part in politics. The Knights of Labor was organized in Philadelphia in 1869, the Federation of Organized Trades in 1881, and the American Federation of Labor in 1886. The latter, under the leadership of Samuel Gompers, had acquired nearly 1.7 million members by 1904, and over 2 million by 1914. Standing apart from these ordinary craft unions were the four railroad brotherhoods, whose members were the best-paid workers in the country. Their diligent efforts finally secured from Congress the enactment of the Adamson Act in 1916, which established for the first time an eight-hour day for all workers in interstate railroad transportation.

Labor had met with mixed success in its effort to organize the American work force. It had suffered a dramatic defeat in the Pullman Strike of 1894, when President Cleveland brought the interest of the national government to weigh against the strikers. The United Mine Workers, who were 100,000 strong after a successful 1897 bituminous-coalfield strike, succeeded in organizing the anthracite fields in Pennsylvania in 1900. But during this same period the American Federation of Labor was unsuccessful in its efforts to organize the steel industry.

Labor had contributed considerably to the support of the Populist movement in the late nineteenth century, but because of improving agricultural conditions that movement had largely spent itself by 1900. As the Populist movement waned, the Progressive movement in all of its manifestations waxed. The latter movement was essentially middle class and urban, with very little support from the labor movement.

One segment of the Progressives were champions of social justice—the idea that the state's police power should be used to alleviate the hardship of the poor and the downtrodden. This philosophy was focused on three particular kinds of laws: child labor laws, minimum wage and maximum hour laws for women, and workmen's compensation laws.

The first laws prohibiting child labor in factories were adopted by New Jersey, New York, and Illinois in the first years of the new century, and during the presidency of Woodrow Wilson a federal law to that effect was adopted in 1916. Laws establishing maximum hours for women were enacted by New York in 1896 and by Massachusetts in 1900, and by 1917 thirty-nine states had followed suit. Minimúm-wage laws for women were likewise enacted by some of the states during the same period, but they proved to be less popular and were ultimately adopted by less than half of the states.

Workmen's-compensation laws were designed to make simpler and more certain the process by which a worker would be compensated for an accident on the job. At first some states had enacted so-called "employers' liability laws," which retained the lawsuit by an employee against an employer as the vehicle for compensation, but took away employers' defenses to the action such as contributory negligence and the fellow-servant doctrine. But states became dissatisfied with the cumbersomeness of this procedure and began shifting to an administrative procedure for awarding compensation. Ten states had set up such systems of workmen's compensation by 1911, and twenty more, together with the federal government, had followed suit by 1916.

Change was thus afoot in the United States at the turn of the century, and it is probably inevitable in a constitutional democracy that some of the manifestations of change will lead to lawsuits about the meaning of statutes or their constitutionality. Litigation before the Supreme Court arising out of the social and political ferment in the country at the time led to a series of cases deciding whether or not the United States Constitution applied to the territories newly acquired from Spain, and to another series of cases involving the constitutionality of minimum-wage laws and other statutory regulations of labor contracts. It is interesting to contrast these two lines of cases. The first, which were regarded as of cardinal importance at the time they were decided, were soon relegated by the march of events to no more than a footnote in constitutional-law casebooks. The second line of cases, on the other hand, produced constitutional doctrine that led to a serious constitutional crisis during the administration of President Franklin Roosevelt. Most of these cases dealt with laws regulating minimum wages and maximum hours that employers must provide for their employees.

Such laws were to meet with an uncertain fate at the hands of the Supreme Court of the United States during the first third of the twentieth century. A statute passed by Utah limiting to ten the number of hours a day that an employee might be required to work in underground mines and in smelters was upheld by the Court in 1898 in the case of *Holden* v. *Hardy*, 169 U.S. 366. A majority of the Court held that the statute was a valid exercise of the state police power, even though it did limit the right of mature adults to contract with one another. The Court distinguished the case of *Allgeyer* v. *Louisiana*, which it had decided the previous year, and which had contained expansive language to the effect that the Due Process Clause of the Fourteenth Amendment protected freedom to contract as well as other forms of liberty. In *Holden*, the Court said:

> This right of contract, however, is itself subject to certain limitations which the state may lawfully impose in the exercise of its police powers. While this power is inherent in all governments, it has doubtless been greatly expanded in its application during the past century, owing to an enormous increase in the number of occupations which are dangerous or so far detrimental to the health of employees as to demand special precautions for their well being and protection. . . . (18 S.C. 388).

Two members of the Court—Justice Rufus Peckham, who had written the Court's opinion in the *Allgeyer* case, and Justice David J. Brewer, who was a nephew of Justice Field, dissented.

Seven years later, in the case of *Lochner* v. *New York*, the Court seemed to reverse its field in what may be fairly described as one of the most ill-starred decisions that it ever rendered. New York had enacted a statute providing that no employer in certain types of occupations, including bakeries, could work his employees more than sixty hours per week. A five-man majority of the Supreme Court, in an opinion written by Justice Peckham, held that such a law unconstitutionally interfered with the freedom of the employer and employee to contract guaranteed them by the Due Process Clause of the Fourteenth Amendment. It described laws such as this, "limiting the hours in which grown and intelligent men may labor to earn their living," as "mere meddlesome interferences with the rights of the individual."

Four members of the Court dissented in two separate opinions, but the dissenting opinion of Justice Oliver Wendell Holmes, Jr., then newly appointed to the Court by President Theodore Roosevelt, is the more lucid and succinct of the two. He said:

> This case is decided upon an economic theory which a large part of the country does not entertain. If it were a question if I agreed with that theory, I should desire to study it further and long before making up my mind. But I do not conceive that to be my duty, because I strongly believe that my agreement or disagreement has nothing to do with the right of a majority to embody their opinions in law. It is settled by various decisions of this Court that state constitutions and state laws may regulate life in many ways which we as legislators might think as injudicious, or if you like as tyrannical, as this, and which, equally with this, interfere with the liberty to contract. . . . The liberty of the citizen to do as he likes so long as he does not interfere with the liberty of others to do the same, which has been a shibboleth for some well-known writers, is interfered with by school laws, by the Post Office, by every state or municipal institution which takes his money for purposes thought desirable, whether he likes it or not. The Fourteenth Amendment does not enact Mr. Herbert Spencer's Social Statics. . . .
>
> A Constitution is not intended to embody a particular economic theory, whether of paternalism and the organic relation of the citizen to the state or of *laissez faire*. It is made for people of fundamentally differing views, and the accident of our finding certain opinions natural and familiar, or novel, and even shocking, ought not to conclude our judgment upon the question whether statutes embodying them conflict with the Constitution of the United States (198 U.S. 75–76).

Rufus Peckham had been appointed to the Supreme Court in 1896 by President Grover Cleveland. As a young man he was elected district attorney of Albany County in New York, and later became a trial judge and then a judge of the highest court of the state of New York. He was active in Democratic party politics, representing the "upstate wing" of the Democratic party. One observer has noted that "perhaps the most urgent task of these up-staters was not defeating the Republicans, but preventing New York City's Tammany Democrats from gaining control of the party machinery in the state." [Skolnick, Richard, "Rufus Peckham," in Friedman and Israel, Vol. 3, p. 1687]

Peckham was on terms of personal friendship with another up-state New York Democrat, Grover Cleveland, and in the very close election of 1884 Cleveland invited Peckham to the Executive Mansion in Albany to join the long election-night vigil. In December 1895, having previously told Peckham, "We'll get you down to Washington yet, Rufus," Cleveland appointed him associate justice of the Supreme Court. Peckham seemed less than enthusiastic about his promotion; he told a friend shortly after the nomination, "If I have got to be put away on the shelf I suppose I might as well be on the top shelf."

"His strong clear features, Roman nose, chiseled chin, unusually long wavy hair and full bushy moustache, both turning silver gray, combined to create a figure of distinction." [Skolnick, op. cit., p. 1695]

Oliver Wendell Holmes, Jr., was by inheritance a Boston Brahmin. He was born in Boston in 1841, entered Harvard at age sixteen, was elected to Phi Beta Kappa, and was a member of the Porcellian and Hasty Pudding clubs. During his senior year, when he was twenty years old, the Confederate forces fired upon Fort Sumter. He enlisted as a private, and graduated from Harvard in June of that year in uniform.

Holmes was commissioned a lieutenant in the 20th Massachusetts Regiment and was wounded at the minor engagement at Ball's Bluff in 1861; he was seriously wounded at Antietam in 1862, and again at Chancellorsville in 1863. No one who has even casually studied his life and work can doubt that these war experiences played a significant part in molding his outlook on life. After being mustered out of the army he entered Harvard Law School in the fall of 1864, graduated from that institution, read law, and was admitted to the Massachusetts bar in 1867. His circumstances were such that he was not required to work for a living, and he had a rather desultory practice of law. He derived more enjoyment from lecturing at the law school and working on his famous treatise *The Common Law*, which was published in 1881. In 1883 he was appointed to the Supreme Judicial Court of Massachusetts, and in 1899 he became chief justice of that court. In 1902 he was appointed by Theodore Roosevelt to the Supreme Court of the United States.

Oliver Wendell Holmes may have been the only justice on the Court at the time of the *Lochner* decision to have been familiar with the book written by the English philosopher Herbert Spencer entitled *Social Statics*. That book was one of several by Spencer embodying the doctrine of Social Darwinism, which attained tremendous popularity both in England and in this country during the last third of the nineteenth century. One of his principal American disciples was William Graham Sumner, a professor of political and social science at Yale College. These men and the doctrine they espoused had an enormous influence on American public opinion during this time:

In the three decades after the Civil War it was impossible to be active in any field of intellectual work without mastering Spencer. [Hofstadter, p. 33]

Social Darwinism taught that the notion of "survival of the fittest" enunciated in Charles Darwin's *Origin of Species* as an explanation for the evolution of life on the planet could be transposed to the world of social and political philosophy.

The most popular catch words of Darwinism, "struggle for existence" and "survival of the fittest," when applied to the life of man in society, suggested that nature would provide that the best competitors in a competitive situation would win, and that this process would lead to continuing improvement. . . . One might, like William Graham Sumner, take a pessimistic view of the import of Darwinism, and conclude that Darwinism could serve only to cause men to face up to the inherent hardship of the battle of life; or one might, like Herbert Spencer, promise that, whatever the immediate hardships for a large portion of mankind, evolution meant progress and thus assured that the whole process of life was tending toward some very remote but altogether glorious consummation. But in either case the conclusions to which Darwinism was at first put were conservative conclusions. They suggested that all attempts to reform social processes were efforts to remedy the irremediable, that they interfered with the wisdom of nature, that they could lead only to degeneration. [Hofstadter, pp. 6–7]

Rufus Peckham's statement in the *Lochner* majority opinion that minimum wage laws for men are "mere meddlesome interference" with individual rights sounds strange to us today, but it sounded a good deal less strange to many people in the United States in 1906 who had been substantially influenced by the doctrines of the Social Darwinists. Indeed, several comments of Oliver Wendell Holmes at other times in his life suggest that he may well have been a Social Darwinist himself; but he insisted that a document like the United States Constitution was not meant to incorporate any one political philosophy.

Three years after its decision in *Lochner,* the Supreme Court decided the case of *Muller* v. *Oregon,* 208 U.S. 412, and unanimously upheld an Oregon law providing that women employed in laundries and factories might not be required to work more than ten hours per day. The case was argued by a prominent Boston attorney, Louis D. Brandeis, and in connection with it he filed what would come to be known as a "Brandeis brief"—emphasizing statistics and commission reports more than judicial precedents. In *Muller,* Justice Brewer's opinion for the Court cited these statistics in Brandeis's brief with approval, and emphasized that the liberty to contract guaranteed by the Fourteenth Amendment was not absolute. *Lochner* was easily distinguished in those days as applying to men, rather than women, and the Court held that whatever might be the case with men, the state could protect women employees from the health hazards of long days in the laundry.

Nearly ten years after *Muller*, the Court decided the case of *Bunting* v. *Oregon*, 243 U.S. 426. That case, too, involved a law enacted by the state of Oregon, which prohibited employees generally from working more than ten hours per day unless they were paid time and a half for the work, in which event they might work up to thirteen hours. The majority of the Court in an opinion by Justice Joseph McKenna upheld this law, relying on statistics as to average hours worked in other countries of the Western world, statistics furnished in a brief authored by young Harvard Law School Professor Felix Frankfurter. Chief Justice White, and Justices Van Devanter and McReynolds, dissented without opinion. The newest justice of the Court, Louis D. Brandeis, who had argued the *Muller* v. *Oregon* case, had been appointed to the Court by President Wilson but took no part in the *Bunting* case because he had been active in its preliminary stages on behalf of Bunting. Perhaps the most interesting fact about the *Bunting* opinion is that it does not even mention the case of *Lochner* v. *New York*. One has visions of Justice Peckham, who had died in 1909, turning over in his grave.

Louis D. Brandeis was born in Louisville, Kentucky, in 1856. He entered Harvard Law School in 1875 without having had any undergraduate college education, and had to earn his living while there by tutoring other students. He completed the course in two years, and set an academic record that still stands. Upon graduation he went into partnership in Boston with his classmate Samuel Warren, and the two had a lucrative and successful private practice of law. But Brandeis was not satisfied with the rewards of the private sector, and proceeded to take on a number of important cases which would today be described as "pro bono" cases. Because of this he was known as the "people's attorney" and he managed to antagonize a number of established business interests.

Brandeis supported Woodrow Wilson for president in 1912, and made numerous speeches on his behalf. It was quite natural that

Wilson, in turn, would appoint Brandeis as an associate justice of the Supreme Court when a vacancy occurred in 1916. The hearings on his confirmation before the Senate Judiciary Committee were extended and contentious; the judgment of history with respect to them seems to have been that opposition was motivated largely, if not entirely, by the fact that Brandeis was viewed as something of a radical and an "outsider" to the American bar establishment, and partly by anti-Semitism. Brandeis was not the first Jew to have been offered a seat on the Supreme Court; that distinction went to Judah P. Benjamin of Louisiana, whom President Millard Fillmore offered to appoint in 1850, but who turned down the offer. But Brandeis was the first Jew to sit on the Court.

Brandeis and Holmes were to sit together on the Supreme Court for sixteen years, until the latter's retirement in 1932. They agreed with one another that the Constitution did not forbid the sort of economic regulation that was one of the fruits of the Progressive movement, and they agreed with one another that the First Amendment to the Constitution protected freedom of speech and freedom of the press in a way that the majority of the Court was not willing to recognize during their tenure. But although their views on constitutional law were remarkably similar, these two great American jurists were quite dissimilar from one another. Brandeis was something of an ascetic, with a crusader's desire to see his version of the right triumph in the world. Holmes was the ultimate skeptic, who had the greatest sort of doubt whether there really was any one version of the right preferable to another. Whether they would have voted together had they sat on the Court in a different era than they did must be regarded as a moot question.

One might have thought that the *Bunting* case, decided in 1917, would have settled the constitutionality of maximum-hour and minimum-wage laws, but such was not to be. In 1923 the Supreme Court decided in the case of *Adkins* v. *Children's Hospital* that a minimum-wage law for women enacted by Congress for the District of Columbia violated the right of freedom to contract on the part of the employer and employee. The Court recognized the constitutionality of maximum-hour laws established by *Bunting,* but held that laws fixing minimum wages were quite different from those fixing maximum hours, and held that the guarantee of women's suffrage by the Nineteenth Amendment had gone far to eliminating the distinction between men and women that had supported the constitutionality of the Oregon law setting maximum hours for women in *Muller*. The majority opinion by Justice George Sutherland quoted extensively from Peckham's opinion in *Lochner*, saying that "subsequent cases in this Court have been distinguished from that decision, but the principles therein stated have never been disapproved" (261 U.S. 550).

Chief Justice Taft and Justices Sanford and Holmes dissented; Justice Brandeis took no part in the case.

Thus after a quarter century of cases deciding the constitutionality of minimum-wage and maximum-hour laws, the Court after shifting back and forth narrowly came down against the constitutionality of most such laws.

In a series of related cases, the Court was dealing body blows to other state and federal legislation that arose out of the Progressive movement. As noted earlier in this chapter, Congress in 1916 followed the lead of virtually all the states and enacted a statute prohibiting the shipment and interstate commerce of goods produced by plants that employed child labor. Although by 1916 virtually all the states had child-labor laws, the efforts to enforce them were uneven, and obviously some sort of federal regulation could add impetus to the state efforts. But shortly after Congress enacted the statute in question, a man named Dagenhart sued in the United States District Court for the District of North Carolina on behalf of himself and his two sons, aged fourteen and sixteen, to enjoin enforcement of the act of Congress on the grounds that his sons were being deprived of their right to contract for their services as they pleased, and on the grounds that Congress's authority to regulate interstate commerce did not reach this far. The Supreme Court upheld this contention by a vote of five to four in the case of *Hammer* v. *Dagenhart*, 247 U.S. 251 (1918). Though the Court had previously sustained child-labor statutes enacted by the states, the majority held that the condition of labor at factories within the states was a matter for regulation by the states rather than for regulation by Congress under the Interstate Commerce Clause. Justice Rufus Day wrote the majority opinion for the Court, and Justices Holmes, McKenna, Brandeis, and Clark dissented.

This was not the first act of Congress inspired by the Progressive movement to have bitten the dust at the hands of the Supreme Court. Congress had earlier forbidden railroads in interstate commerce to require their employees to sign what was called a "yellow-dog" contract: that is, a contract that required as a condition of employment that the employee promise not to join a union during the period of his employment. One William Adair, an agent of the Louisville and Nashville Railroad Company, discharged a locomotive fireman named O. B. Coppage from that employment with the railroad. Coppage sued, contending that he had been discharged because he had refused to sign a yellow-dog contract. When the case reached the Supreme Court, the Court in an opinion by the first Justice Harlan decided that the Fifth Amendment, guaranteeing that the government should not deprive any person of life, liberty, or property without due process of law, forbade Congress to enact this law; just as in *Lochner*, the employees must remain free to contract with their employer on such terms as they chose (*Adair* v. *United States*, 208 U.S. 161 [1908]).

Justices Holmes and McKenna dissented from this decision.

A few years later the Court reached a similar result when it held unconstitutional a Kansas law forbidding an employer to require an employee to enter into a yellow-dog contract as a condition of employment. In this case a man named T. B. Coppage—the reports do not tell us whether he is any relation to O. B. Coppage of *Adair* v. *United States*—was a superintendent of the Frisco Lines in Fort Scott, Kansas. He asked one Hedges, a switchman employed by the Frisco, to either withdraw from the switchmen's union or lose his job. Hedges refused, and T. B. Coppage fired him on behalf of the railroad. The Supreme Court decided in *Coppage* v. *Kansas* that this law was unconstitutional on the basis of its earlier decision in *Adair*. Justice Mahlon B. Pitney of New Jersey spoke for the majority, and Justices Holmes, Day, and Hughes dissented. Justice Pitney for the majority said that the Kansas statute had no "reference to health, safety, morals or public welfare, beyond the supposed desirability of leveling any qualities of fortune by depriving one who has the property of some part" of it.

Arizona had been admitted to the Union in 1912, and its constitutional convention had been dominated by Progressive reformers who had incorporated the initiative, the referendum, and other measures into the proposed constitution. Indeed, President Taft was so opposed to the provision in the Arizona constitution providing that judges might be recalled that he insisted that that provision be deleted before he would support admission of Arizona to the Union. The Arizona legislature had enacted a statute that prohibited the issuance of an injunction in the case of a labor dispute so long as the picketing activities of any striking workers were peaceful. A man named Truax operated a restaurant in Bisbee, Arizona, known as the English Kitchen. Corrigan was one of a group of cooks and waiters who struck the restaurant over wages and working conditions. They picketed outside the restaurant, and advertised in the local newspaper that Truax was "unfair" in his dealings with his workers. Truax went to court to obtain an injunction against this activity, but the Arizona courts held that such an injunction was barred by the Arizona law described above. But Truax took his case to the Supreme Court of the United States, and a majority of that Court said that the statute violated the Equal Protection Clause of the Fourteenth Amendment, because an injunction was available for all other kinds of injury to property or business except those that occurred during a labor dispute. Justices Holmes, Pitney, Brandeis, and Clark dissented from this holding (*Truax* v. *Corrigan*, 257 U.S. 312 [1921]).

Like the Missouri Compromise involved in the *Dred Scott* case, and unlike the subsection of the Judiciary Act of 1789 involved in *Marbury* v. *Madison*, the laws the Court was thus setting at naught were the response of legislators in countless states to keenly perceived and prominently publicized problems of the day. The Court was in the process of sowing a wind, with the whirlwind to be reaped years later.

9

THE
COURT-PACKING PLAN

$\mathscr{D}$uring the seventy-two-year period from 1860 until 1932, only two Democrats had been elected president of the United States: Grover Cleveland and Woodrow Wilson. But Herbert Hoover, the last of the Republican presidents elected during this era, had the misfortune to be chief executive at the time of the Great Depression. The stock-market crash in October 1929 shook the confidence of the business community, weakened the country's financial institutions, and dramatically slowed down industrial expansion. Interacting forces, some national and some worldwide, combined to bring on the Great Depression. Hoover was by no means a "stand-patter," but a cautious progressive who lost the confidence of the majority of the American people during his term. In 1932, Franklin Delano Roosevelt, the Democratic governor of New York, was elected President in a landslide.

Just as Hoover was not a reactionary, Roosevelt was not a doctrinaire liberal. Other than emergency measures taken during his first two years in office, this period was characterized by an effort to reduce federal expenditures and to balance the budget. Other measures of reform included the banking system and the securities markets, and the enactment of the National Industrial Recovery Act. The latter act essentially was designed to end cutthroat competition, raise prices by limiting production, and guarantee a reasonable work week and a living wage to labor. These objectives were to be accomplished by the adopting of codes for all branches of industry and business by committees representing management, labor, and the public. Roosevelt signed the act in June 1933, and in the next year the code-making process was completed. To spur compliance among the thousands of regulated businesses, employers who cooperated were permitted to display a sticker showing a blue eagle—the emblem of the NRA, the National Recovery Administration. Blue eagles appeared in the windows of industrial and commercial establishments throughout the United States, from huge manufacturing plants to small one-man cleaning and pressing shops.

By 1935, the Roosevelt administration was entering into a different phase of the New Deal, in which were passed such far-reaching legislation as the Wagner Act, guaranteeing workers the right to organize and requiring management to bargain with unions, and similar measures. During his first term Roosevelt was able to get from Congress virtually any measure he requested, and the Democratic-controlled Senate and House were accused of being rubber stamps for the Democratic President. But if the legislative and executive branches were working together in complete harmony, there was an understandable fear on the part of the New Dealers that the Supreme Court might not have gotten the message. Charles Evans Hughes, the Chief Justice, had been appointed by President Hoover in 1930; the most senior associate justice, Willis Van Devanter, had been appointed by President Taft in 1911, and the most junior associate justice, Owen Roberts, had been appointed by President Hoover in 1932. Seven members of the Court had been appointed by Republican presidents, and only two by a Democratic president, Woodrow Wilson.

Because it usually takes at least a year, and often two years, from the time a lawsuit is begun in the court where it is filed until the time that a ruling of the Supreme Court may be had on the case, no questions involving New Deal legislation came before the Court in the first two years of Roosevelt's presidency. But in 1935, the Court began to deal with these questions, giving the administration a victory in one important series of cases and a defeat in two others. But if there was any doubt as to which way the judicial wind was blowing, that doubt was resolved on a day that was later known to New Dealers as Black Monday. In one case decided on that day the Court held unanimously that a provision of the Frazier-Lemke Act designed to assist farmers in danger of having their farms foreclosed violated the provision of the Fifth Amendment to the Constitution which provides that "private property shall not be taken for public use without payment of just compensation." There had been debtor-relief laws before this one, but typically they had provided only for a stay of foreclosure proceedings for a brief period of time while the debtor attempted to raise the necessary money to pay off the mortgage. The Frazier-Lemke Act, however, provided for a stay of five years during which the debtor could remain in possession of the property so long as he paid a reasonable rental for it, and at the end of the five-year period the debtor might discharge the mortgage by paying not the face value of the mortgage note but the currently appraised value of the property. The Court held in *Louisville Joint Stock Land Bank* v. *Radford* that however great the urgencies created by the farm depression, Congress could not deprive the mortgage holder of so much of his security without paying compensation for it.

In a second case, *Humphrey's Executor* v. *United States*, which carried a bit of personal affront to President Roosevelt, the Court held by a vote of 8 to 1 that he was not empowered to remove a member of the Federal Trade Commission with whose philosophical outlook he disagreed. Perhaps these two decisions, by unanimous or nearly unanimous Courts, could have been borne, but the third decision rendered on that day declared unconstitutional the National Industrial Recovery Act. Here, too, the Court was unanimous, but the stakes for the New Deal program were a good deal greater.

The case is known as *Schechter Poultry Corporation* v. *United States*, and rapidly acquired the nickname of the "sick-chicken case." A New York wholesale poultry slaughterhouse operator was indicated in New York for violating the minimum-wage and maximum-hour provisions of the "live-poultry" Code of the NRA, and for numerous other code violations including the sale to a butcher of an "unfit chicken"; thus the name "sick chicken."

The Supreme Court in an opinion by Chief Justice Hughes said that the act of Congress delegating authority to the administrator of the National Recovery Administration to promulgate the code had been so vague and general as simply to confer unlimited discretion on the President and the administrator to in effect make laws themselves, contrary to the Constitution. The Court also held that the Schechters' business was so local in nature—they sold their product only to local retailers and butchers, although they purchased it from out of the state—that the Commerce Clause did not authorize Congress to regulate the activity.

This trio of decisions was enough to bring the President himself into action. At an off-the-record press conference later in the week, Roosevelt criticized the decision in the sick-chicken case, and was quoted as saying:

> The issue is going to be whether we go one way or the other. Don't call it right or left; that is just first-year high school language, just about. It is not right or left—it is a question for national decision on a very important problem of government. We are the only nation in the world that has not solved that problem. We thought we were solving it, and now it has been thrown straight in our faces and we have been relegated to the horse-and-buggy definition of interstate commerce.

Administration officials continued to criticize the Court, and the Court continued to invalidate New Deal legislation. In January 1936, it held the Agricultural Act—the New Deal's principal piece of farm legislation—unconstitutional. Here, however, the decision was by a divided vote of 6 to 3, and Justice Stone in a biting dissent made the comment that "[c]ourts are not the only agency of government that must be assumed to have capacity to govern."

In the presidential election of November 1936, Franklin Roosevelt was reelected President by an overwhelming majority. Alfred M. Landon, a Republican candidate, received the electoral votes of only Maine and Vermont, and received a popular vote of roughly nine million as compared to Roosevelt's sixteen million. The Republicans in that year used as one of their arguments for opposing Roosevelt the fact that if he was elected he would undoubtedly be able to fill forthcoming vacancies on the Supreme Court, which was the only branch of the federal government not totally subservient to the New Deal. The Democrats made little of the Court in their campaign, but only a few days after he was inaugurated for a second term—for the first time on January 20 rather than the traditional date of March 4—Franklin Roosevelt proclaimed to the country that he was not going to wait for vacancies on the Court to occur before he sought to remold it to his own image.

On Friday, February 5, 1937, members of the President's Cabinet, the Democratic leadership of both houses of Congress, and the chairmen of the House and Senate Judiciary Committees were summoned to meet with the President in the Cabinet Room of the White House. When Roosevelt entered the Cabinet Room from the Oval Office, he was followed by a secretary who placed a pile of papers at each seat around the table. The papers contained a message to Congress from the President, recommending that the judicial branch of the government be "reorganized." The president explained to the assembled dignitaries that the present Supreme Court had declared unconstitutional one New Deal measure after another, and that it in effect stood as a roadblock to the progressive reforms the country had overwhelmingly indicated in the November election that it wanted. He then spent over an hour reading the message to the Cabinet members and congressional leaders.

The reorganization was to be accompanied by a draft bill providing that for each member of the Supreme Court who was over seventy years of age, and did not elect to retire, the President would be empowered to appoint an additional justice to the Court and thereby enlarge the Court's membership up to a total of fifteen. Since six of the nine members of the Court were then over seventy years of age, if none of them chose to retire upon the enactment of the bill, the President would immediately be authorized to appoint six additional justices to the Court. The President based his case on the argument that the older judges were unable to carry a full share of the Court's workload. The bill also contained other provisions dealing with the lower federal courts, but these were soon lost in the furor resulting from the provision dealing with the enlargement of the Supreme Court.

The measure stunned not only the country but the Democratic leadership in Congress as well. None of them had been privy to the drafting of the plan, which had been a well-kept secret among Roosevelt, his attorney general, Homer Cummings, and one or two trusted assistants of the latter in the Justice Department. At first it appeared that Congress would bow to the President's will in this matter as it had so uniformly done during the President's first term, but then complications developed. The administration strategists would have preferred to have the bill come on for hearings and passage first in the House of Representatives, because the more numerous House members had to face the electorate every two years, and would therefore be more vulnerable to the various pressures that a popular incumbent president can bring to bear on them. But Representative Hatton Sumners, of Texas, the chairman of the House Judiciary Committee, unflinchingly opposed the plan from the moment he heard about it. No sooner had he left the Cabinet Room than he confided to his colleagues, "Boys, here's where I cash in my chips." Because of his influence on the other members of the Judiciary Committee, it was feared that the bill might never be voted out of committee in the House, and therefore the President decided that the issue must first be joined in the Senate. And so it was, from the first part of February until the last part of July.

The President himself would be the chief strategist for the administration forces. Surely no president in modern times had ever stood higher in public esteem than Franklin D. Roosevelt three months after his overwhelming reelection to his second term. Roosevelt was born in 1882 to wealthy landed descendants of the Dutch patroons in the Hudson River Valley, and grew up on the family estate at Hyde Park in Dutchess County, New York. He attended Groton and Harvard without distinguishing himself academically, and studied law at Columbia University Law School in New York without receiving a degree. He married his distant cousin, Anna Eleanor Roosevelt, in 1905, and began a rather desultory practice of law in New York City.

Politics proved to be his first love and his great talent, and he was elected to the New York State Senate in 1910. Woodrow Wilson appointed him assistant secretary of the navy in 1913, and he served throughout Wilson's administration in that capacity. The Democrats nominated him for vice-president as a running mate for Ohio Governor James M. Cox, but the Democratic ticket went down to defeat at the hands of Republican Warren G. Harding. In 1921 he was struck with an attack of polio which permanently paralyzed his legs and required the use of a wheelchair the rest of his life. He courageously fought to regain at least partial use of his legs, and by 1924 he was sufficiently recovered to give a speech at the Democratic convention nominating Alfred E. Smith, governor of New York, for the presidency. By 1928 he was able to discard his crutches in public, and successfully ran for governor of New York. In 1932 he and his supporters successfully battled several other candidates for the Democratic nomination for the presidency.

In February 1937, his massive shoulders, jutting jaw, and air of self-assurance symbolized by his jaunty waving of a cigarette holder made him a perfect subject for both friendly and hostile political cartoonists. He was a man at the zenith of his powers.

Most of the men who occupied the nine seats on the Supreme Court at this time seemed shadowy and two-dimensional compared to Franklin D. Roosevelt. But not Charles Evans Hughes, the Chief Justice. Now seventy-seven years old, he had been by turns a Reform Republican governor of New York and an associate justice of the Supreme Court of the United States from 1910 until 1916. In the latter year he resigned from that position to accept the Republican nomination for the presidency, but was narrowly defeated by Woodrow Wilson. He returned to New York City and a very successful law practice, from which he was lured by President Harding in 1921 to become secretary of state. Upon Harding's death he had again returned to a successful law practice in New York, including many arguments in the Supreme Court; President Hoover had appointed him Chief Justice in 1930.

Charles Evans Hughes was something above medium height with gray hair and a beard best described as Jovian. Central casting could not have produced a better image of a chief justice, and his presence matched his appearance. Felix Frankfurter, who knew them both well, said that in any group that included Franklin Roosevelt and Charles Evans Hughes, they were the dominant figures.

The eight associate justices who sat with Hughes were a varied lot. The four whose legal philosophy was least sympathetic to sustaining New Deal measures were dubbed the "four horsemen": Willis Van Devanter; James C. McReynolds, appointed by Wilson in 1914; George C. Sutherland, appointed by Harding in 1922; and Pierce Butler, appointed by Harding in 1923. All were over seventy years of age, and therefore if the President's Court plan was approved, for each one of them who failed to retire the President could appoint a new associate justice.

On the other side of the bench, jurisprudentially, were three justices regarded as "liberals": Louis D. Brandeis; Harlan F. Stone, appointed by President Coolidge in 1924; and Benjamin Cardozo, appointed by President Hoover in 1932. Of these three only Brandeis was over seventy years of age, and he was seventy-nine. The remaining justice, Owen Roberts, was, along with Chief Justice Hughes, regarded as a "swing man" in the Court's ideological spectrum. He had been appointed by President Hoover in 1930 and was fifty-five years of age.

As national debate over the President's plan mushroomed in the first few weeks after its proposal, members of the Court were urged by radio networks to speak about it, but all refused. While the justices could, ensconced within the walls of their marble palace, safely and properly do this, the members of the Senate where the battle was to be fought could not.

President Roosevelt had not merely been himself reelected in 1936, but had carried with him overwhelming majorities in both houses of Congress. In the Senate the Democrats outnumbered the Republicans seventy-five to eighteen, with an independent and two Farmer-Labor members rounding out the complement of ninety-six. The Republicans to a man were against the President's plan, but their elected minority leader, Charles McNary of Oregon, and senior members such as Arthur Vandenberg of Michigan and William E. Borah of Idaho saw that if the fight over the Court-packing bill was seen as a battle between Republicans and Democrats, the issue would in all probability turn out just as it had in the presidential election a few months earlier. They therefore imposed upon themselves and urged upon their colleagues and other figures in the Republican party a policy of silence. There can be no doubt that the silence on behalf of the Republicans immeasurably strengthened the Democratic opponents of the President's plan.

The leader of the Democratic opposition in the Senate by common consent was Burton K. Wheeler of Montana. Wheeler's credentials for this role were impeccable. Born in Massachusetts, he attended law school at the University of Michigan and then settled in Butte, Montana. He had been elected to the United States Senate in 1922, and reelected in 1928 and 1934. He had been the vice-presidential running mate on Robert M. La Follette, Sr.'s Progressive presidential ticket in 1924, and had been a strong supporter of Roosevelt's campaign for the presidential nomination in 1932 before the Chicago convention. He had been an ardent supporter of Roosevelt's policies during the latter's first term, and had actively campaigned for his reelection in 1936.

What, then, caused Wheeler to break with the administration now? Genuine distaste for the plan was undoubtedly the principal factor; dissatisfaction with the way Democratic patronage in Montana had been handled may also have been a contributing cause. But once enlisted, Wheeler proved to be a formidable opponent.

Because he was not only a Democrat but had been a strong supporter of many of Roosevelt's policies, he could appeal to a broad spectrum of Democrats in the Senate. Senator Millard Tydings of Maryland invited Wheeler and a dozen and a half southern Democrats in the Senate who were likewise opposed to the President's plan to his home for dinner. There they later agreed to follow Wheeler's leadership in the fight. Just as the maximum effect could not have been obtained under the banner of a Republican leader, so it could not have been obtained by a southern Democrat.

Adverse editorial criticism of his programs was nothing new to President Roosevelt, since the great majority of daily newspapers in the United States were controlled by people whom he dubbed "economic royalists." But soon the news columns of these papers were reporting opposition from sources that did not normally voice opposition to New Deal programs, and similar messages were conveyed personally to the President and his strategists. While the President kept the reins of leadership to himself and in a small coterie of associates in the White House, there must of necessity be leadership in favor of the plan in the Senate. This mantle fell in the first instance on Senator Joe Robinson from Arkansas, the Democratic majority leader, and secondarily on the uncertain shoulders of Henry F. Ashurst of Arizona, the chairman of the Senate Judiciary Committee.

Robinson had worked his way up the political ladder in his home state of Arkansas, serving as a member of the House of Representatives and briefly as governor before being elected to the Senate in 1912. Now sixty-five years of age, he had been majority leader in the Senate since 1923 by reason of the almost unvarying adherence of the "solid south" to the Democratic ticket in senatorial elections. He was a big, heavyset man with small eyes and a jutting jaw. He had been a faithful Democratic wheelhorse in the Senate for twenty-four years, and he was not going to stop now, whatever personal reservations he might have about the President's plan. And above all, he had for years nurtured an ambition for a seat on the Supreme Court—an ambition which, he felt, would surely be realized if the President's plan became law.

Arizona's Henry F. Ashurst was a horse of a different color. He was now sixty-two years old, and like Robinson had risen to the powerful position he occupied as chairman of the Senate Judiciary Committee through the seniority system. His middle name was Fountain, and he had a passion for oratory in the old style. "I am a fountain," he said of himself, "not a cistern." He had grown up on the Arizona frontier, but now in Washington he affected the

cutaway-coat garb of a southern statesman. Ashurst announced in
favor of the President's Court plan, but he would prove to be a
weak and unreliable reed for the administration to lean on in the
forthcoming hearings.

Meanwhile, back at the White House, Roosevelt intimates
such as Thomas F. Corcoran and Robert H. Jackson were urging
the President to switch from the justification for the plan that he
stated in his message to Congress to the real justification. The
message drafted by Attorney General Cummings put the need for
Court reorganization entirely on the basis of the age of the incumbent judges. Nothing was said about the present Court's perceived role as a roadblock to the accomplishment of New Deal
reforms. Proponents were troubled by the fact that the oldest justice on the Court, Louis D. Brandeis, was regarded as a sort of
spiritual godfather of the New Deal, and had taken a much
broader view of the congressional power to regulate business than
had some of his younger colleagues. Corcoran and Jackson had
picked a good time to importune the President. Homer Cummings, smug in his knowledge that he alone of major presidential
advisers had played a role in the drafting of the plan, had packed
his bags and left for a Florida vacation. In his absence, the President was persuaded that the justification based on age appeared
disingenuous to the public, and created a suspicion of the President's motives in proposing it. Roosevelt seized the opportunity
of a Democratic victory dinner held at the Mayflower Hotel in
Washington on March 4 to shift from the basis of age to the basis
of constitutional obstructionism in his attack on the Supreme
Court. He delivered a rip-snorting oration outlining the New Deal
efforts to meet the critical problems of farmers, laborers, and the
common man in general, and then told of how the Supreme Court
had declared these plans unconstitutional. Cheered to a fare-thee-
well by the thirteen hundred diners at the Mayflower, he urged
upon his audience and upon the nation his message: "We must
act—now!" Five days later, the night before the Senate Judiciary
Committee hearings on the bill were scheduled to open, he followed up his Mayflower speech with one of his famous "fireside
chats," urging the need for the Court plan and assuring his na-

tionwide audience that he had no desire to be a dictator. The next day the Senate Judiciary Committee, headed by Senator Ashurst, filed into the huge, ornate Caucus Room of the Senate to begin the hearings on the President's bill. The hearing room was packed with hundreds of spectators, reporters, and important administration officials. The first administration witness was Homer Cummings, who, in the tradition of administration witnesses both before and since, read to the assembled multitude a five-thousand-word statement. The next witness was Assistant Attorney General Robert H. Jackson, who made a spirited and articulate defense of the bill on the basis advanced for it by the President in his Mayflower speech—that the Court by unreasonably grudging interpretation of the Constitution was denying the people the right to govern themselves. Succeeding administration witnesses occupied the committee for about two weeks.

Proponents and opponents of the bill viewed the committee hearings differently. To the proponents they were an obstacle to be overcome; thus the administration strategists sought to convince Ashurst, and the opposition as well, that an arrangement should be worked out whereby each side would agree to confine its presentation of witnesses to two weeks. But to the opposition, the hearings were a method of delaying the ultimately crucial vote on the bill in the Senate until public opinion, which they felt was on their side, would have a chance to build up. Washington was rife with speculation at the time as to how the Judiciary Committee members themselves stood on the bill; the consensus was that of its eighteen members, eight favored the bill, eight were opposed to it, and two were undecided. As the administration witnesses wound up the second week of the hearings, Senator Wheeler looked about for a way to put some punch and drama into his testimony as the first opposition witness the following week.

On Thursday, March 18, Wheeler, Senator William King, the ranking Democrat on the Judiciary Committee, and Senator Warren Austin, the ranking Republican on the committee, called upon Chief Justice Hughes and asked him to appear as a witness before the committee to outline the Court's ability to deal with its docket. Even though they sought only factual testimony from Hughes, the Chief Justice said he was unwilling to appear by himself, but would do so if another member of the Court, preferably Justice Brandeis because of his standing as a Democrat and his reputation as a liberal, would accompany him. When Hughes consulted Brandeis, he found that Brandeis was strongly opposed to Hughes or any other member of the Court appearing before the committee. But Brandeis agreed that if the committee were to request the facts from Hughes, it would be entirely proper for him to respond in letter form. Hughes telephoned this response to the senators on the following day. Wheeler had known Justice and Mrs. Brandeis for a long time, and he now called on Brandeis in an effort to obtain testimony from some member of the Court. Brandeis explained to Wheeler the conversation he had had with Hughes, and then said to Wheeler: "You call the Chief Justice. He'll give you a letter." But Wheeler was extremely reluctant to call Hughes, because in 1930 Wheeler had been one of the most vigorous opponents of Hughes's confirmation as Chief Justice; Brandeis, however, not wanting to see the opportunity lost, insisted on telephoning Hughes himself and then handing the telephone to Wheeler. Hughes invited Wheeler to his home, where Wheeler explained to him late that Saturday afternoon that by the following Monday morning he needed a letter explaining how current the Court was in its docket. The letter would be addressed only to the President's original arguments for the Court plan— that the septuagenarian justices were unable to keep abreast of their docket and had fallen badly behind in their work. Hughes was unwilling to address himself to the other arguments in favor of the plan offered by Roosevelt in his March speeches.

Hughes had the letter ready on Sunday, and showed it to Justices Brandeis and Van Devanter, who expressed agreement with its contents and signed it with him. He did not seek approval of the other six justices for the letter. When Wheeler came to the Hughes home Sunday afternoon to pick up the letter, Hughes handed it to him and said: "The baby is born."

Wheeler commenced his testimony as lead-off opposition witness before the Judiciary Committee the next morning, and said that after the attorney general had testified as to the inability of the Supreme Court to keep abreast of its docket, he, Wheeler, had gone "to the only source in this country that could know exactly what the facts were. . . ." As he paused, a hush fell over the Caucus Room, in anticipation of a surprise. Wheeler continued: "And I have here now a letter by the Chief Justice of the Supreme Court, Mr. Charles Evans Hughes, dated March twenty-first, 1937, written by him and approved by Mr. Justice Brandeis and Mr. Justice Van Devanter. Let us see what these gentlemen say about it." Wheeler then read the letter, addressed to him. The letter was couched in factual terms:

> The Supreme Court is fully abreast of its work. When we rose on March 15th (for the present recess) we had heard argument in cases in which certiorari had been granted only four weeks before—February 15th . . . there is no congestion of cases upon our calendar. This gratifying condition has obtained for several years. We have been able for several Terms to adjourn after disposing of all cases which are ready to be heard.

Hughes's letter also contained this observation:

> An increase in the number of Justices of the Supreme Court, apart from any question of policy, which I do not discuss, would not promote the efficiency of the Court. . . . There would be more judges to hear, more judges to confer, more judges to discuss, more judges to be convinced and to decide. The present number of Justices is thought to be large enough so far as the prompt, adequate, and efficient conduct of the work of the court is concerned. . . ." [Pusey, Vol. II, p. 756]

There seems to be little doubt among contemporary observers that the Hughes letter had the effect of a bombshell in the debate over the Court-packing plan. Robert Jackson later said that the Hughes letter was the most significant factor in the defeat of the Court plan. It dealt only with the original arguments made in the presidential message in favor of the plan, but it virtually demolished those arguments. While the arguments later adduced by Roosevelt in his Mayflower speech and fireside chat were not addressed by the Hughes letter, the now-exposed baselessness of the first set of arguments necessarily made the public suspicious of the second set.

Less than two weeks later the first of two successive blows was dealt to the President's plan, and this time by the Supreme Court itself. On Monday, March 29, 1937, the Supreme Court upheld the constitutionality of a Washington state minimum wage law. Two weeks later, it upheld the constitutionality of the National Labor Relations Act, more commonly known as the Wagner Act, which had been passed by Congress in 1935. Both cases were decided by votes of 5 to 4, and in both cases the Chief Justice wrote the Court's opinion. In the case of *Jones & Laughlin* v. *NLRB*, which upheld the constitutionality of the Wagner Act, the Court markedly expanded upon its previous definitions of the scope of congressional authority to regulate commerce among the states. In *West Coast Hotel Company* v. *Parrish*, which upheld the state minimum-wage law, the Court all but abandoned its previous insistence that freedom of contract was protected by the Due Process Clause. Because of the closely divided vote in the Court, there was a feeling among the administration supporters of the President's plan and among Court observers that "two swallows don't make a summer." But if the Court were to adhere to this new tack, much territory in the way of reform legislation desired by the New Deal that had previously seemed out of bounds to Congress was now within reach. The result was that several wavering members of the Senate came to the conclusion that the President's plan, dubious to begin with, was no longer necessary to the accomplishment of the goals of the New Deal, and they privately told Joe Robinson to count them as "no" votes. The Senate committee hearings ended in the last week of April, and the best guess of those in the know was that a majority of the members of the committee opposed the plan and would write a report recommending that it not pass. This feeling was confirmed the following day when three Democrats on the committee—Carl Hatchett of New Mexico, Pat McCarran of Nevada, and Joseph O'Mahoney of Wyoming, announced their opposition. The administration still figured that the count in the full Senate was about forty to forty, with the remainder undecided. The Democratic leaders in the Senate urged some sort of compromise upon the President in view of the recent Supreme Court decisions, but the President confidently refused. Roosevelt summoned Ashurst to the White House, and implied that the Arizona Democrat had killed the Court plan by delay and postponement of the hearings. Publicly, Ashurst still appeared to be a supporter of the plan, saying that an unfavorable report from the Judiciary Committee would in no sense be a fatal blow. But this seeming anticipation of a negative result from a committee overwhelmingly controlled by members of the President's own party was scarcely an encouraging omen for the administration.

Justice Van Devanter had been considering retirement for some time, and he was a good friend of his fellow westerner in the Senate, William E. Borah of Idaho. Borah suggested to Van Devanter that if he was going to retire, he might as well do it at a time when it would help to defeat the Court bill. Van Devanter accordingly picked the morning of May 18, 1937, to call in a wire service reporter covering the Supreme Court and announce that he had moments earlier sent by messenger a letter of resignation to the President. Coincidentally, May 18 was the day on which the Judiciary Committee was to meet and vote on the President's plan, and as the committee convened, Senator Wheeler made sure that each member was aware of the news of the Van Devanter resignation which had just gone out on the ticker tape. The committee, meeting in closed-door session, quickly voted on six variations of the same proposal, designed to save some part of the President's original plan. Each proposal failed, and the committee then by a vote of 10 to 8 adopted a recommendation that the bill "not pass" and approved a report to that effect prepared by its staff. The report concluded that the bill was "a measure which should be so emphatically rejected that its parallel will never again be presented to the free representatives of the free people of America."

Joe Robinson in early June went to the White House for a lengthy meeting with the President and his advisers. Robinson came quickly to the point: By his head count the administration did not have the votes to pass the original Court bill, and its prospects could only go downhill from there on. Robinson urged the President to accept a compromise whereby the new appointments for justices over seventy who did not retire would be limited to one per year. Roosevelt told Robinson to go ahead and negotiate the details so long as the principle of additional justices was in some way preserved. The President confirmed his willingness to compromise in a fencing match with reporters at a news conference early in June.

Suddenly the administration's prospects of passing the bill in this watered-down form improved dramatically. Robinson reported in the middle of June that he had forty-five votes "pro," thirty-nine votes "no," with the remaining twelve uncertain. By the end of the month he told administration leaders that he had the necessary votes to pass the bill, and only a filibuster could defeat it.

On Friday, July 2, 1937, the compromise version of the President's plan was introduced in the Senate. Instead of allowing the President to appoint a new justice for each present member of the Court over seventy, that age was raised to seventy-five; and in addition the bill permitted only one such appointment each year. The "compromise" was something of an illusion, since its enactment would allow Roosevelt to make three appointments to the Supreme Court within a period of six months: one to replace Justice Van Devanter, one new justice for the year 1937, and another new justice for the year 1938. But enough senators saw a difference so as to give the compromise plan a fair prospect of success if the opposition filibuster could be defeated.

Senator Robinson led off the debate for the administration, and was personally in charge of administration strategy in the Senate. During the first week of the debate a heat wave engulfed the eastern United States; in Washington the temperature hovered around 95 degrees each afternoon, and the nationwide death toll from the heat wave was one hundred and fifty. Robinson, sixty-four, overweight, and suffering from a heart condition, was bothered by the heat. He had been the leader of the Senate

Democrats for fourteen years, and now he hoped he was on the verge of taking a seat on the Supreme Court to climax his long career in public life.

In the beginning of the second week of the debate, Robinson complained to Ashurst in the Senate cloakroom of having a sharp pain in his chest. He again complained of such pain on Tuesday, and said he was going home to rest. Home for Joe Robinson was a five-room apartment on the fourth floor of the Methodist Building, located just across Maryland Avenue from the Supreme Court building—the same building in which Sherman Minton lived when he was later appointed a justice. Mrs. Robinson was in Little Rock for the week, and so the senator had the apartment to himself. He retired for the evening reading *The Congressional Record* sitting up in bed, but the next morning when a maid came to fix breakfast for him, he did not appear in the dining room at the usual time. The maid opened the door to his bedroom, and found him sprawled out on the floor dead of a heart attack.

Senator Wheeler that day told reporters that the President should drop his Court plan. It was known to administration leaders that some of the votes pledged to Robinson were personal pledges for past favors done by the majority leader; pledges that would not bind the senators who gave them after his death.

A special funeral train left Washington for Little Rock on Saturday, July 17, carrying thirty-eight members of the Senate, Postmaster General Jim Farley and Vice-President John Nance Garner. On the return trip from Little Rock, Garner held court on the train with bourbon and branch water and talked to nearly every one of the thirty-eight senators. He was convinced that sentiment was shifting against even the President's compromise plan.

When Garner returned to Washington he visited with the President and was asked how he had found the Court situation. In a famous conversation he replied: "Do you want it with the bark on or off, Cap'n?"

Roosevelt replied: "The rough way."

"All right," answered Cactus Jack. "You are beat, you haven't got the votes."

At this point Roosevelt finally capitulated, and instructed

Garner to make the best deal he could to save the plan. This proved in retrospect to be virtually no deal at all. He met with Wheeler and offered him a compromise of a total of two new justices, but Wheeler refused. Garner then met with Senator Ashurst and two other senior Democratic opponents of the President's plan. Garner told Ashurst that the Judiciary Committee should rewrite the President's bill to exclude any reference to the Supreme Court, so that it would deal only with retirement by lower federal judges. A parliamentary plan was worked out designed to superficially save the face of the administration: A motion to recommit the bill would be made in the Senate, which would not expressly refer to the deletion of the provisions with respect to the Supreme Court, but it was understood that when the committee received the bill back it would eliminate those provisions. On Thursday, July 22, Senator Marvel M. Logan of Kentucky rose in the Senate to make the motion to recommit the president's bill. But before a vote could be taken on the measure, Senator Hiram Johnson of California, a Republican who opposed the President's plan, asked whether the new version would include the Supreme Court. Logan tried to reply by indirection, but the elderly California senator would not accept this.

"The Supreme Court is out of the way?" inquired Senator Johnson.

"The Supreme Court is out of the way," acknowledged Senator Logan.

Hiram Johnson then exclaimed, "Glory be to God!" and sat down. After a momentary pause, as if by prearranged signal, the spectators' galleries broke into applause. The President's plan was indeed dead.

The defeat of the Court-packing plan had long-term political consequences for President Roosevelt, the Democratic party, and the nation. But it also constituted a remarkable expression of public feeling about the Supreme Court. Here was a tremendously popular president, reelected months earlier by a landslide electoral and popular vote, who had personally masterminded an effort to remove the Supreme Court as an obstacle to the carrying out of his popular mandate. A House of Representatives which the President's party controlled by a majority of more than four to one declined to take up the President's bill; a Senate in which there were only eighteen Republicans out of a membership of ninety-six ultimately handed the bill a resounding defeat. There is little reason to think that many members of the American public either understood or sympathized with the particular doctrines espoused by the majority of the Court in holding New Deal legislation unconstitutional, but the defeat of the Court-packing plan made it obvious that a majority of the American public did not want even a very popular president to tamper with the Supreme Court of the United States. Whatever the shortcomings of its doctrine in the public mind, its judgments were not to be reversed by the simple expedient of creating new judgeships and filling them with administration supporters.

Supporters of the administration plan were fond of saying that they had lost the battle, but they ultimately won the war: Franklin Roosevelt within four years after the defeat of his Court-packing plan in the Senate was able to name no less than six new justices to the nine-man Court. It is perhaps more accurate to say that had Roosevelt only exercised a little more patience, he could have shaped the character of the Supreme Court in the way that most strong presidents have tried to shape it, without attempting to restructure the institution itself.

10

PRESIDENTIAL APPOINTMENTS TO THE SUPREME COURT

*H*ad Franklin Roosevelt only been more patient—had he but recognized the great wisdom in Henry Ashurst's advice to him—"Time is on your side; *anno domini* is your invincible ally"—he could have avoided the defeat for himself personally and for the Democratic party when the Senate rejected his Court-packing plan, and still have accomplished his goal. Before elaborating on this point, it may be well to define the use of the word *pack*, which seems to me the best verb available for the activity involved despite its highly pejorative connotation. It need not have such a connotation when used in this context; the second edition of Webster's unabridged dictionary defines the verb *pack* as "to choose or arrange (a jury, committee, etc.) in such a way as to secure some advantage, or to favor some particular side or interest." Thus a president who sets out to pack the Court does nothing more than seek to appoint people to the Court who are sympathetic to his political or philosophical principles.

There is no reason in the world why a president should not do this. One of the many marks of genius that our Constitution bears is the fine balance struck in the establishment of the judicial branch, avoiding subservience to the supposedly more vigorous legislative and executive branches on the one hand, and avoiding total institutional isolation from public opinion on the other. The performance of the judicial branch of the United States government for a period of nearly two hundred years has shown it to be remarkably independent of the other coordinate branches of that government. Yet the institution has been constructed in such a way that due to the mortality tables, if nothing else, the public will in the person of the president of the United States—the one official who is elected by the entire nation—have something to say about the membership of the Court, and thereby indirectly about its decisions.

Surely we would not want it any other way. We want our federal courts, and particularly the Supreme Court, to be independent of popular opinion when deciding the particular cases or controversies that come before them. The provision for tenure during good behavior and the prohibition against diminution of compensation have proved more than adequate to secure that sort of independence. The result is that judges are responsible to no electorate or constituency. But the manifold provisions of the Constitution with which judges must deal are by no means crystal clear in their import, and reasonable minds may differ as to which interpretation is proper. When a vacancy occurs on the Court, it is entirely appropriate that that vacancy be filled by the president, responsible to a national constituency, as advised by the Senate, whose members are responsible to regional constituencies. Thus, public opinion has some say in who shall become judges of the Supreme Court.

Whether or not it is, as I contend, both normal and desirable for presidents to attempt to pack the Court, the fact is that presidents who have been sensible of the broad powers they have possessed, and have been willing to exercise those powers, have all but invariably tried to have some influence on the philosophy of the Court as a result of their appointments to that body. Whether or not they have been successful in their attempts to pack the Court is a more difficult question. I think history teaches us that those who have tried have been at least partially successful, but that a number of factors militate against a president's having anything more than partial success. What these factors are can best be illustrated with examples from the history of presidential appointments to the Court.

Very early in the history of the Court, Justice William Cushing, "a sturdy Federalist and follower of Marshall" [Schachner, Vol. II, p. 901] died in September 1810. His death reduced the seven-member Court to six, evenly divided between Federalist appointees and Republican appointees. Shortly after Cushing's death, Thomas Jefferson, two years out of office as president, wrote to his former secretary of the treasury, Albert Gallatin, in these unseemingly gleeful words:

> I observe old Cushing is dead. At length, then, we have a chance of getting a Republican majority in the Supreme Judiciary. For ten years has that branch braved the spirit and will of the Nation. . . . The event is a fortunate one, and so timed as to be a godsend to me.

Jefferson, of course, had been succeeded by James Madison, who, though perhaps less ardently than Jefferson, also championed Republican ideals. Jefferson wrote Madison, "It will be difficult to find a character of firmness enough to preserve his independence on the same Bench with Marshall." [Dunne, p. 77] When he heard that Madison was considering Joseph Story and Ezekiel Bacon, then chairman of the Ways and Means Committee of the House of Representatives, he admonished Madison that "Story and Bacon are exactly the men who deserted us [on the Embargo Act]. The former unquestionably a Tory, and both are too young." [Dunne, pp. 78–79]

President Madison seems to have been "snakebit" in his effort to fill the Cushing vacancy. He first nominated his attorney general, Levi Lincoln, who insisted that he did not want the job and after the Senate confirmed him still refused to serve. Madison then nominated a complete dark horse, one Alexander Wolcott, the federal revenue collector of Connecticut, whom the Senate rejected by the mortifying vote of 24 to 9. Finally, in the midst of a Cabinet crisis that occupied a good deal of his time, Madison nominated Joseph Story for the Cushing vacancy, and the Senate confirmed him as a matter of routine three days later. Story, of course, fulfilled Jefferson's worst expectations about him. He became Chief Justice John Marshall's principal ally on the great legal issues of the day in the Supreme Court, repeatedly casting his vote in favor of national power and against the restrictive interpretation of the Constitution urged by Jefferson and his states' rights school. And Joseph Story served on the Supreme Court for thirty-four years, one of the longest tenures on record.

Presidents who wish to pack the Supreme Court, like murder suspects in a detective novel, must have both motive and opportunity. Here Madison had both, and yet he failed. He was probably a considerably less partisan chief executive than was Jefferson, and so his motivation was perhaps not strong enough. After having botched several opportunities, he finally preferred to nominate someone who would not precipitate another crisis in his relations with the Senate, rather than insisting on a nominee who had the right philosophical credentials. The lesson, I suppose, that can be drawn from this incident is that while for Court-watchers the president's use of his appointment power to nominate people for vacancies on the Supreme Court is the most important use he makes of the executive authority, for the president himself, the filling of Supreme Court vacancies is just one of many acts going on under the "big top" of his administration.

John Marshall was not the only member of the Court to have been appointed in the more than usually partisan atmosphere of a lame-duck presidential administration. In 1840, after the "hard cider and log cabin" campaign, William Henry Harrison, the Whig candidate for president, was elected over Martin Van Buren, the Democratic incumbent. Little more than a week before Harrison would take his oath on March 4, 1841, Justice Phillip Pendleton Barbour of Virginia died suddenly. Two days after Barbour's death Van Buren appointed Peter V. Daniel to be associate justice of the Supreme Court of the United States. A few days later, Martin Van Buren described in a letter to Andrew Jackson, his mentor and predecessor, the appointment of Daniel: "I had an opportunity to put a man on the bench of the Supreme Court at the moment of leaving the government who will I am sure stick to the true principles of the Constitution, and being a Democrat *ab ovo* is not in so much danger of a falling off in the true spirit."

After frantic last-minute maneuvering between the Whig and Democrat factions in the Senate, Daniel was confirmed, and remained an ardent—nay, obdurate—champion of states' rights until his death in 1860.

Abraham Lincoln had inveighed against the Supreme Court's 1857 decision in the *Dred Scott* case during his famous debates with Stephen A. Douglas in 1858 when both sought to be elected United States senator from Illinois. Lincoln lost that election, but his successful presidential campaign two years later was likewise marked by a restrained by nonetheless forceful attack on this decision and by implication on the Court's apparent institutional bias in favor of slaveholders. Within two months of his inauguration, by reason of the death of one justice and the resignation of two others, Lincoln was given three vacancies on the Supreme Court. To fill them he chose Noah Swayne of Ohio, David Davis of Illinois, and Samuel F. Miller of Iowa. All were Republicans who had rendered some help in getting Lincoln elected President in 1860; indeed, Davis had been one of Lincoln's principal managers at the Chicago Convention of the Republican party.

In 1863, by reason of expansion in the membership of the Court, Lincoln was enabled to name still another justice, and he chose Stephen J. Field of California, a War Democrat who had been the chief justice of that state's supreme court. In 1864, Chief Justice Roger B. Taney finally died at the age of eighty-eight, and Lincoln had an opportunity to choose a new chief justice.

At this time, in the fall of 1864, the constitutionality of the so-called "greenback legislation," which the government had used to finance the war effort, was headed for a Court test, and Lincoln was very much aware of this fact. He decided to appoint his secretary of the treasury, Salmon P. Chase, who was in many respects the architect of the greenback legislation, saying to a confidant, "We wish for a Chief Justice who will sustain what has been done in regard to emancipation and the legal tenders. We cannot ask a man what he will do, and if we should, and he should answer us, we should despise him for it. Therefore, we must take a man whose opinions are known" (2 Warren 401).

In all, then, Lincoln had five appointments. How successful was Lincoln at packing the Court with these appointments? The answer has to be, I believe, that he was very successful at first. In the all-important *Prize Cases*, 2 Black 635 (1863), decided in 1863, the three Lincoln appointees already on the Court—Swayne, Miller, and Davis, joined with Justices Wayne and Grier of the Old Court to make up the majority, while Chief Justice Taney and Justices Nelson, Catron, and Clifford dissented. It seems obvious that this case would have been decided the other way had the same justices been on the Court who had decided the *Dred Scott* case six years earlier. Charles Warren, in his *The Supreme Court in United States History*, describes these cases as being not only "the first cases arriving out of the Civil War to be decided by [the Court], but they were far more momentous in the issue involved than any other case; and their final determination favorable to the government's contention was almost a necessary factor in the suppression of the war." [Warren, Vol. II, pp. 380–381].

But immediately after the war, a host of new issues arose which could not really have been foreseen at the time Lincoln made his first appointments to the Supreme Court. The extent to which military tribunals might displace civil courts during time of war or insurrection was decided by the Supreme Court in 1866 in the famous case of *Ex Parte Milligan*, 4 Wall. 2. While the Court was unanimous as to one aspect of this case, it divided 5 to 4 on the equally important question of whether Congress might provide for trial by military commissions during time of insurrection even though the president alone could not. On the latter question, the Lincoln appointees divided two to three.

During the postwar Reconstruction Era, three new amendments to the United States Constitution were promulgated, and the construction of those amendments was also necessarily on the agenda of the Supreme Court. The first important case involving the Fourteenth Amendment to come before the Court was that of the Slaughterhouse Cases, in which the applicability of the provisions of that amendment to claims not based on racial discrimination was taken up by the Court. Of the Lincoln appointees, Justice Miller wrote the majority opinion and was joined in it by Justice Davis, while Chief Justice Chase and Justices Field and Swayne were in dissent.

The ultimate irony in Lincoln's effort to pack the court was the Court's first decision in the so-called Legal Tender Cases, *Hepburn* v. *Griswold,* 8 Wall. 603. In 1870 the Court held, in an opinion by Chief Justice Chase, who had been named Chief Justice by Lincoln primarily for the purposes of upholding the greenback legislation, that this legislation was unconstitutional. Justice Field joined the opinion of the Chief Justice, while the other three Lincoln appointees—Miller, Swayne, and Davis—dissented. Chief Justice Chase's vote in the Legal Tender Cases is a textbook example of the proposition that one may look at a legal question differently as a judge from the way one did as a member of the executive branch. There is no reason to believe that Chase thought he was acting unconstitutionally when he helped draft and shepherd through Congress the greenback legislation, and it may well be that if Lincoln had actually posed the question to him before nominating him as Chief Justice, he would have agreed that the measures were constitutional. But administrators in charge of a program, even if they are lawyers, simply do not ponder these questions in the depth that judges do, and Chase's vote in the Legal Tender Case is proof of this fact.

In assessing Lincoln's success in his effort to pack the Court, it seems that with regard to the problems he foresaw at the time of his first appointments—the difficulties that the Supreme Court might put in the way of successfully fighting the Civil War—Lincoln was preeminently successful in his efforts. But with respect to issues that arose after the war—the use of military courts, the constitutionality of the greenback legislation, and the construction of the Fourteenth Amendment—his appointees divided from one another regularly. Perhaps the lesson to be drawn from these examples is that judges may think very much alike with respect to one issue, but quite differently from one another with respect to other issues. And while both presidents and judicial nominees may know the current constitutional issues of importance, neither

242 William H. Rehnquist

of them is usually vouchsafed the foresight to see what the great issues of ten or fifteen years hence are to be.

By the time Theodore Roosevelt had succeeded to the presidency immediately after the turn of the century, issues arising out of the territorial expansion of the United States following the Spanish-American War and the governmental regulation of trusts and monopolies were issues high on the nation's agenda, issues that had been scarcely spots on the horizon at the time Lincoln appointed Salmon Chase Chief Justice. When President Roosevelt learned of the illness of Associate Justice Horace Gray of Massachusetts in 1902, his attention naturally turned to Chief Justice Oliver Wendell Holmes, Jr., of the Judicial Court of Massachusetts. But he was not going to buy a pig in a poke.

He wrote to his great and good friend Senator Henry Cabot Lodge of Massachusetts, as follows:

Dear Cabot,

". . . Now as to Holmes: if it becomes necessary you can show him this letter. First of all, I wish to go over the reasons why I am in his favor. He possesses the high character and the high reputation both of which should if possible attach to any man who is to go upon the highest court of the entire civilized world. His father's name entitles the son to honor; and if the father had been an utterly unknown man the son would nevertheless now have won the highest honor. The position of Chief Justice of Massachusetts is in itself a guarantee of the highest professional standing. Moreover, Judge Holmes has behind him the kind of career and possesses the kind of personality which make a good American proud of him as a representative of our country. He has been a most gallant soldier, a most able and upright public servant, and in public and private life alike a citizen whom we like to think of as typical of the American character at its best. The labor decisions which have been criticized by some of the big railroad men and other members of large corporations constitute to my mind a strong point in Judge Holmes' favor. The ablest lawyers and greatest judges are men whose past has naturally brought them into close relationship with the wealthiest and most powerful clients, and I am glad when I can find a judge who has been able to preserve his aloofness of mind so as to keep his broad humanity of feeling and his sympathy for the class from which he has not drawn his clients. I think it eminently desirable that our Supreme Court should show in unmistakable fashion their entire sympathy with all proper effort to secure the most favorable possible consideration for the men who most need that consideration.

Finally, Judge Holmes' whole mental attitude, as shown for instance by his great Phi Beta Kappa speech at Harvard is such that I should naturally expect him to be in favor of those principles in which I so earnestly believe. . . .

The majority of the present Court who have, although without satisfactory unanimity, upheld the policies of President McKinley and the Republican party in Congress, have rendered a great service to mankind and to this nation. The minority—a minority so large as to lack but one vote of being a majority—have stood for such reactionary folly as would have hampered well-nigh hopelessly this people in doing efficient and honorable work for the national welfare, and for the welfare of the islands themselves, in Porto Rico and the Philippines. No doubt they have possessed excellent motives and without doubt they are men of excellent personal character; but this no more excuses them than the same conditions excused the various upright and honorable men who took part in the wicked folly of secession in 1860 and 1861.

Now I should like to know that Judge Holmes was in entire sympathy with our views, that is with your views and mine and Judge Gray's, for instance, just as we know that ex-Attorney General Knowlton is, before I would feel justified in appointing him. Judge Gray has been one of the most valuable members of the Court. I should hold myself as guilty of an irreparable wrong to the nation if I should put in his place any man who was not absolutely sane and sound on the great policies for which we stand in public life.

Faithfully yours,
Theodore Roosevelt

P.S.—Judge Gray's letter of resignation to take effect upon the appointment of his successor, or as I may otherwise desire, has just come, so that I should know about Judge Holmes as soon as possible. How would it do, if he seems to be all right, to have him come down here and spend a night with me, and then I could make the announcement on the day that he left after we have talked together? [Roosevelt]

Holmes was duly appointed an associate justice, and largely fulfilled Theodore Roosevelt's expectations of him with respect to the so-called Insular Cases, which were a great issue at that time, although they are scarcely a footnote in a text on constitutional law today. But he disappointed Roosevelt with his dissenting opinion in the *Northern Securities* case, a disappointment Roosevelt is said to have expressed with the phrase: "Out of banana I could have carved a Justice with more backbone than that."

Although Franklin D. Roosevelt was understandably disappointed that he had had no opportunities to fill a vacancy on the Supreme Court during his first term in office, the vacancy occasioned by the retirement of Justice Van Devanter to which he appointed Justice Black was the first of eight vacancies that Roosevelt would have the opportunity to fill during his twelve years as President. There is no doubt that Roosevelt was keenly aware of the importance of judicial philosophy in a justice of the Supreme Court; if he were not, he never would have taken on the institutional might of the third branch with his Court-packing plan. Indeed, when it appeared during the battle in the Senate over the Court-packing bill that a compromise might be achieved in which Roosevelt would be allowed to appoint only two new justices instead of six, he pondered with several of his intimates whom he might choose in a way that he had not felt it necessary to do when he might have had the opportunity to choose six.

Majority Leader Joe Robinson of Arkansas was moved by considerations other than pure party loyalty to lead the fight for the President's Court-packing plan in the Senate. He had long wished to top off his long career of public service with a seat on the high bench, and many knowledgeable Washingtonians assumed that he would certainly be Franklin Roosevelt's first appointment to the Court. Leonard Baker, in his work *Back to Back: The Duel Between*

FDR and the Supreme Court, describes the situation in the Senate this way:

> The day Willis Van Devanter sent his resignation to the White House, Joe Robinson's colleagues considered his appointment as a replacement a sure thing. So did Robinson. He came into the Senate chamber that afternoon with a wide grin on his face and feeling almost jubilant. His fellow senators of both parties, who were also his old and warm friends, swarmed toward him to congratulate him, shake his hand, slap him on the back. Some even called him "Mr. Justice." This situation, the high probability that Joe Robinson would be named to the Court, was one of the reasons Robinson had been able to secure pledges to support the Court bill compromise. His colleagues assumed that the appointment to the Court would be forthcoming as soon as Joe Robinson delivered passage of the Court bill. Some senators, wavering on judicial reform, had decided to go along as a favor to Robinson. They had much affection for him and wanted him to achieve his ambitions. [p. 248]

But Roosevelt's more liberal advisers were already cautioning him about nominating Robinson; he would be sixty-five years old that summer, and it was thought that his outlook as a justice might be more closely akin to the majority of the nine old men than Roosevelt would wish. Assistant Attorney General Robert H. Jackson, who worked closely with him on the plan, told him:

> "I think it would be a great mistake for you to pack the Court and accept additional memberships on it, if you have got to make Joe Robinson one of them. There is only one excuse for packing the Court and that is to change it. You're very likely not to change anything and you will have all the odium of having packed it and being laughed at besides." [Baker, p. 249, quoting Gerhart, pp. 116–117].

About a week after Van Devanter's resignation, Roosevelt was cruising on the Potomac with some of his friends, all of whom except Henry Morgenthau, Jr., secretary of the treasury, had retired belowdecks. Baker describes their conversation in these words:

> "If Brandeis resigns," speculated the President, "whom do you think I should appoint to succeed him—Landis or Frankfurter?" The first reference was to James M. Landis, a brilliant young New Dealer, and the second was to Felix Frankfurter of the Harvard Law School who had been a philosophical mentor to the New Deal.
>
> Morgenthau replied that he considered Landis the better choice.
>
> "Frankfurter would rate a more popular opinion."
>
> Morgenthau agreed, saying: "Yes, I suppose he would, but I believe that the public would have more confidence in Landis."
>
> "Well," said the President, "I think I would have a terrible time getting Frankfurter confirmed."
>
> Morgenthau agreed, commenting that "one of the troubles with Frankfurter is that he is over-brilliant."
>
> A few moments later Morgenthau brought the conversation from the realm of speculation to the immediate problem, the retirement of Willis Van Devanter and the expectation that Joe Robinson would succeed him. "What," he asked the President, "are you going to do about Joe Robinson?"
>
> "I cannot appoint him," announced the President.
>
> "Why not?"
>
> "Because he is not sufficiently liberal."
>
> "I am certainly glad to hear you talk that way," said Morgenthau. "The things that you have done and talked to me about the last ten days have encouraged me tremendously because after all I am a reformer."
>
> Several months later the President returned to the question of appointing Joe Robinson. "If I had three vacancies, I might be able to sandwich in Joe Robinson." But he continued that he had no idea of who was going to resign after Van Devanter, or if anyone would. [Pp. 249–250]

This view is confirmed by observations of then Secretary of the Interior Harold L. Ickes in his diary:

> Mr. Justice Van Devanter, on the nineteenth, sent his resignation to the President, to take effect at the end of this Term of Court. He tipped this off to a favorite newspaper correspondent before his letter could possibly reach the White House.
>
> Not only the enemies of the President's Court plan but many of his friends at once rushed to get behind Senator Joe Robinson, to fill this vacancy. In fact, it seemed to me that the enemies were more interested in booming Robinson than anyone else, and the reason is not far to seek. . . .
>
> I had an appointment with the President just before noon after he had taken cognizance of what was going on on behalf of Robinson. He said to me that if he had three or four appointments to make, it might be alright to appoint Robinson "just to even things up." I told him that I didn't think he could afford to appoint Robinson if his was to be the only appointment, and the President seemed to be emphatically of that opinion. [Ickes, Vol. II]

In rapid succession, as the so-called nine old men retired or died, Franklin Roosevelt appointed first Senator Hugo Black of Alabama, then Solicitor General Stanley Reed of Kentucky, then Professor Felix Frankfurter of Massachusetts, then SEC Chairman William O. Douglas of Connecticut and Washington, then Attorney General Frank Murphy of Michigan. During his third term Roosevelt appointed Attorney General Robert H. Jackson of New York, Senator James F. Byrnes of South Carolina, and law school dean Wiley B. Rutledge of Iowa to the Court. As I have indicated earlier, five of these justices—Black, Reed, Frankfurter, Douglas, and Jackson—remained on the Court at the time of the Steel Seizure Case in 1952.

In the short run the effect of the change in membership on the Court's decisions was immediate, dramatic, and predictable. Social and regulatory legislation, whether enacted by the states or by Congress, was sustained across the board against constitutional challenges that might have prevailed before the Old Court. When Franklin Roosevelt in 1941 elevated Harlan F. Stone from associate justice to Chief Justice in place of Charles Evans Hughes, the periodical *United States News* commented, "The new head of the Court also will find no sharp divergence of opinion among his colleagues." *The Washington Post* echoed the same sentiment when it foresaw "for years to come" a "virtual unanimity on the tribunal." [Mason, *Harlan Fiske Stone*, p. 576]

These forecasts proved to be entirely accurate in the area of economic and social legislation. But other issues began to percolate up through the judicial coffee pot, as they have a habit of doing. The Second World War, which occupied the United States from 1941 until 1945, produced numerous lawsuits about civil liberties. During the war, the Court maintained a fair degree of cohesion in deciding most of these cases, but quite suddenly after the war, the predicted "virtual unanimity" was rent asunder in rancorous squabbling the like of which the Court had never seen before.

A part, but only a part, of the difference was of judicial philosophy. Understandably, seven justices who agreed as to the appropriate constitutional analysis to apply to economic and social legislation might not agree with one another in cases involving civil liberties. These differences manifested themselves infrequently during the war years, but came into full bloom shortly afterward. In a case called *Saia* v. *New York*, 334 U.S. 558 (1948), the Court held by a vote of 5 to 4 that a local ordinance of the city of Lockport, New York, regulating the use of sound trucks in city parks, was unconstitutional. Four of the five justices in the majority were appointees of Franklin Roosevelt, but so were three of the four justices in the minority. Seven months later the Court all but overruled the *Saia* case in *Kovacs* v. *Cooper*, 336 U.S. 53 (1949), with one of the *Saia* majority defecting to join the four dissenters for the *Kovacs* majority. These two cases provide but one of abundant examples of similar episodes in the Court's adjudication during the period from 1945 to 1949.

Thus history teaches us, I think, that even a "strong" president determined to leave his mark on the Court—a president such as Lincoln or Franklin Roosevelt—is apt to be only partially successful. Neither the president nor his appointees can foresee what issues will come before the Court during the tenure of the appointees, and it may be that none has thought very much about these issues. Even though they agree as to the proper resolution of current cases, they may well disagree as to future cases involving other questions when, as judges, they study briefs and hear arguments. Longevity of the appointees, or untimely deaths such as those of Justice Murphy and Justice Rutledge, may also frustrate a president's expectations; so also may the personal antagonisms developed between strong-willed appointees of the same president.

All of these factors are subsumed to a greater or lesser extent by observing that the Supreme Court is an institution far more dominated by centrifugal forces, pushing toward individuality and independence, than it is by centripetal forces pulling for hierarchical ordering and institutional unity. The well-known checks and balances provided by the framers of the Constitution have supplied the necessary centrifugal force to make the Supreme Court independent of Congress and the president. The degree to which a new justice should change his way of looking at things when he "puts on the robe" is emphasized by the fact that Supreme Court appointments almost invariably come one at a time, and each new appointee goes alone to take his place with eight colleagues who are already there. Unlike his freshman counterpart in the House of Representatives, where if there has been a strong political tide running at the time of a particular election there may be as many as seventy or eighty new members who form a bloc and cooperate with one another, the new judicial appointee brings no cohorts with him.

A second series of centrifugal forces is at work within the Court itself, pushing each member to be thoroughly independent of his colleagues. The chief justice has some authority that the associate justices do not have, but this is relatively insignificant compared to the extraordinary independence that each justice has from every other justice. Tenure is assured no matter how one votes in any given case; one is independent not only of public opinion, of the president, and of Congress, but of one's eight colleagues as well. When one puts on the robe, one enters a world of public scrutiny and professional criticism which sets great store by individual performance, and much less store upon the virtue of being a "team player."

James Madison, in his pre-presidential days when he was authoring political tracts, said in *The Federalist*, No. 51:

> But the great security against a gradual concentration of the several powers in the same department, consists in giving to those who administer each department the necessary constitutional means and personal motives to resist encroachments of the others. The provision for defense must in this, as in all other cases, be made commensurate to the danger of attack. Ambition must be made to counteract ambition. The interest of the man must be connected with the constitutional rights of the place.

Madison, of course, was talking about the principles necessary to secure independence of one branch of the government from another. But he might equally well have been talking about principles, at least in the case of the Supreme Court of the United States, designed to weaken and diffuse the outside loyalties of any new appointee, and to gradually cause that appointee to identify his interests in the broadest sense not merely with the institution to which he is appointed, but to his own particular place within the institution. Here again, this remarkable group of fifty-some men who met in Philadelphia in the summer of 1787 seems to have created the separate branches of the federal government with consummate skill. The Supreme Court is to be independent of the legislative and executive branch of the government; yet by reason of vacancies occurring on that Court, it is to be subjected to indirect infusions of the popular will in terms of the president's use of his appointment power. But the institution is so structured that a brand-new presidential appointee, perhaps feeling himself strongly loyal to the president who appointed him, and looking for colleagues of a similar mind on the Court, is immediately beset with the institutional pressures I have described. He identifies more and more strongly with the new institution of which he has become a member, and he learns how much store is set by his behaving independently of his colleagues. I think it is these institutional effects, as much as anything, that have prevented even strong presidents from being any more than partially successful when they sought to pack the Supreme Court.

11

CERTIORARIS: PICKING THE CASES TO BE DECIDED

*S*hortly after the Civil War Congress passed a law providing that the annual term of the Supreme Court should begin on the first Monday in October, and accordingly the first oral argument sessions of the new term of the Court begin on that date. For record-keeping purposes, however, the new term begins on July 1 of each year, and all cases filed on or after that date are numbered accordingly. The work of the Court consists essentially of three different functions: (1) choosing from among more than 4,000 "petitions for certiorari" somewhere around 150 cases in which certiorari is granted; (2) deciding these 150, which includes studying the briefs, hearing oral arguments by the lawyers for the parties, and voting on them at conference; and (3) preparing written opinions supporting the result reached by the majority and separate opinions and dissenting opinions by those justices who do not agree with the reasoning of the majority.

Petitions for certiorari are filed throughout the year and accumulate at a rate of somewhere between eighty and one hundred per week. These petitions are voted on and disposed of in the weekly conferences of the Court, except during a period between the time the Court recesses in July and the time it reconvenes in

254 William H. Rehnquist

October when there are no such conferences. The conferences take place in a room adjacent to the chambers of the chief justice, and are attended only by the justices themselves; they are not open to the public or to other Court personnel.

The Court sits as a body publicly on the bench in the courtroom to hear oral arguments in those cases that are to be decided on the merits in seven two-week sessions each term. The first session, as indicated, falls in October, the second in November, and they continue until the final one beginning sometime in the latter part of April. During each week of oral argument there are two conferences. One is on Wednesday after the justices get off the bench from hearing arguments, at which time the four cases argued the preceding Monday are discussed and voted upon. On Friday, the cases argued the preceding Tuesday and Wednesday are discussed and voted upon, and the pending petitions for certiorari are also disposed of. Between the sessions of oral argument are recesses, most of them two weeks in length, designed to allow the justices to prepare opinions for the Court in cases that have already been argued and voted upon, and to enable them to read briefs and prepare for forthcoming oral arguments. Two recesses, between the December and January sessions of oral argument and between the February and March sessions of oral argument, last four weeks.

When I first came to the Court, on the first Monday in October the justices simply came on the bench, announced to the world that they were back in session, and promptly recessed into conference to dispose of the petitions for certiorari that had accumulated over the summer. But shortly after I arrived, Justice Blackmun pointed out that if the Court were to move the summer certiorari conference, which generally lasts several days, back to the last week of September, it could then begin oral arguments a week earlier and allow an added week in the December recess where the time could be profitably used for working on opinions which by that time would already have been assigned. This suggestion was instantly approved by his colleagues, and we have done business that way ever since.

I have served with eleven different members of the Court in

my fifteen years on the bench, a number which by historical standards is remarkably small considering the length of time I have served. The senior associate justice, and dean in point of time served, when I took my seat on the Court was William O. Douglas. When he finally retired because of ill health in October 1975, he had broken the record for longevity with his service of more than thirty-six years.

Bill Douglas was very much of a maverick throughout his life; at the Court conferences we sometimes had the impression that he was disappointed to have other people agree with his views in a particular case, because he would therefore be unable to write a stinging dissent. He had a brilliant legal mind, but by the time I came to know him as a colleague I think he was somewhat bored with the routine functions of the Court. During all the time that I have been on the Court, it has recessed for the summer somewhere around the first of July and we all make an effort to get our work out by then so that the Court may rise. But Bill Douglas went us one better; he was a very rapid worker, and would invariably have his work all done sometime in early June, when without notification to anyone he would simply leave Washington for his mountain summer home in Goose Prairie, Washington (where my wife, Nan, and I spent several delightful days as guests of Bill and his charming wife, Cathy). There was no phone at the Goose Prairie home, and if Bill wanted to check in with the Court he would go to a pay phone nearby and call his secretary; but there was no way for any of us to communicate directly with him. I remember his once telling Lewis Powell that if he had only seen the latter's dissent in a case that was handed down in the latter part of June he would have joined the dissent rather than the majority opinion!

Potter Stewart, with whom I served from the time I came on the Court until his retirement in June 1981, was born in Jackson, Michigan, in 1915. He attended Yale University and Yale Law School, served in the navy in the Second World War, and practiced in Cincinnati, Ohio, until President Eisenhower appointed him to the Court of Appeals for the Sixth Circuit when he was only thirty-nine years old. Four years later Eisenhower appointed him to the Supreme Court of the United States, where he served for twenty-three years.

Potter Stewart had a very strong feeling for the Court as an institution, and for the way that the Court ought to work. He realized that if all nine justices simply buried themselves in their chambers working only according to their own schedules, without responding to circulations from their colleagues, long and unnecessary delays could ensue. During my time he was unfailingly prompt in advising each colleague of what he proposed to do in response to a circulation from that colleague. He was also, I think, of all the colleagues with whom I have served, the one least influenced by considerations extraneous to the strictly legal aspects of a case—he was, that is, the quintessential judge.

Former Chief Justice Warren E. Burger was born in St. Paul, Minnesota, in 1907. He attended the University of Minnesota, and received his law degree from St. Paul College of Law. He engaged in the private practice of law in St. Paul from 1931 to 1953, and during this time was one of the principal advisers to Harold Stassen, who was governor of Minnesota at an early age and candidate for the Republican nomination for president in 1948 and 1952. Warren Burger served as assistant attorney general in charge of the Civil Division of the Justice Department from 1953 to 1956, at which time President Eisenhower appointed him to the Court of Appeals for the District of Columbia Circuit. President Nixon appointed him Chief Justice of the United States in 1969. He has been a warm and considerate friend of mine since the day I arrived at the Court, and I think he was pleased to have me succeed him as Chief Justice in September, 1986.

William J. Brennan, Jr., at present the senior associate justice, was born in Newark, New Jersey, April 25, 1906. He attended the University of Pennsylvania as an undergraduate and received his law degree from Harvard in 1931. He practiced law in Newark from 1931 to 1949 except for a three-year stint as an officer in the General Staff Corps of the United States Army during World War II. He was successively appointed to the trial, intermediate, appellate and supreme courts of New Jersey, and appointed by President Eisenhower to the Supreme Court in 1956. Bill Brennan and I disagree with one another about a lot of constitutional issues, but his buoyant outlook on life and friendly warmth toward his colleagues ensure that disagreements about the Constitution will not mar personal relationships.

Byron R. White was born in Fort Collins, Colorado, in 1917 and attended the University of Colorado as an undergraduate and received his law degree from Yale Law School. He served in the navy in World War II, and was a Rhodes Scholar at Oxford. He was a law clerk to Chief Justice Vinson and then practiced law in Denver from 1947 until 1960. President Kennedy appointed him deputy attorney general in 1961, and appointed him to the Supreme Court in 1962. Byron is a prominent figure in the history of American sports; he was a nine-letter man at the University of Colorado, played professional football for the Pittsburgh Steelers and the Detroit Lions, and is a member of the Pro Football Hall of Fame. His gruff voice and penetrating questions still strike terror into the hearts of unprepared attorneys arguing orally before the Court the way he used to terrify his football opponents. He wrote more than his share of important opinions for the Burger Court.

Thurgood Marshall was born in Baltimore, Maryland, in 1908. He did his undergraduate study at Lincoln University in Pennsylvania, and received his law degree from Howard University. He entered private practice in Baltimore, and from 1940 until 1962 he was director and counsel of the NAACP Legal Defense and Educational Fund, and was the principal architect of the highly successful legal strategy of that organization which ultimately resulted in the Court's decision outlawing school segregation in *Brown* v. *Board of Education* in 1954. President Kennedy appointed him to the Court of Appeals for the Second Circuit in 1961, President Johnson appointed him solicitor general of the United States in 1965, and to the Supreme Court in 1967. Thurgood is the Court's raconteur; he has a seemingly never-ending fund of droll stories derived from his unique practice.

Harry A. Blackmun was born in Nashville, Illinois, in 1908. He received both his undergraduate degree and his law degree from Harvard University, and served as a law clerk to Judge John

B. Sanborn of the Court of Appeals for the Eighth Circuit. He practiced law in Minneapolis from 1934 to 1950, and then moved to Rochester, Minnesota, where he served as resident counsel for the Mayo Clinic and the Mayo Foundation until 1959. In that year President Eisenhower named him as a judge of the Court of Appeals for the Eighth Circuit, and in 1970 President Nixon nominated him to the Supreme Court of the United States. For more than fourteen years I sat next to Harry on the bench, and we shared an interest in geography trivia which helped to lighten an occasional dull moment.

Lewis F. Powell, Jr., was born in Suffolk, Virginia, in 1907. He received both his undergraduate and his law degree from Washington and Lee University and received an LL.M. from Harvard Law School. He practiced law in Richmond, Virginia, from 1932 to 1971, with a four-year stint in the United States Army Air Force during World War II. He served as president of the American Bar Association in 1964. President Nixon nominated him to the Supreme Court in 1971. Lewis is the ultimate southern gentleman, in the very best sense of that word; at a time when he could have rested on the laurels of a life already rich in public service, he took on the duties of a justice of the Supreme Court.

John Paul Stevens was born in Chicago, Illinois, in 1920. He received his undergraduate degree from the University of Chicago and his law degree from Northwestern University. After serving three years in the United States Navy during the Second World War, he was a law clerk to Justice Wiley Rutledge of the Supreme Court. President Nixon appointed him to the Court of Appeals for the Seventh Circuit in 1970, and President Ford nominated him to the Supreme Court in 1975. John is a man of many talents; in addition to performing his judicial duties, he is an avid tennis player and a tournament contract-bridge player.

Sandra Day O'Connor was born in El Paso, Texas, in 1930. She received her undergraduate degree and her law degree from Stanford University, practiced privately in California and Arizona, served in the Arizona Senate, and as a judge of the Arizona Superior and Intermediate Appellate courts. President Reagan appointed her to the Supreme Court in 1981. Sandra and I were classmates in law school, and my wife, Nan, and her husband, John, were undergraduate classmates there. We go back a long time, and I was overjoyed at her appointment to the Supreme Court.

The newest member of our Court is Antonin Scalia—Nino for short. At the time I was nominated to succeed retiring Chief Justice Burger, President Reagan nominated Nino Scalia to succeed me as an associate justice, and we were both sworn in to our new offices on September 26, 1986. Nino Scalia was born in New Jersey, but grew up in New York City and attended Georgetown University and Harvard Law School. He comes from the academic side of the legal profession, and was a member of the law faculties at the University of Virginia and University of Chicago law schools. He was serving as a judge of the United States Court of Appeals for the District of Columbia Circuit at the time he was appointed to our Court. During his brief tenure he has established a reputation for incisive and persistent questioning of attorneys during oral argument.

Each justice is assigned a series of offices called chambers on the first floor of the Supreme Court building. The assignment of chambers, like virtually every other similar placement, goes by seniority; for example, when Justice Potter Stewart retired in June 1981, and moved to smaller quarters, the senior of any justices who wished to move into Justice Stewart's chambers would have been entitled to do so. As it worked out, Justice John Paul Stevens, then the junior justice, was the only one who wished to move, and he succeeded to Justice Stewart's chambers.

I thought about claiming Justice Stewart's chambers but decided against it. To understand why I did so requires an excursion into the history of the present Supreme Court building. When the new building was first opened at the beginning of the October 1935 term, the justices had been used to working in their homes. They would come to the courtroom in the Capitol building to hear oral arguments, and to hold conferences, but they had law libraries in their homes and did their preparation for argument and conference there. The members of the Court were quite reluctant to abandon these arrangements in 1935, and many of them continued to work out of their homes. The result was that when Justice Hugo L. Black was appointed to the Court in 1937, he was able to claim one of the choice corner chambers even though he was ninth in seniority simply because those senior to him did not wish to change their base of operations from their homes to the rather awesome and impersonal Court building.

When all of the justices had moved to the new building in the late 1930s, each had but one law clerk, and therefore a three-room suite of chambers was completely adequate: one room for the justice, one room for reception of guests, and the secretary, and one room for a law clerk and a messenger. Nine of these three-room suites could be accommodated in one half of the first floor of the Supreme Court building, and because the Court's conference room and the chambers of the chief justice were in the back of the building, it was natural for the chambers of the associate justices to be arranged around the back half of the building also. The views from these offices, at that time looking out largely on rooming houses and the like, were not particularly attractive, but apparently that didn't bother anyone.

As the number of law clerks went from one to two, then from two to three, and finally to four for most of the justices, the three-room suites were no longer adequate. In 1972 the front of the first floor of the building was opened up for use as expanded suites for the four junior justices on the Court, and what had been suites for the chief justice and eight associates in the rear of the building were enlarged to become suites for the chief justice and the four senior associate justices. When I moved from my temporary quarters in Justice Harlan's old chambers (which Justice Jackson had occupied before him) to my new quarters, I was delighted with the dramatic change in my view: From the front window of my office, I now looked out on the Capitol plaza and the dome of the United States Capitol building! I am so fond of this view that I decided not to exchange it for the view from Justice Stewart's old chambers, even though I would have been considerably closer to the conference room had I done so.

Of course, when I became Chief Justice in 1986, I moved from my chambers in the front of the building to the chambers traditionally occupied by the chief justice in the rear of the building. I now have two offices, each of which is about half of the size of my former office, with the Court's conference room situated between them. I have never thought that just because one held an important position it was necessary to have an office the size of the one Italian dictator Benito Mussolini is said to have had, and so I have no complaint about the change. In my present location I am much closer to the conference room and to the courtroom than I was in my old location, and as a result have been more punctual for sessions of the Court and the conference than I was in the past.

I recall that when I was first appointed to the Court in 1972, a young lawyer whom I knew rather casually from church inquired of me whether there might be a position for him on my staff. He said he was not entirely happy with his present employment, and thought he would enjoy a chance to work for me. I asked him if he knew how many lawyers I had on my "staff," and he guessed that there would be somewhere between fifteen and twenty. I told him that the total number of lawyers on my staff was three, and that they were all law clerks who had very recently graduated from law school. He decided he did not want to be a law clerk, but his misunderstanding may be common to many other people who think of the Supreme Court as a rather typical branch of the "government" with its legions of civil-service employees.

The Supreme Court has always been different in this respect; ever since it started out in one room in the basement of the Capitol, it has never tried to assert itself through force of numbers. Many years ago Justice Brandeis was asked why he thought people respected the Supreme Court, and his rather short response was, "Because we do our own work." Though the number of law clerks has increased with the years, the individual justices still continue to do a great deal more of their "own work" than do their counterparts in the other branches of the federal government.

Although I had only two secretaries as an associate justice, I now have three: Janet Barnes, Laverne Frayer, and Barbara Seagle. They are responsible for transcribing my dictation, and handling the voluminous incoming correspondence and telephone calls, and one of them is also available to transcribe dictation of the law clerks. My messenger, Harry Fenwick, has been with me for fifteen years; he serves as a factotum, seeing that the material I wish circulated to the other chambers is copied and taken around, helping with the preparation and serving of meals, and doing a number of other things that make my life easier. Most of my colleagues have four law clerks, but I have three and John Stevens has two, in each case because that is the number we prefer. My law clerks, as do almost all of those of my colleagues, serve one-year terms; they have worked very hard by the end of twelve months and are glad to go on to something else in the profession, and I am convinced that the annual turnover in the chambers is good for me as well as for them.

I spend a fair amount of time picking my law clerks each year, because having good law clerks is a very important factor in the proper functioning of my chambers. As I have mentioned earlier, when I was a law clerk the Ivy League law schools had a virtual monopoly on the jobs, but that is no longer the case either in my chambers or in the chambers of most of my colleagues. In the spring of each year I receive several hundred applications to be a law clerk for the term of the Court commencing the summer of the next year, and I go through the applications myself in an effort to winnow them down to a number between twenty and twenty-five. I look through the résumé for indications that the applicant has done very well in law school. I prefer that the applicant have had a responsible position on the law review, because I think law review is an excellent teaching device whereby one learns to organize, assemble, and develop one's ideas and to work with other people. Service on law review certainly does not teach one to write sparkling or even interesting prose, but it does teach one to organize and logically develop one's train of thought.

Naturally I want law clerks who will get along with me and with whom I will get along, but this is not much of a problem; very few employees would fail to get along with their boss when the job lasts only one year. I also want law clerks who will get along with my secretaries and messenger, since the total population of our chambers is eight, and we all have to work together to be productive. I like law clerks who seem to have a sense of humor, and who do not give the impression of being too sold upon themselves. I ask the new clerks to begin work about the first of July, just at the time the Court will have recessed for the summer. I ask one of the old law clerks to stay for ten days to help break in the new ones, and the Court also conducts orientation sessions for the new law clerks. I like to have mine come aboard in early July because for the next two months they really need address themselves only to petitions for certiorari, and not to preparation for argued cases or drafting of Court opinions or dissents.

As I have said, a petition for certiorari is, stripping away the legal verbiage, a request to the Supreme Court to hear and decide a case that the petitioner has lost either in a federal court of appeals or in a state supreme court. The Supreme Court rules tell a lawyer what a petition for certiorari should contain: a copy of the lower-court opinion that the lawyer wishes to have reviewed, a statement of the legal question or questions that the case presents, and a statement of the reasons why the lawyer thinks the Supreme Court should review his case. A small fraction of the cases we review come to us in ways other than by petition for certiorari, but the difference is not important for the purpose of giving a general sketch of how the Supreme Court operates.

Six members of the Court—I, Justice White, Justice Blackmun, Justice Powell, Justice O'Connor, and Justice Scalia—have pooled our law clerks in order to facilitate the consideration of the petitions for certiorari. The first term in which I served on the Court, there was no "cert pool," and each chambers did all of its own certiorari work as well as its other work. I could not help but notice that my clerks were frequently pressed for time, scrambling between having memos describing the certiorari petitions ready when they should be, and drafts or revisions of Court opinions or dissents ready when they should have been. Justice Powell, who had come on the Court at the same time I had, was also bothered by this phenomenon, and suggested that all the law clerks be pooled for purposes of writing memos describing the facts and contentions in each petition for certiorari. As it turned out, only five members of the Court as it then stood decided to join the pool, but when Justice O'Connor was appointed in 1981 she became the sixth member of the pool.

Each of the twenty-three law clerks in the pool divide among themselves the task of writing memos outlining the facts and contentions of each of the some four thousand petitions for certiorari that are filed each term, and these memos are then circulated to each of the six chambers whose clerks comprise the pool. When the memos come into my chambers, I ask my law clerks to divide them up three ways, and ask each law clerk to read the memo and, if necessary, go back to the petition and response in order to make a recommendation to me as to whether the petition should be granted or denied.

Although our Court otherwise operates by majority rule, as would be expected, the granting of certiorari has historically required only the votes of four of the nine justices. In 1925, the year when Congress allowed the Supreme Court a great deal more discretion in the kinds of cases it would review, the practice of the Court was to grant certiorari if four out of the nine justices wished to hear the case, and that practice has continued to this day.

When I get the annotated certiorari memos from my law clerks, I review the memos and indicate on them the way I intend to vote at conference. I don't necessarily always vote the way I had planned to vote, however; something said at conference may persuade me either to shift from a "deny" to a "grant," or vice versa.

I would guess that somewhere between one and two thousand of the petitions for certiorari filed with the Court each year are patently without merit; even with the wide philosophical differences among the various members of our Court, no one of the nine would have the least interest in granting them. As soon as I am confident that my new law clerks are reliable, I take their word and that of the pool memo writer as to the underlying facts and contentions of the parties in the various petitions, and with a large majority of the petitions it is not necessary to go any further than the pool memo. In cases that seem from the memo perhaps to warrant a vote to grant certiorari, I may ask my law clerk to further check out one of the issues, and may review the lower court opinion, the petition, and the response myself.

During the time I am away from my chambers in the summer, and there are no conferences, the certiorari memos are mailed to me and I review them there and return them to my chambers. During the summer the petitions for certiorari simply accumulate, and by the time we have our annual September conference, which starts the week before the "first Monday in October," as many as a thousand petitions for certiorari will be waiting. These are disposed of at the September conference in the same manner that petitions for certiorari are disposed of at our regular conferences.

Shortly before each conference at which the Court will consider petitions for certiorari, the chief justice sends out a list of the petitions he wishes to have discussed. After the chief's "discuss list" has come around, each of the associate justices may ask to have additional cases put on this list. If at a particular conference there are one hundred petitions for certiorari on the conference list, the number discussed at conference will range from fifteen to thirty. The petitions for certiorari that are not discussed at conference are denied without any recorded vote.

Whether or not to vote to grant certiorari strikes me as a rather subjective decision, made up in part of intuition and in part of legal judgment. One factor that plays a large part with every member of the Court is whether the case sought to be reviewed has been decided differently from a very similar case coming from another lower court: If it has, its chances for being reviewed are much greater than if it hasn't. Another important factor is the perception of one or more justices that the lower-court decision may well have been both an incorrect application of Supreme Court precedent or of general importance beyond its effect on these particular litigants.

I have on occasion described the certiorari process to groups interested in the work of the Court, and find occasional raised eyebrows at one or more of its aspects. Recently I was asked whether or not the use of the law clerks in a cert pool didn't represent the abandonment of the justices' responsibilities to a sort of internal bureaucracy. I certainly do not think so. The individual justices are of course quite free to disregard whatever recommendation the writer of the pool memo may have made, as well as the recommendation of his own law clerks, but this is not a complete answer to the criticism. It is one thing to do the work yourself, and it is another thing to simply approve the recommendation of another person who has done the work. But the decision as to whether to grant certiorari is a much more "channeled" decision than the decision as to how a case should be decided on the merits; there are really only two or three factors comprised in the certiorari decision—conflict with other courts, general importance, and perception that the decision is wrong in the light of Supreme Court precedent. Each of these factors is one that a well-trained law clerk is capable of evaluating, and the justices, of course, having been in the certiorari-granting business term after term, are quite familiar with many of the issues that come up. I must say I would feel entirely different about a system that assigned the preparation of "bench memos"—memoranda that summarize the contention of the parties and recommend a particular result in an argued case—to one law clerk in a large pool of law clerks.

Another criticism I have heard voiced is that the great majority of petitions for certiorari are never even discussed at conference and are simply denied without being taken up by the justices as a group. I do not think this is a valid criticism. For the sixty years since the enactment of the Certiorari Act of 1925, there have been significant ideological divisions on the Court, such that one group of justices might be inclined to review one kind of case, and another group of justices inclined to review another kind of case. When one realizes that any one of nine justices, differing among themselves as they usually do about which cases are important and how cases should be decided, may ask that a petition for certiorari be discussed, the fate of a case that is "dead listed" ("dead listing" a case is the converse of putting a case on the "discuss list") is a fate well deserved. It simply means that no one of the nine justices thought the case was worth discussing at conference with a view to trying to persuade four members of the Court to grant certiorari. It would be a totally sterile exercise to discuss such a case at conference since no justice would be a proponent of granting it and it would end up being denied in less time than it takes to write this paragraph.

Examination of the certiorari process naturally brings up the question of the precise role of the Supreme Court of the United States in our country's legal system. Many would intuitively say that the task of the "highest court in the land" is to make sure that justice is done to every litigant, or some similarly general and appealing description. The Supreme Court of the United States once played a role in the federal system corresponding fairly closely to that description, but the days when it could do so are long gone.

The first Congress in 1789 established the Supreme Court of the United States, and lower federal courts which were essentially trial courts. In the lower courts witnesses testified, documents were received in evidence, and at the close of the trial the judge or the jury ruled in favor of one of the parties and against the other. Congress provided that appeals from these decisions should lie to the Supreme Court of the United States, and the task of the latter Court in these early days was to do what any other appellate court traditionally does: make sure that the trial was fairly conducted, that the judge correctly applied the law, and that the evidence supported the result reached by the lower court. In its earlier days, as I have previously indicated, the Supreme Court did not have a great deal to do as an appellate court—for several decades it sat in Washington for only a few weeks a year, hearing appeals from the lower federal courts and from state supreme courts. Indeed, the justices spent far more of their time circuit riding to sit as trial judges in the geographic circuits to which they were assigned than they did as appellate judges in Washington.

But this rather easygoing picture changed before the Civil War, and the Supreme Court justices had to spend more of their time sitting as appellate judges and still found themselves falling behind in their docket. After the Civil War, court congestion increased. Congress expanded the jurisdiction of the lower federal courts, so that they could hear types of cases they had previously been denied the authority to hear. Congress began to enact regulatory legislation, which created new kinds of lawsuits that could be brought in the federal courts. Finally, both the commercial activity and the population of the United States continued to increase dramatically, and both of these kinds of growth naturally caused more litigation. By 1890 it took three and one half years between the time a case was first docketed in the Supreme Court and the time it was orally argued before the justices. Court congestion is not often a major concern of Congress, but these extreme delays caused the legal profession to rise up in righteous indignation, and in 1891 Congress responded by creating the federal circuit courts of appeals.

The federal circuit courts of appeals were regional federal appellate courts. Congress provided that in cases where the federal trial courts had jurisdiction not because of a federal question involved in the case but only because one of the parties was a citizen of one state and the other a citizen of another, appeal from the decision of the trial court would lie not to the Supreme Court of the United States, but to the federal court of appeals in the geographic region in which the trial courts lay. Review of the decision of the court of appeals could not be had automatically in the Supreme Court, but only if the Supreme Court agreed to review the decision.

Other acts of Congress in the early part of this century, culminating in the Certiorari Act of 1925, further limited the access of parties to Supreme Court review. After 1925, review not only of diversity cases but of most federal-question cases decided by the federal trial courts was to be had as a matter of right not in the Supreme Court but in the federal courts of appeals. Further review by the Supreme Court was made to depend on the discretionary decision of that court to hear the case. Chief Justice William Howard Taft was one of the architects of the Certiorari Act of 1925, and his biographer, Henry F. Pringle, summarizes his view of the role of the Supreme Court in these words:

It was vital, he said in opening his drive for the Judges' Bill, that cases before the Court be reduced without limiting the

function of pronouncing "the last word on every important issue under the Constitution and the statutes of the United
States." A supreme court, on the other hand, should not be a
tribunal obligated to weigh justice among contesting parties.

"They have had all they have a right to claim," Taft said,
"when they have had two courts in which to have adjudicated
their controversy." [Pringle, Vol. II, pp. 997–998]

There are thousands of state-court judges in this country at
the present time, and hundreds of federal judges. Each of these
has sworn to uphold the Constitution and laws of the United
States, and the overwhelming majority of these judges are capable
of applying settled law to the facts of the cases before them, and
eager to do so. Occasionally, these trial judges make mistakes,
but the federal courts of appeals sit to correct these mistakes
within the federal system, and state appellate courts sit to do the
same in every state system. It would be a useless duplication of
these functions if the Supreme Court of the United States were to
serve simply as an even higher court for the correction of errors in
cases involving no generally important principle of law. The Supreme Court, quite correctly in my opinion, instead seeks to pick,
from the several thousand cases it is annually asked to review,
those cases involving unsettled questions of federal constitutional
or statutory law of general interest.

Ever since I have been on the Court, we have heard somewhere around one hundred fifty cases each year on the merits,
and I know of no member of the Court or student of the Court
who feels that we ought to try to hear more cases than this. Each
year we find more than enough cases to meet the demanding standards for Supreme Court review, and must turn down many that
several of the justices, although not a sufficient number to grant
certiorari, think do meet the standard for review. We are
stretched quite thin trying to do what we ought to do—in the
words of Chief Justice Taft, pronouncing "the last word on every
important issue under the Constitution and the statutes of the
United States"—without trying to reach out and correct errors in
cases where the lower courts may have reached an incorrect result, but where that result is not apt to have any influence beyond
its effect on the parties to the case.

12

HOW THE COURT DOES ITS WORK: ORAL ARGUMENT

*T*he time that elapses between the grant of certiorari in a case and its oral argument depends upon the time of year at which certiorari is granted and the state of the Court's calendar. Usually a case granted review in September will be argued in January or February, but a case granted review in June will not be argued until December. Several weeks before the oral argument is scheduled, the briefs filed by the parties are available to the justices to read. Court rules rigorously prescribe the form and contents of the brief: The briefs must be printed on relatively small pages in a particular type of print, they must have indexes listing each case or other authority cited, and they must not exceed fifty pages in length. Even the colors of the briefs are prescribed: The brief of the petitioner (the party who seeks to overturn the lower-court judgment) must have a blue cover, and the brief of the respondent (the party who seeks to support the judgment of the lower court) must have a red cover. The Court will also receive briefs from *amici curiae*, "friends of the Court" in a case; these briefs cannot exceed thirty pages, and they must have a green cover. All of this may seem highly ritualistic until it is remembered that the bundle of briefs that a justice pulls out in a particular case may well include eight or ten separate briefs, and it is very handy to be able to identify them by color without having first to read the legends on the cover.

Each justice prepares for oral argument and conference in his own way. Several of my colleagues get what are called bench memos from their law clerks on the cases—bench memos being digests of the arguments contained in the briefs and the law clerk's analysis of the various arguments pro and con. I do not do this, simply because it does not suit my own style of working. When I start to prepare for a case that will be orally argued, I begin by reading the opinion of the lower court which is to be reviewed. I find this a good starting point because it is the product of another court, like ours sworn to uphold the Constitution and the laws, and presumably not biased against either party to the case. I then read the petitioner's brief, and then the respondent's brief. Meanwhile, I have asked one of my law clerks to do the same thing, with a view to our discussing the case.

I let my law clerks divide up the cases among themselves according to their own formula. Since there are usually twenty-four cases for each two-week session of oral argument, this means that each law clerk will end up with eight cases for which that clerk is responsible. I think that most years my clerks have divided up the cases with a system something like the National Football League draft, in which those morsels viewed as more choice are taken first in rotation, with the cases viewed as the dregs left until the end.

When the law clerk and I are both ready to talk about the case, we do just that; sometimes walking around the neighborhood of the Court building, sometimes sitting in my chambers. I tell the law clerk some of my reactions to the arguments of the parties, and am interested in getting the clerk's reactions to these same arguments. If there is some point of law involved in the case that doesn't appear to be adequately covered by the briefs, I may ask the law clerk to write me a memorandum on that particular point. Either before or after I talk about the case with the law clerk, I also go back and read several of our previous opinions that are relied upon by one side or the other. If it is a recent opinion, it is quite easy to imagine that you remember what was said without having to look at it again, but this often turns out to be exactly that: imagination, rather than reality.

I have used this process pretty much since the time I first came to the Court, but when the process I have just described came to an end, I used to wonder what I should do next. If it was an important constitutional question, it obviously deserved extended and deliberate consideration, and I felt there was obviously more that I should do. I would then begin reading decisions from other courts, and cases from our Court that were only tangentially related to the one to be argued; I even set aside a particular time at which I would simply sit down and "think" about the case. None of these backup procedures seemed to advance me much toward my goal; it is much easier to read what someone else has said about a particular legal problem than to try to figure out what *you* think about it. Then I began to realize that some of my best insights came not during my enforced thinking periods in my chambers, but while I was shaving in the morning, driving to work, or just walking from one place to another. This phenomenon led me to revise my approach to preparation for argued cases by sharply cutting down on collateral reading in most of them, and simply allowing some time for the case to "percolate" in my mind.

After I finished reading the lower-court opinion and briefs, reading the controlling precedents, and talking to the law clerks, I would simply go on to the next item of business. I did that not because I had finally reached a conclusion about the case, but with the idea that I now knew enough that thoughts about it would probably occur between then and the time for conference discussion and voting. They might come in a chance bit of conversation with a colleague; they might come some night while I was lying awake in bed; they might come during oral argument. But once I had made myself sufficiently familiar with the case, come they inevitably did. Probably the most important catalyst for generating further thought was the oral argument of that *case*.

The only publicly visible part of the Supreme Court's decision process is the oral argument. It is the time allotted to lawyers for both sides to argue their positions to the judges who will decide their *case*. In our Court, it takes place in the courtroom of the Supreme Court building fourteen weeks out of each year; two weeks each in the months of October through April. During weeks of oral argument, the Court sits on the bench from ten o'clock in the morning until noon, and from one o'clock until three, on Monday, Tuesday, and Wednesday. On each of these days it hears four cases, allotting one half hour to the lawyers for each side in the four cases that it will hear that day. Oral arguments are open to the public, and one can generally find in the newspaper what cases are going to be argued on a particular day.

In the fifteen years that I have been on the Court, the presentation of each side of a case has been limited to one half hour except in cases of extraordinary public importance and difficulty. Three hours were allowed in *United States* v. *Nixon* in 1974, for example, and two hours for *Bowsher* v. *Synar* in 1986. But the limit of one hour per case is of recent origin. When I was a law clerk, in the early 1950s, the Court had two different dockets, the "regular" docket and the "summary" docket. The more difficult cases were assigned to the regular docket, and the lawyer for each side in such a case was allowed one hour to present his argument. Cases thought to be simpler were assigned to the summary docket, and in these cases the lawyer for each side was allowed only half an hour. By the time I was appointed to the Court, this distinction had been abolished. My experience during my tenure as a justice convinces me that by and large our present rules for oral argument are about right. There may be an extremely rare case which because of both its importance and its complexity requires more than an hour for oral argument, but in such cases the Court is generally willing to grant additional time. The Supreme Court of the United States does not generally review evidentiary matters, and so the only questions before us in a given case are pure questions of law. Even these are sometimes limited to one or two in number by the order granting certiorari. A good lawyer should be able to make his necessary points in such a case in one half hour.

It was not always so, however. If we go back in time one hundred seventy or so years to February 4, 1824, to the little courtroom in Washington where the great case of *Gibbons* v. *Ogden* is about to be argued to the Court, there are no rules limiting the length of oral argument and counsel take full advantage of this fact. The oral argument in that case was opened by Daniel Webster, who began at 11:00 o'clock in the morning. Webster argued for two and one half hours in an "excessively crowded" courtroom. Thomas J. Oakley, counsel for Ogden, followed, and spoke for an hour on February 4, and for the entire court day of February 5. Thomas Emmet spent the whole of the third day, February 6, and two hours of February 7, delivering his argument. And the arguments were finally closed on the eighth by William Wirt for the appellant *Gibbons*. Five full Court days—four hours each day—were devoted to the argument of this important case.

One senses from reading contemporary accounts of the arguments in *Gibbons* v. *Ogden* that the judges had genuine respect, even awe, for some of the counsel who appeared before them; and the lawyers had equal respect for some of the judges. A New York correspondent described William Wirt, one of the advocates in *Gibbons* v. *Ogden*, in these words:

> His voice is powerful, his tones harmonious, and his enunciation clear and distinct. . . . His arguments are constantly enlivened by classical allusions and flashes of wit. Many a dry cause, calculated to fatigue and weary, is thus rendered interesting to the spectator as well as to the Court. . . . [Warren, p. 600]

Daniel Webster himself wrote of his feelings at the opening of the argument in the *Gibbons* case:

> I can see The Chief Justice as he looked at that moment. Chief Justice Marshall always wrote with a quill. He never adopted the barbarous invention of steel pens. . . . And always, before counsel began to argue, the Chief Justice would nib his pen; and then, when everything was ready, pulling up the sleeves of his gown, he would nod to the counsel who was to address him, as much as to say "I am ready; now you may

go on." I think I never experienced more intellectual pleasure then arguing a novel question to a great man who could appreciate it and take it in; and he did take it in, as a baby takes in its mother's milk. [Warren, p. 603]

It may be that reporters then were less cynical than they are now, or that lawyers and judges were more effusive in expressing their praise for one another. Or it may be that there were giants among us then who are present no longer. Perhaps there are so many other forms of public entertainment and amusement that now compete for our attention that neither Daniel Webster nor John Marshall would inspire any particular awe in this latter part of the twentieth century. Whatever the reason, oral argument of a case before the Court today is much more restricted in time than it was in the days of *Gibbons* v. *Ogden*.

Lawyers often ask me whether oral argument "really makes a difference." Often the question is asked with an undertone of skepticism, if not cynicism, intimating that the judges have really made up their minds before they ever come on the bench and oral argument is pretty much of a formality. My answer is that, speaking for myself, it does make a difference: I think that in a significant minority of the cases in which I have heard oral argument, I have left the bench feeling different about the case than I did when I came on the bench. The change is seldom a full one-hundred-and-eighty-degree swing, and I find that it is most likely to occur in cases involving areas of law with which I am least familiar.

There is more to oral argument than meets the eye—or the ear. Nominally, it is the hour allotted to opposing counsel to argue their respective positions to the judges who are to decide the case. Even if it were in fact largely a formality, I think it would still have the value that many public ceremonies have: It forces the judges who are going to decide the case and the lawyers who represent the clients whose fates will be affected by the outcome of the decision to look at one another for an hour, and talk back and forth about how the case should be decided.

But if an oral advocate is effective, how he presents his position during oral argument *will* have something to do with how the case comes out. Most judges have tentative views of the case when they come on the bench, and it would be strange if they did not. A judge will have read the briefs filed by the parties, and probably have talked to one of his law clerks about the case, or have received a written memorandum from the law clerk on the case. A judge who had not prepared at all for oral argument might be more "open-minded," but it would be the open-mindedness of ignorance, not of impartiality.

But a second important function of oral argument can be gleaned from the fact that it is the only time before conference discussion of the case later in the week when all of the judges are expected to sit on the bench and concentrate on one particular case. The judges' questions, although nominally directed to the attorney arguing the case, may in fact be for the benefit of their colleagues. A good oral advocate will recognize this fact, and make use of it during his presentation. Questions may reveal that a particular judge has a misunderstanding as to an important fact in the case, or perhaps reads a given precedent differently from the way in which the attorney thinks it should be read. If the judge simply sat silent during the oral argument, there would be no opportunity for the lawyer to correct the factual misimpression or to state his reasons for interpreting the particular case the way he does. Each attorney arguing a case ought to be much, much more familiar with the facts and the law governing it than the judges who are to decide it. Each of the nine members of our Court must prepare for argument in four cases a day, on three successive days of each week. One can do his level best to digest from the briefs and other reading what he believes necessary to decide the case, and still find himself falling short in one aspect or another of either the law or the facts. Oral argument can cure these shortcomings.

On occasion of course we get lawyers who do not come up to even the minimum level of competence in representing their client before our Court, either from lack of training and ability or, even worse, lack of preparation. But the great majority of advocates who appear before us exceed the minimum level of competence one might expect, and most of them are far above average in the profession. In my day as a law clerk, it seemed to me that criminal defendants were not as capably represented as they might have been, because at that time the so-called "criminal lawyer" was often possessed of a second-rate education and second-rate abilities. But that is no longer true today with the proliferation of public defender and similar offices which attract bright and able younger lawyers. The truly outstanding advocate before our Court is still a great rarity, as he is presumably before every court: the lawyer who knows the law, knows the facts, can speak articulately, but who knows that at bottom first-rate oral advocacy is something more than stringing together as many well-constructed relevant sentences as is possible in one half hour.

We who sit on the bench day after day to hear lawyers practice this art are bound to become, whether we like it or not, connoisseurs of its practitioners. Rather than try to draw up a long list of do's and don'ts for the oral advocate, I have tried in the following paragraphs to catalog some of the species of practitioners who have argued before the Court in my time.

The first is the lector, and he does just what his name implies: He reads his argument. The worst case of the lector is the lawyer who actually reads the brief itself; this behavior is so egregious that it is rarely seen. But milder cases read paraphrases of the brief, although they train themselves to look up from their script occasionally to meet the judges' eyes. Questions from the judges, instead of being used as an opportunity to advance one's own arguments by response, are looked upon as an interruption in the advocate's delivery of his "speech," and the lawyer after answering the question returns to the printed page at exactly where he left off; returns, one often feels, with the phrase "as I was saying" implied if not expressed. One feels on occasion that at the conclusion of his argument the lector will say, "Thus endeth the lesson for today."

The lector is very seldom a good oral advocate. It would be foolish for a lawyer to stand before an appellate court with *nothing* written out to guide his presentation, but the use of notes for reference conveys a far different effect from the reading of a series of typed pages. The ultimate purpose of oral argument, from the point of view of the advocate, is to work his way into the judge's consciousness and make the judge think about the things that the advocate wishes him to think about. One of the best ways to begin this process is to establish eye contact with as many of the judges as possible, and this simply can't be done while you are reading your presentation.

An oral advocate should welcome questions from the bench, because a question shows that at least one judge is inviting him to say what he thinks about a particular aspect of the case. A question also has the valuable psychological effect of bringing a second voice into the performance, so that the minds of judges, which may have momentarily strayed from the lawyer's presentation, are brought back simply by this different sound. But the lector is apt to receive fewer questions than a better advocate just because he seems less willing than other lawyers to take the trouble to carefully answer the questions. When he has finished reading a presentation to the Court, all he has done is to state a logical and reasoned basis for the position he has taken on behalf of his client before the Court; but this much should have been accomplished in his briefs. If oral argument provides nothing more than a summary of the brief in monologue, it is of very little value to the Court.

The second species of oral advocate who comes to my mind is what I shall call the debating champion. He has an excellent grasp of his theory of the case and the arguments supporting it, and with the aid of a few notes and memorization can depart from the printed page at will. But he is so full of his subject, and so desirous of demonstrating this to others, that he doesn't listen carefully to questions. He is the authority, and every question from the bench is presumed to call for one of several stock answers, none of which may be particularly helpful to the inquiring judge. He pulls out all the stops, welcomes questions, and exudes confidence; when he has finished and sat down, one judge may turn to another and say, "Boy, he certainly knows his subject." But simply showing how well you know your subject is not the same as convincing doubters by first carefully listening to their questions and then carefully answering them.

The third species of oral advocate I shall simply call "Casey Jones." This lawyer has a complete grasp of his subject matter, *does* listen to questions, tries to answer them carefully, and does not read from any prepared text. He is a good oral advocate, but falls short of being a top-notch oral advocate because he forgets about the limitations of those he is trying to convince. The reason I call him Casey Jones is because he is like an engineer on a nonstop train—he will not stop to pick up passengers along the way.

He knows the complexities of his subject, and knows that if he were permitted to do so he could easily spend an hour and a half arguing this particular case without ever repeating himself. He is probably right. For this reason, in order to get as much as possible of his argument into half an hour, he speaks very rapidly, without realizing that when he is arguing before a bench of nine people, each of them will require a little time to assimilate what he is saying. If the lawyer goes nonstop throughout the thirty minutes without even a pause, except for questions, even able and well-prepared judges are going to be left behind. To become a truly first-rate oral advocate, this lawyer must simply learn to leave the secondary points to the brief, to slow down his pace of speaking, and to remember that the lawyer who makes six points, of which three are remembered by the judges, is a better lawyer than a lawyer who makes twelve points, of which only one is remembered by the judges.

Next we come to the spellbinder, who is fortunately today much more of a rara avis than even in the days when I was a law clerk. The spellbinder has a good voice, and a good deal of that undefinable something called "presence" which enables him to talk *with* the Court rather than talk *to* the Court. This species of oral advocate has much going for him, but he tends to let his natural assets be a substitute for any careful analysis of the legal issues in the case. He is the other side of the coin from Casey Jones, who won't let up on legal analysis long enough to give the judges even a mental breathing spell. The spellbinder's magniloquent presentation of the big picture could be copied in part with profit by Casey Jones, but the thorough attention to the subject of the latter could be copied by the spellbinder. The spellbinder's ultimate weapon is his peroration, or at least so he thinks. A florid peroration, exhorting the Court either to save the Bill of Rights from the government or to save the government from the Bill of Rights, simply does not work very well in our Court.

These are but a few of the varied species of oral advocates that have come before our Court in my time. If we were to combine the best in all of them, we would of course have the All American oral advocate. If the essential element of the case turns on how the statute is worded, she will pause and slowly read the crucial sentence or paragraph. She will realize that there is an element of drama in an oral argument, a drama in which for half an hour she is the protagonist. But she also realizes that her spoken lines must have substantive legal meaning, and does not waste her relatively short time with observations that do not advance the interest of her client. She has a theme and a plan for her argument, but is quite willing to pause and listen carefully to questions. The questions may reveal that the judge is ignorant, stupid, or both, but even such questions should have the best possible answer. She avoids table pounding and other hortatory mannerisms, but she realizes equally well that an oral argument on behalf of one's client requires controlled enthusiasm and not an impression of *fin de siècle* ennui.

One of the common misapprehensions about practice before the Supreme Court, which I heard often during my days in private practice in Phoenix and still hear since I have been on the Court, is that if one has business before the Supreme Court of the United States it is best to retain a "Washington lawyer" or a "Supreme Court specialist." The first of these statements is simply not true, and the second is true only in a very limited sense.

During particular times in the history of the Supreme Court, there has been a very definite "Supreme Court bar," consisting of lawyers who follow the work of the Court closely, and appear before the Court regularly year in and year out. Daniel Webster and his colleagues at the bar did this in the days of John Marshall and Roger Taney; Reverdy Johnson, William Evarts, and Matthew

Carpenter did it in the days of Salmon P. Chase and Morrison Waite; and Charles Evans Hughes and John W. Davis did it in the days of William Howard Taft. Whether any of these lawyers had any special influence upon the Court I do not know, but apparently a number of clients thought so or they would not have been retained in so many cases.

Based on personal observation during my sixteen years of service on the Court, I am quite firmly of the belief that there is no such Supreme Court bar at the present time. With the exception of the attorneys in the office of the solicitor general of the United States, who of course are not available to represent private clients, it is quite remarkable if a single lawyer argues more than one or two cases a year before us. This is not to say that there are not lawyers in law firms who follow the Court's work carefully, and have their share of cases before the Court; but that "share" simply is not very large.

Our Court is naturally more likely to be influenced by a good brief than a bad brief, and by a good oral argument than by a bad oral argument. But I think I can state categorically that it is not the least bit likely to be influenced by the fact that the brief is signed, or the oral argument is made, by a lawyer who practices in Washington rather than somewhere else. Nor is it the least bit likely to be influenced by the fact that the brief is signed, or the oral argument made, by a well-known lawyer from a large firm anywhere in the country as opposed to a little-known lawyer from a small firm anywhere in the country. Advocacy before our Court is preeminently a *carrière ouverte aux talents* in the very best tradition of that phrase.

It must be apparent from the foregoing paragraph that I do *not* mean to say that it makes no difference whom a client retains to represent him before our Court. It makes a great deal of difference, but that difference lies not in the geographic location of the lawyer, or his reputation, but in the kind of performance he puts on in any particular client's behalf. A lawyer in Prescott, Arizona, who knows very little about Supreme Court cases and makes equally little effort to find out about them in the process of preparing a brief in the Supreme Court will be of little use to the client. But a Washington lawyer of similar ignorance and laziness will be of equally little use to the client. Every lawyer who stands up and begins to argue orally before our Court is presumed by us to be capable of doing full justice to the client's cause. That presumption may be rebutted, but if so it will be only as a result of the lawyer's performance, and not because of any lack of reputation or experience as a Supreme Court advocate.

Probably the most difficult thing for an oral advocate to do is to realize that when the judges start out hearing his argument, they are probably much less interested in his case than he is. I think that anything one does frequently and regularly—and the case of an appellate judge hearing oral arguments surely qualifies on both scores—is bound to bring a sense of *déjà vu* to the doer. When I argued orally on appeal before the Supreme Court of Arizona or the Court of Appeals for the Ninth Circuit and, in one instance, in the Supreme Court of the United States, I had spent considerable time preparing for my argument and it was a high point of at least the day on which I argued. My adrenaline was up, and I sat like a greyhound in the slip waiting for my chance to begin. After the one argument I made before the Supreme Court of the United States when I was an assistant attorney general in the Justice Department, I was drenched with sweat.

I do not think my attitude or experience is unusual for advocates, but over a career of seventeen years of practice and a considerable amount of oral advocacy, I don't think I ever realized how different was the perspective of the judges to whom the case was being argued from that of the lawyer who was doing the arguing. The justices of our Court are responsible, diligent public officials, but there is no way that one can get "up" for four cases a day, three days a week, in the same way that a lawyer can get "up" for his solo performance in one of those twelve cases.

This difference in the perspective of the lawyer who is arguing the case from the perspective of the judges who are deciding it can, I think, be illustrated by the following parable. When I practiced law, like other lawyers I would see clients or witnesses in my office, and sometimes many years later one of these people would recognize me on the street and have to introduce themselves because I did not remember them. I gradually came to realize that while interviewing witnesses and talking to clients was a routine part of my life, a visit to a lawyer's office was a highly unusual event for the client or the witness. I suppose that is why they remembered the event and I didn't.

In the time since I have been a judge, I am often disturbed by the fact that at a bar-association meeting for a law school a lawyer will come up to me, introduce himself, and say that he argued the case of *Smith* v. *Jones* in our Court the previous year. His face may look vaguely familiar, but I will often have no recollection at all of his having argued that particular case. At first this sort of occurrence bothered me greatly, because to this day I can remember the names and faces of every single appellate judge *I* argued before during my time practicing law. Why, I thought to myself, has it all changed now that I am on the bench? Again, I think the answer is the same as before; to the lawyer, arguing the case in a particular court is a highly unusual event, and one he will therefore remember; to a judge, hearing an oral argument of a case in his court is not an unusual event, and therefore he does not tend to remember the individual participants.

I will round off the parable by recalling an experience I had about fifteen years ago when the American Bar Association met in London in 1971. My wife and I and three children decided to take in the bar-association meeting and travel some in Europe, and we flew from Washington to London on a charter flight. The charter flight was due to return some three and one half weeks later from Amsterdam to Washington, and it was scheduled to depart Amsterdam at two o'clock in the afternoon. Our family, and virtually everybody else who was scheduled to return, showed up in plenty of time, but it turned out that the plane was having mechanical difficulty. The passengers were told to come back in an hour, and given a ticket for a free drink. Four times this happened, and by early evening we had not only frustrated, angry passengers, but passengers who had had too much to drink, and some very nasty incidents were barely avoided. To this day, more than fifteen years later, I still remember the face of the airline "passenger representative" who presided over all of this, although I am sure to him it was all in a day's work and he would have no recollection whatsoever of the various passengers who were scheduled to board that charter flight fifteen years ago. The client remembers the lawyer; the lawyer remembers the judge; the judge remembers the passenger agent.

13

HOW THE COURT
DOES ITS WORK:
DECIDING THE CASES

*P*otter Stewart, with whom it was my privilege to sit as a member of the Court for nearly ten years, passed on to me more than one bit of sound advice in the years when I was the junior member of the Court. I remember his saying that he thought he would never know more about a case than when he left the bench after hearing it orally argued, and I have found that his statement also holds true for me. When one thinks of the important ramifications that some of the constitutional decisions of the Supreme Court have, it seems that one could never know as much as he ought to know about how to cast his vote in a case. But true as this is, each member of the Court must cast votes in about one hundred and fifty cases decided on the merits each year, and there must come a time when pondering one's own views must cease, and deliberation with one's colleagues and voting must begin.

That time is each Wednesday afternoon after we get off the bench for those cases argued on Monday, and Friday for those cases argued on Tuesday and Wednesday. During most of the year the Friday conferences begin at 9:30 A.M., but after the conclusion of oral arguments they begin at 10:00 A.M. because there are no longer argued cases as well as petitions for certiorari to be discussed. A buzzer sounds—or, to put it more accurately, is supposed to sound—in each of the nine chambers five minutes before the time for conference, and the nine members of the Court then congregate in the Court's conference room next to the chambers of the Chief Justice. We all shake hands with one another when we come in, and our vote sheets and whatever other material we wish to have are at our places at the conference table. Seating at this long, rectangular table is strictly by seniority: the Chief Justice sits at one end of the table, and Justice Brennan, the senior associate justice, sits at the other end of the table. Unlike those ranged along the sides of the table, we have unrestricted elbow room. But even along the sides of the table, the seating remains by seniority: the three associate justices next in seniority sit along one side, and the four associates having the least seniority sit along the opposite side. Thus there are three levels of elbow room around the conference table: excellent, so far as the Chief Justice and Justice Brennan are concerned; good, so far as Justices White, Marshall, and Blackmun are concerned; and fair to middling with respect to Justices Powell, Stevens, O'Connor, and Scalia.

To one and all familiar with the decision-making process in other governmental institutions, the most striking thing about our Court's conference is that only the nine justices are present. There are no law clerks, no secretaries, no staff assistants, no outside personnel of any kind. If one of the messengers from the Marshal's Office who guard the door of the conference knocks on the door to indicate that there is a message for one of the justices, the junior justice opens the door and delivers the message. The junior justice is also responsible for dictating to the staff of the clerk's office at the close of the conference the text of the orders that will appear on the Court's order list issued on the Monday following the conference.

I think that the tradition of having only the justices themselves present at the Court's conference is a salutary one for more than one reason. Its principal effect is to implement the observation of Justice Brandeis, previously quoted, that the Supreme

Court is respected because "we do our own work." If a justice is to participate meaningfully in the conference, the justice must himself know the issues to be discussed and the arguments he wishes to make. Some cases may be sufficiently complicated as to require written notes to remind one of various points, but any extended reading of one's position to a group of only eight colleagues is bound to lessen the effect of what one says. This is less important in the second part of the conference, devoted to the discussion of petitions for certiorari, than it is to that part of the conference devoted to the discussion of cases that have been orally argued, because the discussion of the former is much less elaborate than the discussion of the latter. With respect to petitions for certiorari, if the Chief Justice has put the case on the discuss list, he leads off the discussion with a statement of why he thought the case should be brought to the attention of the conference, and usually will indicate that he thinks certiorari should be granted. The discussion then proceeds around the table from the senior associate justice to the junior justice, with each indicating a vote to either grant review or to deny review. If one of the associate justices has put the case on the discuss list, that justice leads off the discussion by giving his reasons for wanting the case discussed, and indicating whether he votes to grant or deny review. In all cases in which there have been four or more votes to grant certiorari, the Court's order issued on Mondays carries a written order granting certiorari.

In discussing cases that have been argued, the Chief Justice begins by reviewing the facts and the decision of the lower court, outlining his understanding of the applicable case law, and indicating either that he votes to affirm the decision of the lower court or to reverse it. The discussion then proceeds to Justice Brennan and in turn down the line to Justice Scalia. For many years there has circulated a tale that although the discussion in conference proceeds in order from the Chief Justice to the junior justice, the voting actually begins with the junior justice and proceeds back to the Chief Justice in order of seniority. I can testify that, at least during my fifteen years on the Court, this tale is very much of a myth; I don't believe I have ever seen it happen at any of the conferences that I have attended.

The time taken in discussion of a particular case by each justice will naturally vary with the complexity of the case and the nature of the discussion which has preceded his. The Chief Justice, going first as he does, takes more time than any one associate in a typical case, because he feels called upon to go into greater detail as to the facts and the lower-court holding than do those who come after him. Justice Brennan, who frequently disagrees with me (and also disagreed with Chief Justice Burger) in important constitutional cases, and is therefore the first to state the view of the law with which he agrees, also frequently takes more time than the other associates. The truth is that there simply are not nine different points of view in even the most complex and difficult case, and all of us feel impelled to a greater or lesser degree to try to reach some consensus that can be embodied in a written opinion that will command the support of at least a majority of the members of the Court. The lack of anything that is both previously unsaid, relevant, and sensible is apt to be frustrating to those far down the line of discussion, but this is one of the prices exacted by the seniority system. With occasional exceptions, each justice begins and ends his part of the discussion without interruption from his colleagues, and in the great majority of cases by the time Justice Scalia is finished with his discussion, it will be evident that a majority of the Court has agreed upon a basis for either affirming or reversing the decision of the lower court in the case under discussion.

When I first went on the Court, I was both surprised and disappointed at how little interplay there was between the various justices during the process of conferring on a case. Each would state his views, and a junior justice could express agreement or disagreement with views expressed by a justice senior to him earlier in the discussion, but the converse did not apply; a junior justice's views were seldom commented upon, because votes had been already cast up the line. Like most junior justices before me must have felt, I thought I had some very significant contributions to make, and was disappointed that they hardly ever seemed to influence anyone because people did not change their votes in response to my contrary views. I thought it would be desirable to have more of a round-table discussion of the matter after each of us had expressed our views. Having now sat in conferences for fifteen years, and risen from ninth to seventh to first in seniority, I now realize—with newfound clarity—that while my idea is fine in the abstract it probably would not contribute much in practice, and at any rate is doomed by the seniority system to which the senior justices naturally adhere.

Each member of the Court has done such work as he deems necessary to arrive at his own views before coming into conference; it is not a bull session in which off-the-cuff reactions are traded, but instead a discussion in which very considered views are stated. We are all working with the same materials, dealing with the same briefs, the same cases, and have heard the same oral argument; unlikely as it may seem to the brand-new justice, the point that he seizes upon has probably been considered by some of the others and they have not found it persuasive. It is not as if we were trying to find a formula for squaring the circle, and all of those preceding the junior justice had bumblingly admitted their inability to find the formula; then suddenly the latter solves the riddle, and the others cry "Eureka! He has found it." The law is at best an inexact science, and the cases our Court takes to decide are frequently ones upon which able judges in lower courts have disagreed. There simply is no demonstrably "right" answer to the question involved in many of our difficult cases.

Until the past term, I had sat in conference only under Chief Justice Burger; three of the associate justices sitting at present—Justices Brennan, White, and Marshall—also sat in conference under Chief Justice Warren. Chief Justice Burger presided for seventeen years, and so all of us became used to a particular form and style of conference. But there is good reason to think that the conferences of past Courts may have been quite different from that of the Burger Court.

I have heard both Justice Felix Frankfurter and Justice William O. Douglas describe the conferences presided over by Chief Justice Charles Evans Hughes in which they sat, and I have heard

Justice Douglas describe the conferences presided over by Chief
Justice Harlan F. Stone. These two styles of conference were apparently much different. Chief Justice Hughes has rightly been
described as Jovian in appearance, and, according to Frankfurter,
he "radiated authority." He was totally prepared in each case,
lucidly expressed his views, and said no more than was necessary.
In the words of Justice Frankfurter, you did not speak up in that
conference unless you were very certain that you knew what you
were talking about. Discipline and restraint were the order of
the day.

Understandably, some of the justices appointed by President
Franklin Roosevelt in the last part of Hughes's tenure resented
the tight rein imposed by the latter—imposed albeit only by example. Hughes was succeeded as Chief Justice by Harlan F.
Stone in 1941. Stone was one of those who had disliked the taut
atmosphere of the Hughes conference, and he opened up the
floor to more discussion. But, according to Justice Douglas, Stone
was unable to shake his role as a law-school professor, and as a
result he led off the discussion with a full statement of his own
views, then turned over the floor to the senior associate justice;
but at the conclusion of the latter's presentation Stone took the
floor once more himself to critique the analysis of the senior associate. The conference totally lost the tautness it had under
Hughes, and on some occasions went on interminably.

The conferences under Chief Justice Burger were somewhere
in between those presided over by Hughes and those presided
over by Stone. Since I have become Chief Justice, I have tried to
make my opening presentation of a case somewhat shorter than
Chief Justice Burger made his. I do not think that conference
discussion changes many votes, and I do not think that the impact
of the Chief Justice's presentation is necessarily proportional to its
length. I do not mean to give the impression that the discussion
in every case is stated in terms of nine inflexible positions; on
occasion one or more of those who have stated their views toward
the beginning of the discussion, upon seeing that those views as
stated are not in agreement with those of the majority, may indicate a willingness to alter those views along the lines of the think-

ing of the majority. But there is virtually no institutional pressure to do this; dissent from the views of the majority is in no way discouraged, and one only need read the opinions of the Court to see that it is practiced by all of us.

I feel quite strongly a preference for the Hughes style over the Stone style insofar as interruptions of conference discussion are concerned. I think it is very desirable that all members of the Court have an opportunity to state their views before there is any cross-questioning or interruption, and I try to convey this sentiment to my colleagues. But the Chief Justice is not like the speaker of the House of Representatives; it would be unheard of to declare anyone out of order, and the Chief Justice is pretty much limited to leading by example. On rare occasions questioning of a justice who is speaking by one who has already spoken may throw added light on a particular issue, but this practice carries with it the potential for disrupting the orderly participation of each member of the Court in the discussion. At the end of the discussion, I announce how I am recording the vote in the case, so that others may have the opportunity to disagree with my count if they believe I am mistaken.

The upshot of the conference discussion of a case will, of course, vary in its precision and detail. If a case is a relatively simple one, with only one real legal issue in it, it will generally be very clear where each member of the Court stands on that issue. But many of the cases that we decide are complex ones, with several interrelated issues, and it is simply not possible in the format of the conference to have nine people answering either yes or no to a series of difficult questions about constitutional law. One justice may quite logically believe that a negative answer to the very first of several questions makes it unnecessary to decide the subsequent ones, and having answered the first one in the negative will say no more. But if a majority answers the first question in the affirmative, then the Court's opinion will have to go on and discuss the other questions. Whether or not the first justice agrees with the majority on these other issues may not be clear from the conference discussion. The comment is frequently heard during the course of a discussion that "some things will have to be worked out in the writing" and this is very true in a number of cases. Oral discussion of a complex case will usually give the broad outlines of each justice's position, but it is simply not adequate to fine-tune the various positions in the way that the written opinion for the majority of the Court, and the dissenting opinions, eventually will. The broad outlines emerge from the conference discussion, but often not the refinements.

So long as we rely entirely on oral discussion for the exposition of views at conference, I do not see how the conference could do more than it now does in refining the various views on a particular issue in a case. I understand that judges of other courts rely on written presentations circulated by each judge to his colleagues before the conference discussion; this practice may well flush out more views on the details of a case, but the need to reconcile the differences in the views expressed still remains. There is also a very human tendency, I believe, to become more firmly committed to a view that is put in writing than one that is simply expressed orally, and therefore the possibility of adjustment and adaptation might be lessened by this approach. At any rate, we do not use it, and I know of no one currently on our Court who believes we should try it.

Our conference is a relatively fragile instrument, I believe, which works well for the purpose to which we put it, but which also has very significant limitations. Probably every new justice, and very likely some justices who have been there for a while, wish that on occasion the floor could be opened up to a free-swinging exchange of views with much give-and-take rather than a structured statement of nine positions. I don't doubt that courts traditionally consisting of three judges, such as the federal courts of appeals, can be much more relaxed and informal in their discussion of a case they have heard argued. But the very fact that we are nine, and not three, or five, or seven, sets limits on our procedure. We meet with one another week after week, year after year, to discuss and deliberate over some of the most important legal questions in the United States. Each of us soon comes to know the general outlook of his eight colleagues, and on occasion I am sure that each of us feels, listening to the eight others, that he has "heard it all before." If there were a real prospect that extended discussion would bring about crucial changes in position on the part of one or more members of the Court, there would be a strong argument for having that sort of discussion even with its attendant consumption of time. But my sixteen years on the Court have convinced me that the true purpose of the conference discussion of argued cases is not to persuade one's colleagues through impassioned advocacy to alter their views, but instead by hearing each justice express his own views to determine therefrom the view of the majority of the Court. This is not to say that minds are never changed in conference; they certainly are. But it is very much the exception, and not the rule, and if one gives some thought to the matter this should come as no surprise.

The justices sitting in conference are not, after all, like a group of decision-makers who are hearing arguments pro and con about the matter for the first time. They have presumably read the briefs, they have heard the oral arguments of the lawyers who generally know far more about the particular case than the justices do, and they have had an opportunity to discuss the case with one or more of their law clerks. The party who wishes to have the decision of the lower court reversed has attempted to show the Court, by citation of relevant case law and statutes, how and why this should be done; the party who wishes to sustain the judgment of the lower court has made a similar effort on behalf of his point of view. The conference of our Court is the penultimate stage in our decision-making process, and we have all been dealing with much the same arguments on both sides of the case since first we began to consider it. The fact that one or more justices feels very strongly about his view of the case is no indication that other justices who may be less hortatory in their discussion feel less strongly about their views. All in all, I think our conference does about all that it can be expected to do in moving the Court to a final decision of a case by means of a written opinion.

During a given two-week session of oral argument, we will have heard twenty-four cases. By the Friday of the second week we will have conferred about all of them. Now the time comes for assignment to the various members of the Court of the task of preparing written opinions to support the result reached by the majority.

In every case in which the Chief Justice votes with the majority, he assigns the case; where the Chief Justice has been in the minority at conference, the senior associate justice in the majority assigns the case. Although one would not know it from reading the press coverage of the Court's work, the Court is unanimous in a good number of its opinions, and these of course are assigned by the Chief Justice. Since the odds of his being in a minority of one or two are mathematically small, he assigns the great majority of cases in which there is disagreement within the Court but which are not decided by a close vote. When the conference vote produces three or even four dissents from the majority view, the odds of course increase that the Chief Justice will be one of the dissenters; I have during my tenure received assignments not only from the Chief Justice, but from Justice Douglas, Justice Brennan, Justice White, and Justice Marshall. Sometimes the assignments come around during the weekend after the second week of oral argument, but sometimes they are delayed until early the following week. Since there are nine candidates to write twenty-four opinions, the law of averages again suggests that each chambers will ordinarily receive three assignments.

I know from the time during which I was an associate justice how important the assignment of the cases is to each member of the Court. The signed opinions produced by each justice are to a very large extent the only visible record of his work on the Court, and the office offers no greater reward than the opportunity to author an opinion on an important point of constitutional law. When I was an associate justice I eagerly awaited the assignments, and I think that my law clerks awaited them more eagerly than I did. Law clerks serve for only one year, and if I was assigned seventeen or eighteen opinions during the course of the year, each of the law clerks would have an opportunity to work on five or six opinions. My law clerks were always in high hopes that one of the cases on which they had worked or in which they were really interested and regarded as very important would be assigned to me. Unfortunately, they were frequently disappointed in this respect, because not every one of the twenty-four cases argued during a two-week term is both interesting and important.

Now that I am Chief Justice, of course, I have the responsibility for assigning the writing of opinions for the Court in cases where I have voted with the majority. This is an important responsibility, and it is desirable that it be discharged carefully and fairly. The Chief Justice is expected to retain for himself some opinions that he regards as of great significance, but he is also expected to pass around to his colleagues some of this kind of opinion. I think it also pleases the other members of the Court if the Chief Justice occasionally takes for himself a rather routine and uninteresting case, just as they are expected to do as a result of the assignment process. At the start of the October 1986 term I tried to be as evenhanded as possible as far as numbers of cases assigned to each justice, but as the term goes on I take into consideration the extent to which the various justices are current in writing and circulating opinions that have previously been assigned.

Because of my method of working with my law clerks, if I assign myself three cases after a given sitting, ideally they should include one worked on by each of my three law clerks. Unfortunately, there are so many other considerations to be factored into the assignment process that this is one to which I can give little weight, and so if the cases I assign myself should consist of two worked on by one law clerk and one worked on by another law clerk, the problem is resolved inside chambers.

It would of course be possible for the law clerk who worked on two cases to first go to work with me on the first of these two cases, and then when he had a written opinion ready to circulate in that case to start working with me on the second case. But experimentation with this method has satisfied me that it causes too much delay in getting to work on the drafting of the second opinion, and so I ask the law clerk who worked on two of the assigned cases to give up one of them to the law clerk who worked on none of the cases that we were assigned. This requires the latter to plunge in to work on a case that may not greatly interest him, and on which he has done little or no previous work, and there is therefore time necessarily lost while he familiarizes himself with the law on the facts of the case. But one law clerk is quite willing to lend another a helping hand, and this solution seems the best one to me.

I sit down with the law clerk who is now responsible for the case, and go over my conference notes with him. My conference notes are unfortunately not as good as they should be because my handwriting, always poor, has with advancing age become almost indecipherable to almost anyone but me. But the combination of the notes and my recollection of what was said at conference generally proves an adequate basis for discussion between me and the law clerk of the views expressed by the majority at conference, and of the way in which an opinion supporting the result reached by the majority can be drafted. After this discussion, I ask the law clerk to prepare a first draft of a Court opinion, and to have it for me in ten days or two weeks.

I know that this sort of deadline seems onerous to the new crop of law clerks when, after the October oral argument session, they undertake the first drafting of an opinion for me. I am sure that every law clerk coming to work for a justice of the Supreme Court fancies that the opinion he is about to draft will make an important contribution to the jurisprudence of the Supreme Court, and in the rare case he may be right. But with this goal in mind the law clerk is all too apt to first ponder endlessly, and then write and rewrite, and then polish to a fare-thee-well. This might be entirely appropriate if his draft were a paper to be presented in an academic seminar, or an entry in a poetry contest. But it is neither of these things; it is a rough draft of an opinion embodying the views of a majority of the Court expressed at conference, a rough draft that I may very well substantially rewrite. It is far more useful to me to get something in fairly rough form in two weeks than to receive after four or five weeks a highly polished draft that I feel obligated nonetheless to substantially revise. It is easy in October, when the work of the Court is really just starting up for the term, to imagine that there is an infinite amount of time in which to explore every nuance of a question and to perfect the style of every paragraph of the opinion. But, as I learned long ago, and as the law clerks soon find out, there is not an infinite amount of time. By the last week in October, we are already busy preparing for the November oral-argument session, at the end of which we will be assigned two or three more cases in which to prepare opinions for the Court. I feel very strongly that I want to keep as current as I possibly can with my work on the Court, in order not to build up that sort of backlog of unfinished work that hangs over one as an incubus throughout the remainder of the term.

When I receive a rough draft of a Court opinion from a law clerk, I read it over, and to the extent necessary go back and again read the opinion of the lower court and selected parts of the parties' briefs. The drafts I get during the first part of the term from the law clerks require more revision and editing than the ones later in the term, after the law clerks are more used to my views and my approach to writing. I go through the draft with a view to shortening it, simplifying it, and clarifying it. A good law clerk will include in the draft things that he might feel could be left out, simply to give me the option of making that decision. Law clerks also have been exposed to so much "legal writing" on law reviews and elsewhere that their prose tends to stress accuracy at the expense of brevity and clarity. Frank Wozencraft, who was my predecessor as assistant attorney general for the Office of Legal Counsel in the Justice Department, imparted to me a rule of thumb that he used in drafting opinions, which I have used since: If a sentence takes up more than six lines of type on an ordinary page, it is probably too long. This rule is truly stark in its simplicity, but every draft I review is subjected to it. Occasionally, but not often, a draft submitted by a law clerk will seem to me to have simply missed a major point I think necessary to support the conclusion reached by the majority at conference; I will of course rewrite the draft to include that point.

The practice of assigning the task of preparing first drafts of Court opinions to law clerks who are usually just one or two years out of law school may undoubtedly and with some reason cause raised eyebrows in the legal profession and outside of it. Here is the Supreme Court of the United States, picking and choosing with great care one hundred and fifty of the most significant cases out of the four or five thousand presented to it each year, and the opinion in the case is drafted by a law clerk! I think the practice is entirely proper: The justice must retain for himself control not merely of the outcome of the case, but of the explanation for the outcome, and I do not believe this practice sacrifices either.

I hope it is clear from my explanation of the way that opinions are drafted in my chambers that the law clerk is not simply turned loose on an important legal question to draft an opinion embodying the reasoning and the result favored by the law clerk. Quite the contrary is the case. The law clerk is given, as best I can, a summary of the conference discussion, a description of the result reached by the majority in that discussion, and my views as to how a written opinion can best be prepared embodying that reasoning. The law clerk is not off on a frolic of his own, but is instead engaged in a highly structured task which has been largely mapped out for him by the conference discussion and my suggestions to him.

This is not to say that the clerk who prepares a first draft does not have a very considerable responsibility in the matter. The discussion in conference has been entirely oral, and as I have previously indicated, nine oral statements of position suffice to convey the broad outlines of the views of the justices but do not invariably settle exactly how the opinion will be reasoned through. Something that sounded very sensible to a majority of the Court at conference may, when an effort is made to justify it in writing, not seem so sensible, and it is the law clerk who undertakes the draft of the opinion who will first discover this difficulty. The clerk confronting such a situation generally comes back to me and explains the problem, and we discuss possible ways of solving it. It may turn out that I do not share the clerk's dissatisfaction with the reasoning of the conference, in which event I simply tell him to go ahead. If the objection or difficulty he sees is also seen as such by me, we then undertake an exploration for alternative means of writing the same passage in the draft. Similarly, the conference discussion may have passed over a subsidiary point without even treating it; it is not until the attempt is made to draft a written opinion that the necessity of deciding the subsidiary question becomes apparent. Here again, we do the best we can, recognizing that the proof of the pudding will be the reaction of those who voted with the majority at conference when they see the draft Court opinion.

When I have finished my revisions of the draft opinion, I return it to the law clerk, and the law clerk then refines and on occasion may suggest additional revisions. We then send the finished product to the printer, and in short order get back printed copies with the correct formal heading for the opinion.

When the Supreme Court first began to hand down written opinions in the last decade of the eighteenth century, the author of the opinion was designated, for example, "Cushing, Justice." This style was followed until the February 1820 term of the Court when it was replaced by the form, for example, "Mr. Justice Johnson" as the author of the opinion. This style endured for more than one hundred and fifty years, indeed until a year or two before Justice O'Connor was appointed to the Court in 1981. In 1980 Justice White with great prescience suggested to the conference that since in the very near future a woman justice was bound to be appointed, we ought to avoid the embarrassment of having to change the style of designating the author of the opinion at that time by doing it before the event. The conference was in entire agreement, and very shortly thereafter, without any explanation, the manner of designating the author of the opinion became simply, for example, "Justice Brennan." Our desire to avoid later embarrassment was only partially successful, however; the very first day on which opinions in the new style were handed down, *The New York Times* carried a story devoted to the change of style under the by-line of its astute Supreme Court correspondent, Linda Greenhouse.

I have always felt that opinions coming back in printed form are vastly impoved over the draft sent to the printer even though the latter has not changed a word in the draft. There is something about seeing a legal opinion in print that makes it far more convincing than it was in typescript. I have the feeling that if we circulated our drafts to the other justices in typescript, we might get many more criticisms than we do with the printed product.

At any rate, circulate them to the other chambers we do, and we wait anxiously to see what the reaction of the other justices will be, especially those justices who voted with the majority at conference. If a justice agrees with the draft and has no criticisms or suggestions, he will simply send a letter saying something such as "Please join me in your opinion in this case." If a justice agrees with the general import of the draft, but wishes changes to be made in it before joining, a letter to that effect will be sent, and the writer of the opinion will, if possible, accommodate the suggestions. The willingness to accommodate on the part of the author of the opinion is often directly proportional to the number of votes supporting the majority result at conference; if there were only five justices at conference voting to affirm the decision of the lower court, and one of those five wishes significant changes to be made in the draft, the opinion writer is under considerable pressure to work out something that will satisfy the critic, in order to obtain five votes for the opinion. Chief Justice Hughes once said that he tried to write his opinions clearly and logically, but if he needed the fifth vote of a colleague who insisted on putting in a paragraph that did not "belong," in it went, and let the law reviews figure out what it meant.

But if the result at conference was reached by a unanimous or a lopsided vote, a critic who wishes substantial changes in the opinion has less leverage. I willingly accept relatively minor suggestions for change in emphasis or deletion of language that I do not regard as critical, but resist where possible substantial changes with which I do not agree. Often much effort is expended in negotiating these changes, and it is usually effort well spent in a desire to agree upon a single opinion that will command the assent of a majority of the justices.

The senior justice among those who disagreed with the result reached by the majority at conference usually undertakes to assign the preparation of the dissenting opinion in the case if there is to be one. In the past it was a common practice for justices who disagreed with the opinion of the Court simply to note their dissent from the opinion without more ado, but this practice is very rare today. The justice who will write the dissent notifies the au-

thor of the opinion and the other justices of his intention to prepare a dissent, and will circulate that opinion in due course.
Perhaps it would be a more rational system if, in a case where a
dissent is being prepared, all of those, except the opinion writer,
who voted with the majority at conference, as well as those who
dissented, would await the circulation of the dissent, but in most
cases this practice is not followed. One reason for the current
practice is probably that for one reason or another dissents are
usually circulated weeks, and often months, after the majority
opinion is circulated. A justice who was doubtful as to his vote at
conference, or who has reservations about the draft of the Court
opinion, may tell the author that he intends to await the dissent
before deciding which opinion to join. But this is the exception,
not the rule; ordinarily those justices who voted with the majority
at conference, if they are satisfied with the proposed Court opinion, will join it without waiting for the circulation of the dissent.

At our Friday conferences the first order of business is the
decision as to what opinions are ready to be handed down. The
Chief Justice goes in order, beginning with Justice Scalia, and will
ask him if any of his opinions are ready to be handed down. If all
of the votes are in in a case where he has authored the draft of the
Court's opinion, he will so advise the conference, and unless
there is some objection, his opinion for the Court will be handed
down at one of the sittings of the Court the following week. On
that day, the Clerk's Office will have available at 10:00 A.M. for
anyone who wishes it copies of Justice Scalia's opinion in that
particular case. Meanwhile, the first order of business after the
Court goes on the bench will be the announcement by Justice
Scalia of his opinion from the bench. He will describe the case,
summarize the reasoning of the Court, announce the result, and
announce whatever separate or dissenting opinions have been
filed. The decision-making process has now run full circle: A case
in which certiorari was granted somewhere from six months to a
year ago has been briefed, orally argued, and now finally decided
by the Supreme Court of the United States.

14

THE COURT
IN ITS THIRD CENTURY

*I*t is relatively easy to describe in one or two sentences the role of the Supreme Court of the United States in our nation's system of government. Congress and the president enact laws, the president executes the laws, and the Supreme Court decides cases arising under those laws or under the United States Constitution. In a case properly brought before it, the Court must decide whether or not a particular challenged law violates the Constitution, or whether or not an individual claiming injury by the government has had his constitutional rights violated. Simply reading such a description in a textbook, one might wonder why such an institution should create any controversy.

Yet the readers of the earlier chapters of this book will understand why the Court has been controversial. Placed in the context of the United States political history, it has had a great deal to say about whether the political solutions to major national problems devised by the legislative and executive branches would be allowed to proceed. One does not wonder at Oliver Wendell Holmes, Jr., writing shortly after he went on the Court that "we are quiet here, but it is the quiet of a storm center." Nor does one wonder at Robert H. Jackson, writing in the aftermath of the defeat of the Roosevelt Court-packing plan, stating his view that:

> As created, the Supreme Court seemed too anemic to endure a long contest for power. . . .

Yet in spite of its apparently vulnerable position, this Court has repeatedly overruled and thwarted both the Congress and the Executive. It has been in angry collision with the most dynamic and popular Presidents in our history. Jefferson retaliated with impeachment; Jackson denied its authority; Lincoln disobeyed a writ of the Chief Justice; Theodore Roosevelt, after his Presidency, proposed recall of judicial decisions; Wilson tried to liberalize its membership; and Franklin D. Roosevelt proposed to "reorganize" it. [Jackson, pp. ix–x]

As Jackson suggests, the Court did not reach its present eminence in our system of government without a struggle. Great Britain, from which most of the colonists had emigrated, had in 1787 a court system in which the judges, once appointed, were independent of both the crown and of Parliament, but the English courts had no power then—and they have no power today—to declare an act of Parliament unconstitutional. But the framers of the United States Constitution quite clearly had in mind something different from the British system: They wanted the judges to be independent of the president and of Congress, but in all probability they also wanted the federal courts to be able to pass on whether or not legislation enacted by Congress was consistent with the limitations of the United States Constitution. The framers reconciled in a somewhat roughhewn way the need for an anti-majoritarian institution such as the Supreme Court to interpret a written constitution within a broader system of government basically committed to majority rule. Yet it is doubtful that the framers fully envisioned the extent to which the Court would become embroiled in the great political issues that troubled the nation as it grew from thirteen states on the Atlantic seaboard in 1789 to today's nation spanning a continent and more. Alexander Hamilton in his "Federalist Paper No. 78" described the judicial branch of the federal government as one that "will always be the least dangerous to the political rights of the Constitution" because it "has no influence over either the sword or the purse; no direction either of the strength or the wealth of the society." If John Jay could spend a year in England during his six-year tenure as

Chief Justice, and Oliver Ellsworth could spend nearly a year in France during his five-year stint in that office, could the Court itself ever amount to much?

Not only did the Court lack the power of the purse and of the sword, but it was to prove to be more than once the object of jealous scrutiny by the executive and legislative branches of the federal government. President Franklin Roosevelt failed in his effort to pack the Court in 1937, but in the midst of that battle the Court significantly altered its constitutional doctrine in a way that served to placate its opponents. Long before this historic confrontation, however, there were other episodes of attempts to bully the Supreme Court on the part of the popularly elected branches.

The first of these occasions was during Thomas Jefferson's first term as President, when his Republican party had succeeded in seizing control of both the presidency and the Congress from the Federalists as a result of the election of 1800. Samuel Chase, a Federalist appointee from Maryland, had antagonized the Republicans by his partisan charges to grand juries in Baltimore, and by his conduct in several cases tried under the Alien and Sedition Acts. Jefferson wrote one of the Republican leaders in the House of Representatives, Joseph Nicholson, asking him whether Chase's conduct should go "unpunished" (4 Malone 467). Jefferson hastened to add that it was better that he should not interfere, but Nicholson took the hint. Articles of impeachment against Justice Chase were voted by the House of Representatives in 1804, and when Jefferson learned of this, he commented, "Now we have caught the whale, let us have an eye to the shoal." [Warren, p. 293]

Rightly or wrongly, many contemporary observers viewed the proceedings against Chase as but one step in an assault on the entire judicial branch of the government. While the articles were pending and Chase was awaiting trial, John Marshall had privately proposed that Congress be granted authority to overrule judicial decisions on constitutional questions. One of his biographers attributes this suggestion to Marshall's extreme fear of the Chase impeachment proceedings.

Almost the whole month of February 1805 was occupied by the presentation of evidence in the Chase trial, and the proceedings were watched with great interest by all. One of the leading historians of the Supreme Court of this era wrote that:

> The profound effect produced upon the course of American legal history by the failure of the Chase impeachment can hardly be overestimated; for it is an undoubted fact that, had the effort been successful, it was the intention of the Republicans to institute impeachment proceedings against all the judges of the Court. . . . But the mere fact of an intention to impeach all the judges was not the most serious feature of the situation. Its gravest aspect lay in the theory which the Republican leaders in the House had adopted.
>   . . . They contended that impeachment must be considered a means of keeping the Court in reasonable harmony with the will of the nation, as expressed through Congress and the executive, and that a judicial decision declaring an Act of Congress unconstitutional would support impeachment and the removal of a judge, who thus constituted himself an instrument of opposition to the course of government. [Warren, p. 293]

The party lineup in the Senate at this time was twenty-five Republicans and nine Federalists. From this fact it was clear that if the vote in the Senate went on strictly party lines, the Republicans could obtain the twenty-three votes for the two-thirds majority required to convict. But the party lines did not hold; Chase had been charged on several separate articles, and the most votes mustered against him were on the article based on the charge to the grand jury in Baltimore, on which nineteen senators voted to find him guilty and fifteen voted to find him not guilty. At the conclusion of the trial in the Senate Vice-President Aaron Burr announced that Chase had been acquitted, and the other justices presumably breathed a sigh of relief.

A similar episode of what might be called legislative bullying occurred immediately after the Civil War, when Congress was in the hands of the Radical Republicans. This faction greatly feared that some of the measures it wished to enact into law might be held unconstitutional by the Supreme Court.

Congress at this time was so antipathetic to President Andrew Johnson that it enacted a law providing that no vacancies should be filled on the Supreme Court until the membership of the Court, which was then ten, should have decreased to seven. This law very effectively deprived Andrew Johnson of any opportunity to appoint to vacancies on the Court during his single four-year term. But this measure only avoided the possibility that Johnson would change the philosophy of the then existing Court by future appointments; it did nothing to prevent the Court as it then stood from declaring unconstitutional some of the sweeping Reconstruction legislation Congress had enacted in 1867. Many impartial observers thought that these laws, which placed most of the South under military government, had major constitutional flaws in them.

William H. McCardle, the editor of a newspaper in Vicksburg, Mississippi, had been vituperative in his criticism of the acts of the Reconstruction government in the South and in Mississippi in particular. The commanding general of the military district embracing Mississippi ordered McCardle arrested and confined in November 1867, to be held for trial before a military commission on charges that his editorials incited insurrection, disorder, and violence, that they libeled some of the figures in the military government, and that they "impeded reconstruction." McCardle sought habeas corpus in the federal circuit court in Mississippi, claiming that his arrest and detention were in contravention of the Constitution and laws of the United States.

In November 1867, McCardle's case was heard in the United States circuit court in Jackson, Mississippi, and that court ruled against McCardle's constitutional claims. The judge did conclude his opinion by stating that he was "gratified that the law has provided a direct appeal to the Supreme Court . . . where any error I may have committed can be corrected." [Fairman, *History of the Supreme Court*, p. 439]

The constitutional questions in the case were indeed significant. Could Congress establish military government and military tribunals in a previously seceded state of the Union after the war was over? Not only was the relationship between Congress and the states involved, but the right of McCardle to a jury trial, which would have obtained under the Bill of Rights had he been tried in a civil court. The case was soon docketed in the Supreme Court, and in January 1868, a majority of the Court granted a motion to advance the case on the calendar and set argument for the first week of March 1868. At that time the Court heard argument for four days, because each side had been allowed six hours, as opposed to the normal two hours, to present its argument. On one of the days of argument the proceedings were interrupted because Chief Justice Salmon P. Chase was obligated to preside over the Senate while it constituted itself a court of impeachment to try President Andrew Johnson. Thus two significant tests of the strength of the Radical Republicans in Congress were going forward at the same time.

Jeremiah Black, who had been attorney general in Buchanan's Cabinet, argued for McCardle. He contended, as might be expected, that Congress could not simply turn the state of Mississippi into a military district in time of peace. The *Milligan* case, decided only a little over a year before, previously established, he argued, that no one could be deprived of his right to trial by jury so long as the civil courts sat and did business. Matthew Carpenter, soon to be a senator from Wisconsin, argued for the government that Congress in passing the Reconstruction Act of 1867 had made a judgment on an essentially political question, which could not be challenged in the courts. After hearing from these and other distinguished counsel in the case, the Court concluded the arguments on March 9 and the case was submitted for decision. On March 21 the Court apparently reached the case at conference, but voted to postpone decision because of legislation that was speeding its way through Congress.

This legislation was designed to repeal the law giving the Supreme Court the right to hear appeals from the circuit courts in habeas corpus cases, and it had passed both the House of Representatives and the Senate on March 12. President Johnson vetoed the bill, but his veto was overridden by both houses of Congress and the bill became law on March 27, 1868. Now a brand-new issue was presented in the McCardle case: Could Congress divest the Supreme Court of jurisdiction over a case that had been already argued and submitted for decision?

The Supreme Court adjourned on April 6 of that year, and at that time ordered that the McCardle case be put over until the next term without any decision. Jeremiah Black in a letter to Howell Cobb, a Georgia colleague in the Buchanan Cabinet, expressed his outrage at the Court's knuckling under: "The Court stood still to be ravished and did not even hallo while the thing was getting done." [Quoted in Fairman, *History of the Supreme Court*, p. 478]

That part of the press sympathetic to the Democrats joined in this cry. The *Louisville Courier Journal* editorialized that the Court had not "possessed half the nerve that belongs to many a justice of the peace." The *Richmond Enquirer and Examiner* deplored the "cowardice" of the Supreme Court. [Fairman, *History of the Supreme Court*, p. 479]. But letters to editors from members of the Supreme Court bar defended the Court's course of action.

The ultimate disposition of the McCardle case by the Supreme Court was somewhat anticlimactic, perhaps because most people felt they had seen the handwriting on the wall when the Court refused to decide the case in 1868. In March 1869, the Court heard argument on the question posed by the act of Congress depriving jurisdiction in the case, and the following month Chief Justice Chase delivered a unanimous opinion holding that that law had indeed accomplished its purpose: Article III of the Constitution gave Congress the power to make exceptions to the Supreme Court's appellate jurisdiction, and the Court could not inquire into the motive with which Congress enacted such exceptions.

Yet despite its lack of the power of the purse or the sword, and despite its occasional retreat in the face of antagonistic popularly elected branches of government, the Court has grown steadily in prestige and authority throughout the two centuries of its existence. It has not hesitated to rule against a president or against Congress when it has thought the Constitution required such a ruling. The Steel Seizure Case described in detail in Chapter 3 was a stinging rebuff to President Truman. In its decision in *United States* v. *Nixon* in 1974, the Court held that even the president could be required to turn over relevant evidence in connection with a Court proceeding, and President Nixon resigned from office immediately after this decision was handed down. In the case of *Chadha* v. *Immigration and Naturalization Service*, decided in 1983, the Court held unconstitutional the so-called "legislative veto," whereby Congress attempted to reserve to itself the authority to overrule determinations made by an agency within the executive branch pursuant to a statute already enacted into law. This device represented Congress's quite legitimate concern with the necessity of delegating broad authority to the executive branch to "fill in the blanks" of statutes that it enacted, and that had been incorporated in one form or another in literally dozens of statutes enacted over a period of many years.

There can be no doubt that with decisions like these the Supreme Court has established the judicial branch as a full partner in the tripartite system of federal government ordained by the Constitution. This is not to say that there may not be future confrontations between the popularly elected branches and the Court, but such confrontations will find the Court enjoying a large measure of public trust by reason of its overall performance during the two centuries of its existence.

But the necessity to repel boarders from the popularly elected branches of government is not the only difficulty the Court faces in carrying out its duties of constitutional interpretation. It has always been beset by temptations to be too timid on the one hand, or too bold on the other, in passing on the constitutionality of laws enacted by Congress or by the state legislatures. The temptation to be too timid comes not only because of attacks from the president and Congress or denunciations in the press. It also arises because judges have often had a background in politics and frequently share many of the same sentiments as possess members of the executive and legislative branches of government. In 1896 the Court decided in the case of *Plessy* v. *Ferguson* that a Louisiana statute that required railroads to provide separate passenger cars for whites and blacks did not violate the Equal Protection Clause of the Fourteenth Amendment. The Court said that so long as the facilities provided were equal, the requirement that the races be separated did not discriminate against blacks at the expense of whites. From the perspective of the present day it seems that this decision was extraordinarily insensitive to the onus blacks must have felt as a result of enforced segregation, and the *Plessy* decision was overruled in substance nearly sixty years later by the decision in *Brown* v. *Board of Education*.

During the Second World War, the Supreme Court decided in the case of *Korematsu* v. *United States* that a United States citizen of Japanese ancestry could be criminally prosecuted for failure to obey an order of a military commander in California requiring such citizens to be removed from their homes against their will and sent to "relocation centers." This decision was rendered while the United States was at war with Japan and cannot be dealt with as categorically as the decision in *Plessy* v. *Ferguson*. But a governmental order classifying people solely on the basis of race without any inquiry into disloyalty in a particular case undoubtedly strains the bounds of the Constitution even in time of war.

But there is an equally great danger on the other side that the Court will expand beyond their fair meaning some of the provisions of the Constitution that restrict governmental authority, and thereby impair not individual rights but the principle of majority rule. Two of the cases described in detail in the preceding chapters are examples of this propensity on the part of the Court: the *Dred Scott* case decided just before the Civil War, and the *Lochner* case decided shortly after the turn of the century. Charles Evans Hughes referred to the *Dred Scott* case as "a self-inflicted wound," and he was surely correct: There is no pressure on the Court from any political branch to expand constitutional guarantees and thereby limit governmental authority; mistakes in this direction come not from any caution induced by creditable political threats to the Court's autonomy but by the Court's mistaking its own views of policy for the restrictions contained in the Constitution. The justices of the Supreme Court were not appointed to roam at large in the realm of public policy and strike down laws that of-fend their own ideas of what laws are desirable and what laws are undesirable. The Greek philosopher Plato long ago suggested that the best form of government might be one in which a country was ruled by a group of very wise kings, who would not in any way be responsible to public opinion. During the Constitutional Convention in 1787 it was proposed that the Supreme Court be granted a power to "revise" laws passed by Congress, but the convention rejected this proposal. Justices of the Supreme Court have a great deal of authority, but it is not an authority to weave into the Constitution their own ideas of what is good and what is bad. Learned Hand, one of our country's outstanding judges, had this to say about such judges:

> For myself I would find it most irksome to be ruled by a bevy of Platonic Guardians, even if I knew how to choose them, which I assuredly do not. If they were in charge, I should miss the stimulus of living in this society where I have, at least theoretically, some part in the direction of public affairs. Of course, I know how illusory would be the belief that my vote determined anything; but nevertheless when I go to the polls I have a satisfaction in the sense that we are all engaged in a common venture. [Hand, pp. 73–74]

But having said this, it becomes a question of belling the cat. How is a disinterested observer to know when the Court is working within the bounds of the Constitution, and when it is going beyond those bounds to impose on the country its own views in the guise of constitutional doctrine; how is such an observer to know, on the other hand, when the Court is properly deferring to legislative and executive judgment, and when it is supinely refusing to uphold quite valid claims of individual right? Countless students of the Court have devoted an enormous amount of prose to attempt to answer these questions, with what success I shall leave it to others to determine. But for the general reader a few rather commonplace observations may prove useful.

It is perfectly evident that those who drafted the Constitution in Philadelphia in 1787 contemplated that their work would endure for a considerable period of time, and that often they deliberately spoke in generalities to avoid a sort of temporal parochialism. Travel at the end of the nineteenth century was by stagecoach, and goods were transported in sailing ships. The steamboat would not appear for twenty-five years, the railroad would not appear for forty years, and the automobile and the airplane came much later. But no serious student of the subject would claim that the constitutional grant of authority to Congress to regulate "commerce among the several states" was limited to the regulation of sailing ships and stagecoaches, to the exclusion of steamboats, railroads, automobiles, and airplanes. We may again turn to the felicitous language of Justice Holmes to make the point:

> When we are dealing with words that also are a constituent act, like the Constitution of the United States, we must realize that they have called into life a being the development of which could not have been foreseen completely by the most gifted of its begetters. It was enough for them to realize or to hope that they had created an organism; it has taken a century and has cost their successors much sweat and blood to prove that they had created a nation (*Missouri* v. *Holland*, 252 U.S. 416 [1920]).

At the close of the Civil War, Congress propounded and the states ratified the Thirteenth, Fourteenth, and Fifteenth Amendments to the United States Constitution. The Fourteenth Amendment provides that no state shall "deny to any person within its jurisdiction the equal protection of the laws." The principal reason for the inclusion of this language in the amendment was to deal with the so-called Black Codes enacted by the states of the former Confederacy, which explicitly and in no uncertain terms prevented blacks from voting, serving on juries, being witnesses in court, possessing firearms, and acquiring liquor. No doubt state laws of this kind deprived blacks of the "equal protection of the laws" guaranteed by the Fourteenth Amendment, but what other kinds of laws came within the purview of this clause? Justice Miller, writing the opinion of the Court in the Slaughterhouse Cases, had said with respect to the Equal Protection

Clause, "We doubt very much whether any action of a state not directed by way of discrimination against the Negroes as a class, or on account of their race, will ever be held to come within the purview of this provision."

But more than a century of decided cases since that time has given the lie to Justice Miller's statement; numerous other laws, which were not directed at blacks at all, have been held to violate the Equal Protection Clause of the Fourteenth Amendment. Though Congress may have had a particular situation, such as the Black Codes in the southern states, uppermost in its mind when it drafted the amendment, the amendment spoke in general terms of protecting "persons" against denial of "equal protection of the laws" and it seems entirely fair to apply the amendment more broadly than Justice Miller would have. But the problem at which the amendment was directed—the Black Codes—is bound to shed some light on what Congress meant and the states understood by the words "equal protection of the laws."

The Supreme Court thus has considerable latitude to interpret the meaning of constitutional language such as "commerce among the several states" and "equal protection of the laws." But the very breadth of the language, and the consequent breadth of interpretation that is permissible, may lead judges to feel that the sky is the limit when it comes to imposing their solutions to national problems on the popularly elected branches of the government and on the people. Every judge who has sat on a case involving a constitutional claim must have surely experienced the feeling that the particular law being challenged was either unjust, or silly, or vindictive. It is unfortunately all too easy to translate these visceral reactions into a determination to find some way to hold the law unconstitutional. Judges are no more immune than other mortals to the phenomenon described long ago by John Stuart Mill:

> The disposition of mankind, whether as rulers or as fellow-citizens, to impose their own opinions and inclinations as a rule of conduct on others, is so energetically supported by some of the best and by some of the worst feeling incident to

human nature, that it is hardly ever kept under restraint by anything but want of power. . . . [J. S. Mill, *On Liberty*]

The Supreme Court has on occasion been referred to as the conscience of the country, but I think this description has a considerable potential for mischief. If no more is meant by it than that the Supreme Court insofar as it upholds the principles of the Constitution is the conscience of the country, it is of course quite accurate. But the phrase is also subject to the more sweeping interpretation that the justices of the Supreme Court are to bring to bear on every constitutional question the moral principles found in each of their individual consciences. Yet to go beyond the language of the Constitution, and the meaning that may be fairly ascribed to the language, and into the consciences of individual judges, is to embark on a journey that is treacherous indeed. Many of us necessarily feel strongly and deeply about the judgments of our own consciences, but these remain only personal moral judgments until in some way they are given the sanction of supreme law. Again I turn to Justice Holmes:

Certitude is not the test of certainty. We have been cock sure of many things that were not so. . . . One cannot be wrenched from the rocky crevices into which one is thrown for many years without feeling that one is attacked in one's life. What we most love and revere generally is determined by early associations. I love granite rocks and barberry bushes, no doubt because with them were my earliest joys that reach back through the past eternity of my life. But while one's experience thus makes certain preferences dogmatic for oneself, recognition of how they came to be so leaves one able to see that others, poor souls, may be equally dogmatic about something else. And this again means skepticism. [Holmes, "Natural Law," p. 311]

Another oft-heard description of the Supreme Court is that it is the ultimate protector in our society of the liberties of the individual. Again, this phrase describes an important role of the Supreme Court, but by ignoring other equally important functions of the Court, it has its own potential for mischief. It is a fairly short leap from this language to a feeling that the United States Constitution is somehow "vindicated" every time a claim of individual right against government is upheld, and is not vindicated whenever such a claim is not upheld. But this, of course, cannot be the case. The role of the Supreme Court is to uphold those claims of individual liberty against the government that it finds are well founded in the Constitution, and to reject other claims of individual liberty against the government that it concludes are not well founded. Its role is no more to exclusively uphold the claims of the individual than it is to exclusively uphold the claims of the government: It must hold the constitutional balance true between these claims. And if it finds the scales evenly balanced, the long-standing "presumption of constitutionality" to which every law enacted by Congress or a state or local government is entitled means that the person who seeks to have the law held unconstitutional has failed to carry his burden of proof on the question.

It has always seemed to me that this presumption of constitutionality makes eminent good sense. If the Supreme Court wrongly decides that a law enacted by Congress is constitutional, it has made a mistake, but the result of its mistake is only to leave the nation with a law duly enacted by the popularly chosen members of the House of Representatives and the Senate and signed into law by the popularly chosen president. But if the Supreme Court wrongly decides that a law enacted by Congress is not constitutional, it has made a mistake of considerably greater consequence; it has struck down a law duly enacted by the popularly elected branches of government not because of any principle in the Constitution, but because of the individual views of desirable policy held by a majority of the nine justices at that time. Every time a claim of constitutional right is asserted by an individual or a group against a legislative act, the principle of majority rule and self-government is placed on one side of the judicial scale, and the principle of the individual right is placed on the other side of the scale. The function of the Supreme Court is, indeed, to hold the balance true between these weights in the scale, and not to consciously elevate one at the expense of the other. Opinions may differ as to whether in a particular case the Supreme Court has read the Constitution too expansively, or too narrowly. So long as the Court is involved, as it has been throughout its two centuries of existence, in helping to decide what kind of laws shall govern us, it is bound to draw criticism from those who are offended by its rulings.

But far more important than the fact that the Court has on occasion made rather demonstrable errors of both omission and commission during this time is the fact that it and the country have survived these mistakes and the Court as an institution has steadily grown in authority and prestige. In the light of the temptations that naturally beset any human being who becomes a judge of the Supreme Court, the truly remarkable fact is not that its members may have on infrequent occasions succumbed to these temptations, but that they have by and large had the good judgment and common sense to rise above them in the overwhelming majority of the cases they have decided. The framers of our system of government may indeed have built perhaps better than they knew. They wanted a Constitution that would check the excesses of majority rule, and they created an institution to enforce the commands of the Constitution. But wary of unchecked power in the judiciary as in all other branches of government, they gave the president with the consent of the Senate the power to appoint members of the Court, and the people by extraordinary majority the right to amend the Constitution. They limited the Court to deciding actual cases and controversies that were brought before it, and they left it partially dependent upon the popularly elected branches of government for the enforcement of its mandates. Two hundred years of experience now tell us that they succeeded to an extraordinary degree in accomplishing their purpose. We cannot know for certain the sort of issues with which the Court will grapple in the third century of its existence. But there is no reason to doubt that it will continue as a vital and uniquely American institutional participant in the everlasting search of civilized society for the proper balance between liberty and authority, between the state and the individual.

TABLE
OF CASES

BIBLIOGRAPHY

Alsop, Joseph, and Turner Catledge. *The 168 Days*. New York: Doubleday, Doran & Company, 1938.

Baker, Leonard. *Back to Back: The Duel Between F.D.R. and the Supreme Court*. New York: The Macmillan Company, 1967.

Beltz, Herman. *Reconstructing the Union*. Ithaca, N.Y.: Cornell University Press, 1968.

Bowen, Katherine Drinker. *Yankee from Olympus*. Boston: Little, Brown & Company, 1944.

Bowers, Claude G. *The Tragic Era*. Cambridge, Mass.: Houghton Mifflin Company, 1929.

Cleveland, Frederick A., and Fred Wilbur Powell. *Railroad Promotion and Capitalization in the United States*. New York: Arno Press, 1981.

Dunne, Gerald T. *Justice Joseph Story*. New York: Simon & Schuster, 1970.

Fairman, Charles. *Mr. Justice Miller and the Supreme Court 1862–1890*. Cambridge: Harvard University Press, 1939.

Fairman, Charles. *History of the Supreme Court of the United States: Reconstruction and Reunion 1864–88 (Part One)*. New York: The Macmillan Company, 1971.

Frank, John P. *Justice Daniel Dissenting: A Biography of Peter V. Daniel, 1784–1860*. Cambridge: Harvard University Press, 1964.

Friedman, Leon, and Fred L. Israel, eds. *The Justices of the United States Supreme Court 1789–1978*. (5 Vols.) New York: Chelsea House Publishers, 1980.

Gerhart, Eugene C. *Robert H. Jackson*. Indianapolis: The Bobbs-Merrill Company, Inc., 1958.

Goulden, Joseph. *Korea: The Untold Story of the War*. New York: Times Books, 1982.

Hand, Learned. *The Bill of Rights*. Cambridge, Mass.: Harvard University Press, 1958.

Haskins, George L., and Herbert A. Johnson. *Foundations of Power: John Marshall, 1801–1815*. New York: The Macmillan Company, 1981.

Haw, James, Francis Beirne, Rosamond Beirne, and R. Samuel Jett. *Stormy Patriot: The Life of Samuel Chase*. Baltimore: Maryland Historical Society.

Hawgood, John A. *America's Western Frontiers*. New York: Alfred A. Knopf, 1967.

Hicks, John D. *The Populist Revolt*. Lincoln, Neb.: University of Nebraska Press, 1961.

Hofstadter, Richard. *Social Darwinism in American Thought*. Rev. ed. New York: George Braziller, Inc., 1959.

Holmes, Oliver Wendell, Jr. *The Common Law and Other Writings*. Birmingham, Ala.: The Legal Classics Library, 1982.

Hughes, Charles Evans. *The Supreme Court of the United States*. New York: Columbia University Press, 1928.

Ickes, Harold L. *The Secret Diary of Harold L. Ickes*. 3 vol. New York: Simon & Schuster, 1954.

Jackson, Robert H. *The Struggle for Judicial Supremacy*. New York: Alfred A. Knopf, 1941.

The Junior League of Washington, ed. Thomas Froncek. *The City of Washington*. New York: Alfred A. Knopf, 1977.

Link, Arthur S. *American Epoch*. New York: Alfred A. Knopf, 1955.

Loth, David. *Chief Justice: John Marshall and the Growth of the Republic*. New York: W.W. Norton and Company, 1949.

McReynolds, Edwin C. *Missouri*. Norman, Okla.: University of Oklahoma Press, 1962.

Malone, Dumas. *Jefferson and His Time*, Vol. IV. Boston: Little, Brown and Company, 1970.

Marcus, Maeva. *Truman and the Steel Seizure Case: The Limits of Presidential Power*. New York: Columbia University Press, 1977.

Mason, Alpheus Thomas. *Brandeis: A Free Man's Life*. New York: The Viking Press, 1946.

Mason, Alpheus Thomas. *Harlan Fiske Stone: Pillar of the Law*. New York: Viking Press, 1956.

Nevins, Allan. *Ordeal of the Union*, Vol. II. New York: Charles Scribner's Sons, 1947.

Nevins, Allan. *The Emergence of Lincoln*. New York: Charles Scribner's Sons, 1950.

Oliver, Andrew. *The Portraits of John Marshall*. Charlottesville, Va.: University of Virginia Press, 1977.

Pringle, Henry F. *Life and Times of William Howard Taft*. 2 vol. Hamden, Conn.: Shoe String Press, 1965.

Pusey, Merlo L. *Charles Evans Hughes*. (2 Vols.) New York: The Macmillan Company, 1951.

Ripley, William Z. *Railroad Rates and Regulations*. New York: Longmans, Green and Co., 1912.

Roosevelt, Theodore. *The Letters of Theodore Roosevelt*, ed. Elting E. Morison. Cambridge, Mass.: Harvard University Press, 1951.

Schachner, Nathan. *Thomas Jefferson*. New York: Appleton-Century-Crofts, 1951.

Swisher, Carl Brent. *Roger B. Taney*. Hamden, Conn.: Archon Books, 1961.

Swisher, Carl Brent. *Stephen J. Field: Craftsman of the Law*. Washington: The Brookings Institution, 1930.

Swisher, Carl Brent. *The Taney Period, 1836–64*. New York: The Macmillan Company, 1974.

Warren, Charles. *The Supreme Court in United States History*. (3 Vols.) Boston: Little, Brown & Company, 1923.

INDEX